W9-BXT-006

ANIMALS AND THE MORAL COMMUNITY

# ANIMALS AND THE MORAL COMMUNITY

## MENTAL LIFE, MORAL STATUS, AND KINSHIP

Gary Steiner

COLUMBIA UNIVERSITY PRESS    NEW YORK

COLUMBIA UNIVERSITY PRESS

*Publishers Since 1893*

NEW YORK   CHICHESTER, WEST SUSSEX

Library of Congress Cataloging-in-Publication Data

Steiner, Gary, 1956–

Animals and the moral community : mental life, moral status, and kinship / Gary Steiner.

p. cm.

Includes bibliographical references and index.

ISBN 978-0-231-14234-2 (cloth : alk. paper)—ISBN 978-0-231-51260-2 (e-book)

1. Consciousness in animals.   2. Animal psychology.   3. Animal welfare—Moral and ethical aspects.   I. Title.

QL785.25.S74 2008

179′.3—dc22

2008008299

∞

Columbia University Press books are printed on permanent and durable acid-free paper.

This book is printed on paper with recycled content.

Printed in the United States of America

c  10  9  8  7  6  5  4  3  2  1

*For Pindar, who teaches me every day about the meaning of kinship*

# CONTENTS

# PREFACE

In all essential respects, *the animal* is absolutely identical with us. . . . The difference lies merely in the accident, the intellect, not in the substance which is the will. The world is not a piece of machinery and animals are not articles manufactured for our use.
— SCHOPENHAUER, "On Religion"

There is a long and regrettable history of thinking in the West according to which human beings are morally superior to animals and hence enjoy the prerogative to use animals for whatever purposes they see fit. A predominant tendency in this thinking is to suppose that our putatively superior intellect entitles us to treat animals as if they were created to satisfy our desires. Some philosophers have argued for human moral superiority on the grounds that animals possess certain cognitive capacities but lack reason, while others have maintained that animals are devoid of cognitive capacities and are subject entirely to instinct. In both cases the grounding assumption is that capacities such as language and abstract thought, which enable us to relate to the distant future and remote past and to engage in conceptualization and planning, confer on us a unique status: that of the central and most important being in creation. Even Schopenhauer, who recognized that animals are identical to human beings in striving to flourish according to their natures, succumbs to this anthropocentric prejudice when he asserts that "it is the mind . . . that makes man lord of the earth."[1]

In recent years philosophers and ethologists have begun to challenge this prejudice by taking seriously the idea of animal cognition and by emphasizing the continuities rather than the differences between the mental lives of human beings and animals.[2] According to the dominant traditional logic, a being's moral status is a function of the cognitive skills that being possesses; human beings possess the highest moral status in virtue of their rational and linguistic capacities, whereas animals possess an inferior moral status in virtue of lacking these capacities. Recently this logic has begun to shift: it is increasingly common for philosophers to argue that animals possess much more sophisticated cognitive abilities than was previously recognized, and that animals therefore enjoy a higher moral status than was previously thought.

Thinkers who endorse this newer logic continue to subscribe to the old assumption that superior cognitive abilities are the basis for superior moral status. In their zeal to elevate the moral status of animals, such thinkers, if only unwittingly, attribute more sophisticated mental capacities to animals than they actually seem to possess. In particular, such thinkers tend too often to assume that mental life is an all-or-nothing affair—that a being either possesses all the capacities of rationality, such as reflective self-consciousness, or that it possesses none of them. To the extent that it is implausible to explain many sorts of animal behavior on the basis of blind instinct, the thinking goes, the only reasonable alternative is to attribute to animals sophisticated capacities such as conceptual thought and predicatively structured mental states such as belief.

In the first half of this book I challenge this line of thinking on the grounds that most if not all animals seem to lack the capacity for abstract thought. It is in virtue of abstract, conceptual thought that humans are able to form complex plans and intentions, and to represent to themselves moments of time far removed from the present. Because animals cannot communicate with us through language, we can never be certain about the precise nature of animal experience. This problem is compounded by the fact that different animals have different types of experience. Hence we must be careful in making generalizations to the effect that all animals experience the world in exactly the same way. Nonetheless, some tentative generalizations can be made and put to the test in empirical observations of and encounters with animals.

A common basis in contemporary thought for attributing rational capacities to at least some animals is physiological similarity and evolutionary continuity between humans and animals. It seems plausible to suppose that there are basic similarities between human and animal experience. But in making this supposition, we need not rush to assume that animals are rational. Another way to approach the problem is to recognize that a great many human mental operations and behaviors occur at a sub- or pre-rational, pre-linguistic level, and that this level of experience is really what makes animals most like us from a cognitive standpoint. After examining some key debates in contemporary philosophy and ethology concerning the nature of animal cognition, I conclude the first half of this book by sketching a theory of the mental lives of animals that appeals to Humean associations rather than to conceptual and predicative abilities in the endeavor to account for animal behavior. The closer an animal lies to the putative dividing line between human and nonhuman, the less this model will apply to that animal; empirical observation and reflections on evolutionary continuity suggest that some animals, particularly apes and dolphins, are capable of highly sophisticated mental operations that more closely resemble human cognition than do the mental operations of other animals. But animals more typically seem not to possess such capacities, and in the case of those animals there is a need for a model of mental life that does not take its bearings from human rationality.

The other major theme I take up in this book is the proper basis for establishing the moral status of animals. I reject the traditional prejudice that moral status is in any way a function of cognitive capacities. I argue instead that sentience —the capacity to experience pleasure and suffer pain—is a sufficient condition for equal consideration in the moral community. But instead of proceeding on utilitarian or traditional animal rights grounds, I argue that sentience is a capacity shared by all beings for whom the struggle for life and flourishing *matters*, whether or not the being in question has a reflective sense of which things matter or how they matter. Sentient beings, both human and nonhuman, have a kinship relation to one another that binds them together in a moral community in which neither can properly be said to be superior or inferior to the other. One of the greatest challenges for this theory of kinship is how to affirm it without sacrificing the achievements of liberal political theory. In a society in which our sensibilities have been shaped for millennia by the idea of absolute human superiority over animals, how can we be brought to acknowledge our fundamental moral obligations toward animals without being forced to do so through absolutist totalitarian means? I conclude the second half of this book with a discussion of how this might be achieved.

The questions of mental life and moral status bear upon one another in ways that I first examined in *Anthropocentrism and Its Discontents*.[3] In that book my primary concern was to trace the history of anthropocentric thinking about animals, from the epic Greeks to the present, as a propaedeutic to a rethinking of the mental lives and the moral status of animals. In the chapters that follow I offer such a rethinking in the hope that it will contribute to the effort to liberate animals from a regime of subjection and suffering that has gone largely unquestioned for thousands of years.

# ACKNOWLEDGMENTS

Writing this text has primarily been a work of solitude, but several individuals have offered important advice and feedback along the way. I am grateful to Colin Allen, Marc Bekoff, Valéry Giroux, Michael James, Larry Kay, Marc Lucht, Elaine Steiner, James Steiner, Red Watson, and Markus Wild for their valuable contributions to my understanding of the issues addressed in this book. I very much appreciate the enthusiasm and support of Wendy Lochner at Columbia University Press. My greatest debt of thanks goes to Gary Francione, whose pioneering work on animals has been an inspiration to me and whose critical engagement with my own work has been indispensable.

ANIMALS AND THE MORAL COMMUNITY

CHAPTER ONE

# Arguments Against Rationality in Animals

## THE CONTROVERSY

The African greater honey guide is a bird that eats wax from honey-combs but is unable to open bee nests on its own. It is dependent on humans—and, in some cases, other animals—to open the nests so that it can eat the honeycomb. The honey guide has developed a symbiotic relationship with humans, who benefit from the relationship by obtaining honey from the nests. When the honey guide finds a nest that is of interest to it, it emits a series of "churring" sounds within hearing range of a human being. When the human approaches, the honey guide flies to another location, typically a tree branch, closer to the nest and continues churring while fanning its tail conspicuously and waiting for the human to catch up to it. When the honey guide has come close to the nest, it waits for the human to approach, open the nest, and depart with some of the honeycomb. Then the honey guide comes down to the nest and feeds on the remains of the honeycomb. Such guiding behavior can last up to an hour and traverse distances of up to a mile.[1]

It is tempting to describe the behavior of the honey guide as pur-posive conduct: the honey guide wants honeycomb, knows where the honeycomb is located, knows that human beings (or certain ani-mals) want honey and can open the hive, and knows that it can lure a human being toward the nest with its churring and hopscotching behavior. (Or, if the honey guide does not know these things, it at least believes them.) The honey guide has a plan, and it can carry out this plan over a long distance and a good stretch of time. It has con-scious intentions and acts in accordance with these intentions by employing knowledge that it has acquired about, among other things, the tendencies and behavior of human beings. One might even go so far as to say that the honey guide communicates with hu-man beings by emitting its churring sounds, and (according to some reports) that human beings communicate with the honey guides along the way by whistling and banging on trees as they follow the birds.

What is really going on in the subjective experience of the honey guide? Is it consciously entertaining plans and intentions, and does it possess explicit states of knowledge, belief, and desire that guide its behavior? Or is there reason to believe, as researcher Herbert Friedmann maintains, that "there is no occasion whatsoever to as-sume anything involving planning or intelligence on the bird's part" and that, on the contrary, "the behavior is wholly on an instinctive level"?[2] Friedmann believes that the behavior is purely instinctive because the course of guiding can be highly erratic and occasionally leads not to a hive but to an animal. If the behavior were conscious and intentional, we would expect the bird to pursue its course more directly and to lead humans consistently to hives rather than to other objects. And yet to attribute this elaborate array of behaviors to the black box of "instinct" seems to beg the question: What is the subjective experience of the honey guide really like? Appeals to in-stinct beg this question by deferring altogether the question of con-scious mental states; in extreme cases such appeals deny animal consciousness entirely.

Another bird, the piping plover, engages in an activity known as the "broken-wing display." When a potential predator comes close to the plover's young in the nest, the plover lures the intruder away from the nest by fluttering and dragging its outstretched wings along the ground, as if to suggest it had a broken wing. The plover may emit loud squawks while exhibiting this behavior to attract the intruder's attention. Once the intruder has followed the plover away from the nest—often hundreds of meters—the plover takes off and returns to the nest and its young, leaving the potential predator far away. The case of the plover, like that of the honey guide, involves luring behavior; but unlike the the honey guide the plover appears to be engaging in deliberate deception. From the standpoint of human experience, deception is a sophisticated form of conduct that requires not only the ability to have beliefs and desires but also the ability to distinguish between truth and falsity and the capacity to induce another agent to believe something that is false—in other words, to conceal from another agent one's true intentions. The ability to deceive thus seems to require elaborate cognitive powers, including the ability to contemplate and manipulate the beliefs of another agent. I must be able to think of the other agent as an agent much like myself, albeit one whose interests are at odds with my own. If the piping plover is consciously endeavoring to deceive predators, does the plover possess all this cognitive equipment? The ethologist Carolyn Ristau observes that "for a plover to be intentional it must be shown to have mind states. An intentional creature will have beliefs and knowledge, and it will act in accordance with them. Its behavior, such as a broken-wing display, will not simply appear, like a reflex or a fixed action pattern, only in the presence of very specific stimuli. An intentionalist plover would be aware of its goal, and alters its behavior in ways appropriate to achieve its goal."[3] Ristau notes that plovers are able to distinguish between safe versus dangerous intruders, are sensitive to different aspects of the environment (including the attention paid by intruders to the nest area), and modify their behavior in accordance with changes in the behavior of the intruder pursuing them. This leads Ristau tentatively to propose that plovers are intentional creatures.

Of all the features of animal behavior, the one that lends the greatest support to the attribution of consciousness and intentional action is "the plasticity of . . . behavior in response to different environmental conditions."[4] If an organism reacts to stimuli in a strictly rule-governed way allowing for no variation in response, the reaction appears to be involuntary and unconscious and an explanation in terms of instinct may appear perfectly reasonable. If, however, the organism's behavior shows variation and innovation in response to contingencies in the environment, the explanation of the behavior in terms of instinct seems to beg the question; appealing to the vocabulary of mental representation, assessment, and choice appears far more appropriate in such cases. It seems particularly appropriate in cases of deception. How, otherwise, would we explain the behavior of my friend's border collie, Chelsea, who often lures the other dogs in the house away from the favored spot on the bed by barking and running toward the back door, behaving in the same manner as when she hears a potential intruder outside? When the other dogs run to the back door, my friend opens the door and all the dogs except Chelsea run outside to check for an intruder, at which point Chelsea bolts back to the bedroom and takes up the favored spot on the bed. It is not absolutely essential to employ the vocabulary of intention in explaining such behavior; in some cases it is possible to offer an explanation in terms of conditioning or instinct. As the behavior becomes more sophisticated or innovative, however, nonintentional explanations become increasingly implausible.

To wonder what the mental lives of animals are really like is to ask a question to which science can never offer a definitive answer. This is so because "inner" mental life can never be a direct object of scientific investigation. At best we can draw inferences about subjective experience on the basis of observed behavior and physiological processes. Until fairly recently the study of animal behavior was dominated by a behavioral method that eschewed appeals to subjective experience and focused exclusively on outward, observable behavior. This was entirely in keeping with respect for the limits of science, which must confine itself to matters of logical demonstration and empirical observation. As the recent study of animal behavior has become increasingly congenial to the study of animal cognition, it has begun to erode the boundary between science and speculation by making descriptions of subjective mental states a key goal of its investigations.[5]

The move from behavioral to cognitive ethology signals an increased willingness to acknowledge that animals have rich inner lives. The problem for cognitive ethology is twofold: How can we endeavor to characterize the mental lives of animals, and what is the mental life of a given animal like? At this point in the study of animal behavior, much of the problem is methodological: What sorts of vocabulary are appropriate in describing the subjective awareness of animals—for example, is it legitimate to speak of "animal minds"— and what constitutes a legitimate inference about subjective awareness given certain observed behaviors? Given that very few if any animals can use language to inform us about their inner states, how are we to make determinations about what it is like to be a certain animal? To what extent is our own experience a useful guide in characterizing the mental lives of animals?

In the contemporary debates about animal cognition, advocates of one extreme and increasingly unpopular viewpoint maintain that the subjective experiences of animals, if indeed there are any, are fundamentally more primitive than those of human beings. Exponents of this view maintain that attributions of such cognitive capacities as beliefs and intentions to animals are at best a heuristic device, that is, that such attributions facilitate the prediction and control of animal behavior, quite apart from the question whether such attributions truly reflect the nature of animal cognition. Extreme exponents of this approach suggest that animal "cognition" is nothing more than computerlike information processing involving no subjective awareness whatsoever.[6] Others hold the view that animals do have mental states, but that these states fall far short of human rationality—that animals are locked in the immediacy of perception and lack the capacity for beliefs, desires, concepts, reflection, deliberation, and free choice. On this view, which has a long tradition in the history of Western philosophy, perceptions, desires, and inclinations in animals function as strict causes.[7] Animals are unable to step back from these experiences and evaluate them. For example, when a sheep sees a wolf, the sheer perception of the wolf causes the sheep to run away. Unable to contemplate the wolf as a wolf and to consider whether running away is the best course of action, the sheep simply automatically runs away. The sheep's "belief" that the wolf poses a threat and its "desire" to run away are both understood functionally: we see the sheep run away, so we describe the sheep as having "wanted" to run away. Since the sheep has no sense of itself as a self among other selves, it cannot relate to the wolf—or to the idea of a threat, or that of running away—as such. To say that the sheep "wants" or "chooses" to run away from the wolf is simply to project onto the sheep's behavior the sort of teleological reasoning that we would employ in responding to the threat the wolf would pose to us.

Such an account of the sheep's behavior bears the traces of the behavioristic thinking that has long dominated Western thought concerning the cognitive capacities of animals. The shift from behavioral to cognitive ethology has been inspired, in large part, by the recognition that a key assumption of the Western philosophical tradition is highly questionable, namely, that because animals lack the capacity for language, they lack all related cognitive capacities, such as the capacity to form beliefs, desires, intentions, and concepts. Recent studies of apes have shown that chimpanzees, bonobos, and gorillas possess sophisticated cognitive and communicative capacities; recent ethological investigations have also found communicative abilities in vervets, dolphins, and some other animals. Darwin's suggestion that the differences between human beings and animals are merely matters of degree rather than kind did much to prepare the way for these ethological insights. It has become increasingly commonplace for ethologists and philosophers to appeal to evolutionary continuity and physiological similarity as grounds for concluding that animals have mental lives that resemble our own in important respects.[8]

The shift to cognitive ethology goes far beyond the acknowledgment that at least some animals seem to possess the capacity for linguistic communication. The old prejudice that only linguistic beings can possess such states as beliefs and desires has been increasingly abandoned in favor of the view that animals need not be linguistic, at least not in the specifically human sense, in order to be capable of mental states such as belief. As ethologists chip away at what was once taken to be an insuperable boundary between humans and nonhuman animals, it has become increasingly difficult to deny the existence of sophisticated communicative capacity in at least some animals.

Much recent work has focused on the communicative and cognitive abilities of animals that lie very close to the human-animal boundary. Here and in the following two chapters I will focus on the more difficult question of the mental lives of animals that do *not* lie near the putative boundary between human and nonhuman. What sorts of mental capacities are characteristic of, say, a dog, a cat, a lizard, or a sparrow? Naturally the capacities will not be identical in all these animals, but some generalizations can be made when it comes to such questions as whether the honey guide "believes" that the human helpers will follow it, or whether Chelsea "intends" that the other dogs be fooled by her false-alarm call at the back door. Do animals experience and evaluate the world in terms of beliefs, desires, and intentions? Given that human beings possess such cognitive capacities, should we conclude, by analogy, that animals possess them too?

Cognitive ethologists acknowledge that analogy is the only methodological tool available when it comes to drawing inferences about the mental lives of animals. Douglas Candland notes that in the endeavor to describe the mental processes of a dog such as Chelsea, "the mind of my dog is inextricably bound to my mind, for I have no way to create its mind other than by applying the categories of my own." It thus seems unavoidable that we must at least begin by attributing to Chelsea certain beliefs and intentions. But, given the unavoidable necessity of thinking about animal consciousness in terms of our own, Candland stresses that "we must deny the arrogance of thinking that we are objective and devote our attention to examining our own categories and thereby the power and weakness of our human natures."[9] Even if we start by attributing such categories as belief, desire, and intention to animals, we must then reflect on our own mental lives and ask whether and to what extent our own actions are best accounted for through appeals to conscious states such as belief. Are my actions always—or even typically—motivated by explicit beliefs, desires, and intentions? If I hear a noise on my front porch that I am accustomed to associating with the arrival of the morning paper, I might form an explicit belief that the morning paper has arrived. But there are many situations—the arrival of the morning paper may be one—in which it may not seem plausible to account for my actions on the basis of explicit states such as belief. For example, when I go out for a walk it does not seem plausible to attribute to me the belief that the sidewalk will bear my weight or the desire to place one foot in front of the other. By the same token, when I am working in the garden on a hot day and stop to take a drink from the hose, it need not occur to me consciously that I want to take a drink.

Philosophers, particularly those in the phenomenological tradition, have struggled to characterize these sorts of experiences in human beings. It does not seem accurate to say that such experiences are "unconscious" in the strict psychoanalytical sense because that would suggest that my actions are caused by motivations that remain unconscious in virtue of being threatening or otherwise unacceptable to me. It seems more apposite to describe these sorts of situations as ones in which I am so fully absorbed in the task at hand that I am not thinking—nor do I need to think—consciously and explicitly about what I am doing. Martin Heidegger describes this form of conduct in terms of engaged practice. Here we relate to things transparently, without explicit reflective awareness in terms of which we sometimes relate to motivations, projects, and things in our world.[10] In our everyday dealings we do not proceed on the basis of explicit beliefs, desires, concepts, and intentions, yet we are always able to step back from our immersion in a task and reflectively characterize it in terms of such explicit intentional states as belief and desire. On Heidegger's view, unless a problem or obstacle presents itself that hinders the progress of a given project (e.g., a broken or missing tool), there is generally no occasion for moving from the mode of engaged practice to the level of detached, reflective awareness. Moreover, Heidegger criticizes the cognitivist orientation of

Cartesian-Kantian philosophy for treating detached states of aware-ness, such as belief and desire, as if they were typical of human men-tal life. He argues that this orientation has given rise to a distorted picture of the subjective experiences of humans, and that the task of phenomenology is to provide a richer and more accurate conception of human experience.

The phenomenological attempt to characterize a mode of en-gaged practice that underlies explicit, formally structured mental states has important implications for reflections on the mental lives of animals. It opens up the possibility that animals relate to the world not by means of formal states, such as belief and desire, but in terms of a kind of engaged practice of their own. On this view, a key difference between human beings and animals is that whereas hu-man beings can always shift from engaged practice to such formally structured mental states as beliefs and desires—particularly when we seek to explain our actions to ourselves or others—animals (at least those *not* close to the human-animal boundary) can never break out of the mode of engaged practice.

Gadamer follows his teacher Heidegger in characterizing the dif-ference between humans and animals in the following way:

> In contrast with all other living beings, the human understand-ing of world [Welt] is characterized by *freedom from the environment* [*Umweltfreiheit*]. . . . Animals can leave their environment and wander the entire earth, but in doing so they cannot break free of their confinement in the environment. For humans, on the other hand, going beyond the environment is a going-beyond toward the world and signifies not an abandonment of the envi-ronment but rather a different relationship to it, a free, dis-tanced relation that is always realized linguistically.[11]

On Heidegger's view, to say that animals are incapable of language is not simply to claim that they lack the capacity for speech and hu-man grammar but that animals are incapable of engaging in acts of interpretation, which, among other things, requires the ability to re-late to units of meaning *as* units of meaning. Human freedom consists in the capacity to question and evaluate the events and possibilities that confront us in our environment, and this, in turn, enables us to construct a meaningful world through acts of interpretation. It also enables us to reflect on objects, meanings, mental states, and the like "as such"—which is to say that we can relate to different courses of action *as* different courses of action, and to ourselves as individual selves among other selves. The "detachment" of which Gadamer speaks in characterizing human freedom is not the detached contemplation of such cognitive states as belief and desire. Rather, it refers to the fact that we can, already in engaged practice, distinguish different possibilities or meanings from each other and entertain them *as* meanings or possibilities. On the basis of this ability, which Heidegger describes as the "hermeneutical 'as' of interpretation," we are able to step back even further to a more detached and formal specification of our relationship to ourselves and things in our environment by employing the "apophantic 'as'" of predication.[12] Central to Heidegger's conception of human experience is the conviction that we do not typically relate to the world in terms of such formal states as belief and desire but can do so when we step out of engaged practice and reflect on the situation. For Heidegger a key mistake of cognitivist theories of mind is that they characterize the immediacy of engaged experience as if it took the same form as the detached reflection that seeks to characterize engaged practice.

On Heidegger's view, the possession of the "as such" in both the hermeneutical and apophantic senses is denied to animals, which are confined within the narrow boundaries of the immediate pursuit of food and shelter, the imperative to procreate, and the need to defend themselves against predators.[13] Heidegger's distinction between humans and animals in terms of the "as" reflects the dual influence of Stoic and Kantian thought, according to which even at the level of immediate perceptual awareness there is a difference between human and animal experience. On this view, human experience is not simply animal perception "plus" formal cognitive or linguistic abilities; rather, the possession of these abilities fundamentally informs the nature of human perception. In adopting this view, Heidegger, like Kant and the Stoics before him, takes a stand on the question of the relationship between the experience of humans and that of animals, namely, that there is a fundamental difference between the subjective awareness of human beings and that—assuming there is any—of animals. Contemporary thinkers such as John McDowell go so far as to deny animals any subjectivity whatsoever, granting them only a comparatively dim "proto-subjective perceptual sensitivity to features of the environment" such as an immediate sensitivity to pain or fear.[14] For McDowell animals possess no understanding because they are incapable of employing concepts to organize their experience. For Heidegger animals lack the "as" on the basis of which humans are able to have a free, meaningful encounter with the world even prior to conceptual abstraction and predicative description of things and events.

## INTENTIONALITY AND CONCEPTS

These reflections return us to the question of the nature of animal awareness and, in particular, to the question whether animals are capable of experiencing the world in anything like the way in which human beings experience it. The debate between Kantian thinkers such as McDowell and phenomenological thinkers such as Heidegger concerning human experience centers on the question whether our experience is fundamentally informed by concepts and structured in terms of such states as belief and desire or whether, at a more fundamental level, our experience is preconceptual and pre-predicative. As regards animals, the additional question is whether they are capable of relating to the world in either of these ways, or whether the nature of their subjective experience is such that they are fundamentally unable to relate to the world freely. To relate to the world freely is to be able to take a stand on it that goes beyond considerations of material need, as humans do when engaging in such activities as art, literature, and philosophy. Heidegger and McDowell agree that animals are strictly confined within their environments in the sense that they are incapable of relating to anything other than the demands of material existence.

But even if this is true, it may still be the case that there is something that it is like to be an animal of a given kind. This is the point that Thomas Nagel makes in "What Is It Like to Be a Bat?" Nagel takes it as a given that animals such as bats have a subjective encounter with the world, even though that encounter is almost certainly very unlike our own due to differences in perceptual apparatus. To say that an animal "has conscious experience *at all* means, basically, that there is something it is like to *be* that organism. . . . We believe that these experiences also have in each case a specific subjective character, which it is beyond our ability to conceive."[15] To say that an animal possesses conscious awareness is to say that it has a point of view, quite apart from the question whether it can employ concepts or have beliefs and desires. Many cognitive ethologists are quick to reject Nagel's challenge to the possibility of conceiving of the nature of animal awareness because it threatens to undermine the prospect of developing scientifically rigorous theories of animal awareness.[16] This simply reminds us that science cannot provide a definitive account of the nature of animal experience, any more than it can hope to provide a definitive account of the human condition. Nagel's discussion also sheds light on the limits of analogy in the endeavor to understand animal consciousness. It may prove to be a mistake to characterize animal minds in terms of beliefs, desires, and conceptual ability, just as it may prove erroneous to consider these capacities to be central and typical in human experience.

Since most of the investigative work on animal awareness that has been done in philosophy and ethology has focused on these capacities, a consideration of these investigations is essential to understanding the central disagreements in the contemporary debates concerning animal awareness. It is also important to focus on these capacities because they lie at the core of our conception of agency. To be an agent in a legal, social, or moral sense is to be capable of assessing one's interests, the consequences of one's actions, and one's relationship to other individuals. It is to be able to take up points of view other than one's own, and to assess the impact that one's choices will have on others as well as on oneself. To be an agent is to be autonomous, that is, capable of governing oneself by employing one's reason. Even if we make many of our choices in a pre-reflective manner, without explicitly entertaining reasons, we are nonetheless capable of giving a rational account of our actions. Doing so enables us not only to explain our motivations to others but, just as important, to hold our own motivations up to rational scrutiny and hence alter our conduct where reason demands it. We consider healthy adults to be autonomous and hence responsible for their actions. By the same token, we accord them certain rights in virtue of their autonomy, in particular the right to engage in acts of self-determination, provided that these acts do not interfere with the corresponding rights of others. To take the question of animal rights seriously, we must examine the question of agency in animals. Even if there are reasons not to impose obligations of responsibility on animals, there may well be reasons to accord them rights, as we do in the cases of children and so-called marginal human beings (e.g., the comatose or severely mentally impaired).

Contemporary debates about the mental capacities of animals center on two interrelated questions, namely, whether animals are capable of intentional states and whether animals are capable of conceptual abstraction. Intentional states are mental states with propositional content, such as beliefs, desires, hopes, and fears. Many philosophers argue that human action proceeds on the basis of intentional states. On this view, when I perform a given action I do so because I have particular beliefs and desires. When I believe something, I always believe that P, where P is some content with predicative form; for example, I believe that the Giants are the best team in major league baseball this season, or I believe that my car is in the garage. When I want something, I always want that P; for example, the intentional structure of "I want to go to the store" is "I want that I go to the store." To be capable of intentionality in this sense, a being must be capable of engaging in acts of predication and must be able to contemplate mental representations with propositional content (which content is predicative by definition). Thus, if animals are capable of intentionality, they must be capable of forming and contemplating representations with propositional content. An intentional creature will possess beliefs and knowledge; in pursuing its goals, it will be able to alter its behavior in accordance with its beliefs and knowledge.

To attribute intentionality to a being is thus to say a great deal about the nature of its experience. Intentional beings have goals, beliefs, and an ability to monitor and correct their own behavior in accordance with new information. Moreover, if a being's experiences are intentional, a strong case can be made that even that being's perceptual experiences have propositional content. On this view, there is a basic distinction between sensation and perceptual experience; the latter involves concepts that permit me to structure or organize my sensations into a coherent, meaningful experience. For example, John Searle argues that "visual experiences have propositional Intentional contents,"such that when I see a yellow car, I see a yellow car and not an array of bits of color that I can subsequently identify as a car. "The content of the visual experience is equivalent to a whole proposition," in this case (that) there is a car in front of me.[17]

McDowell presents a comparable analysis of the intentionality of perceptual experience. He relies on Kant's statement in the *Critique of Pure Reason* that "thoughts without content are empty, intuitions without concepts are blind."[18] Kant argues that the only way to have a coherent experience of the world is to subject the raw data of sensation to the form imposed by our mind's conceptual apparatus. A concept is "something universal that serves as a rule" in the sense that it provides us with a specific way of organizing our sensations.[19] The system of concepts in our understanding enables us to synthesize our experience into a totality that can be grasped as a totality. Thus, concepts enable our understanding to synthesize what Kant calls a "manifold" of sense-data (e.g., bits of visual data) into a unified experience of an object (a yellow car) that is located in a coherent causal nexus with other objects and events.

It is on the basis of this Kantian reasoning that McDowell argues that "the content of perceptual experience is conceptual."[20] Concepts are tools of the understanding, which Kant also calls spontaneity. On McDowell's view, "mere animals do not come within the scope of the Kantian thesis." If "intuitions without concepts are blind," then animals, which fundamentally lack concepts, must in an essential sense be "blind": "In the absence of spontaneity, no self can be in view, and by the same token, the world cannot be in view either." Animals obviously have perceptions, but they do not have perceptual *experience*; they are incapable of "exercising spontaneity [and] deciding what to think and do."[21] McDowell follows Kant in supposing that the ultimate capacity for unifying our experience is apperception, which brings a self into view by framing each individual experience as *my* experience, that is, as the experience of this one selfsame agent of experience in contrast with other agents of experience. Since animals lack the faculty of spontaneity, of which apperception is the highest moment, they lack the stable sense of self that lies at the core of any coherent, conceptualized experience of the world. On McDowell's view, by attributing some kind of subjective awareness to animals, Nagel "treat[s] what is only a proto-subjectivity as if it were a full-fledged subjectivity."[22]

Implicit in Kant's discussion of the understanding is the idea that intentional states involve concepts. To have a belief that P is to be committed to the truth of a particular propositional content; it is to be convinced that a particular property is truly predicable of a particular subject.[23] "Rationality requirements on what attitudes should be taken in given circumstances are requirements that operate at the level of concepts. . . . One cannot formulate such requirements without the notion of a concept."[24] When I assert that the car is yellow, I am giving linguistic expression to my conviction (i.e., my "attitude") about a thought that involves the concepts of "car" and "yellow," specifically the thought that yellow is predicable of this car. In this sense, "concepts are constituents of so-called intentional states (beliefs, desires, etc.): for instance, the thought that there is a squirrel in the tree is constituted by a structured arrangement of the concepts of squirrel, tree, and in-ness."[25]

On this view, even to be able to identify the subject of this propositional content *as* a car I must have a concept of car. A concept is mental content that is separate from the particulars to which it pertains. "To have a concept of X where the specification of X is not exhausted by a perceptual characterization, it is not enough just to have the ability to discriminate $X$'s from non-$X$'s. One must have a representation of $X$ that abstracts away from the perceptual features that enable one to identify $X$'s."[26] Simply to distinguish, say, blue from red does not require having a concept. To form a concept, one must abstract away from the properties that distinguish different members of a certain class and produce a mental representation of what the members of the class have in common. [27] One can imagine a dog being able to discriminate between bones and non-bones, or between tasty and non-tasty food, without having the concept of bone, food, or tasty. To see a squirrel in a tree, a dog does not need any concepts. Gottlob Frege suggests that a dog can stare at an individual object, such as the moon, without having the concept of 'one'.[28] But to have the thought or belief that the moon is one isolated entity, or that a squirrel is in the tree, the dog would need a variety of concepts.[29] To have any kind of belief about a squirrel, at the very least the dog would need a mental representation of squirrel-ness that transcends all the particular experiences of squirrels that the dog has had, and on the basis of which the dog would be able to predicate certain properties of this particular squirrel (such as that it is in this tree). Moreover, this concept would derive some of its meaning from the ways in which it is related to other concepts that the dog possesses.

Thus, the question whether animals are capable of intentionality devolves in important part on the question whether they are capable of conceptual abstraction. In examining philosophers' views on these two interrelated questions, we need to bear in mind Searle's distinction between cases of "*intrinsic intentionality*, which are cases of actual mental states, and . . . *observer-relative ascriptions of intentionality*, which are ways that people have of speaking about entities figuring in our activities but lacking intrinsic intentionality." Intentionality is legitimately attributable only to beings with semantically significant inner states. Yet in everyday discourse we often attribute beliefs and desires to all sorts of non-intentional beings such as computers and car engines (e.g., "the computer thinks I haven't entered my pin number" or "the car doesn't want to start"). "These are ascriptions of intentionality made to entities that lack any mental states, but in which the ascription is a manner of speaking about the intentionality of the observers."[30] We make such ascriptions because "it is very difficult for human beings to accept non-animistic, non-intentionalistic forms of explanation. . . . The idea that there are mechanical explanations that cite no intentionality is a very hard idea to grasp."[31]

Daniel Dennett proposes that attributions of intentionality to entities such as thermostats are perfectly acceptable because they facilitate explanation.[32] But Dennett is not concerned with understanding the inner mental lives of animals, humans, or anything else; he is simply interested in the prediction and explanation of the behavior of various systems. In pursuing this end, he is content to attribute to intentional states the "putative" status of "idealized fictions in an action-predicting, action-explaining calculus."[33] On Dennett's view, the idea of irreducible mental content or what Searle calls "intrinsic intentionality" is simply a version of the ghost in the machine.

To take Dennett's position is to assume too hastily that inner mental states are nothing more than "idealized fictions" and to place too much confidence in the power of functional explanations to capture the essence of experience. One need only reflect on one's own experience, on one's encounters with other humans, and on one's observations of and encounters with animals to recognize both the legitimacy and the importance of Searle's distinction. There does indeed appear to be something it is like to be an animal. To what extent can we hope to characterize the "aboutness" of animal experience, and what are the best terms to use in describing it?

## ARGUMENTS AGAINST INTENTIONALITY AND CONCEPTS IN ANIMALS

In recent years a number of philosophers have roundly rejected the idea that animals are capable of intentionality. These thinkers are reaffirming a prejudice that extends far back into the history of Western philosophy. It is evident particularly in Aristotle, the Stoics, the medieval Christian philosophers, and Descartes, all of whom maintained that animals are incapable of language and thought. Descartes's views have had the greatest impact on contemporary thinkers. Descartes argues that animals are biological machines with absolutely no inner mental states whatsoever. He bases his view on the dual assumption that animals cannot use language in meaningful and innovative ways and that animals do not show any flexibility in their behavior but instead behave like clocks.[34] We now know that both of these assumptions are false. It is tempting to suppose that if Descartes were alive today, he would not have been able to advance the view of animals that he articulated almost four hundred years ago.

Even though few if any contemporary philosophers or ethologists maintain that animals are simply biological machines, a number of these thinkers still adhere to the Cartesian view that animals are incapable of rationality. Bernard Williams argues that we can ascribe beliefs "to non-language-using animals . . . in the course of explaining a great deal of [their] behavior," but that animals cannot really have beliefs because they lack the requisite concepts. At best, animals have beliefs "in a somewhat impoverished sense"; at worst, we are simply projecting "an enormous amount of anthropomorphic apparatus" in attributing concepts and beliefs to animals.[35] On Williams's view, animals completely lack what Searle calls intrinsic intentionality; our attribution of concepts and beliefs to the animal simply reflects our own intentionality and our own proclivities in explaining animal behavior. In this respect Williams's view is much like that of Dennett, who suggests that in the interest of explaining animal behavior we tend to attribute cognitive apparatus to animals that they simply do not seem to possess. In the case of the bird exhibiting the broken-wing display, Dennett states that "it is unlikely in the extreme that any feathered 'deceiver' is an intentional system" with sufficient intelligence to have expectations and beliefs, at least those regarding the mental states of other animals. "We start, sometimes, with the hypothesis that we can assign a certain rationale to (the 'mind' of) some individual creature, and then we learn better; the creature is too stupid to harbor it. We do not necessarily discard the rationale; if it is no coincidence that the 'smart' behavior occurred, we pass the rationale from the individual to the evolving genotype."[36] In other words, if the deceptive behavior appears to be more than accidental, we attribute the intentionality not to the individual bird but to its genetic constitution—which is essentially to call the behavior instinctive.

There are cases of animal behavior for which this kind of explanation seems entirely appropriate, in particular those in which the behavior is rigid and does not change in response to conflicting information. Ants have a mechanistic response to oleic acid: when they smell it on another ant, they take that ant to be dead regardless of whether there is conflicting evidence, such as movement in the supposedly dead ant. "Ants will remove from the nest anything that has oleic acid painted on it, including other live ants. Although the ants get other information that would tend to count against the assessment that the acid-treated conspecific is dead (they are, for instance, capable of detecting its motion), they are incapable of using this information to modify their removal response."[37] Similarly, crabs and sand wasps exhibit certain rigidly fixed forms of behavior. Serotonin plays a significant role in the aggressiveness of crabs; even those crabs that would normally back down from a fight with a superior adversary will become highly combative when researchers inject serotonin into their hemolymph.[38] A sand wasp will dig a hole in the ground in which to lay its eggs. Then it will paralyze a grasshopper or caterpillar and place it in the hole so that the hatched larvae can feed off it. When the wasp brings a paralyzed insect to the hole, the wasp leaves the insect at the entrance and inspects the hole for unwanted parasites. Researchers have found that if they move the paralyzed insect even a few centimeters while the wasp is inspecting the hole, instead of bringing the insect into the hole the wasp will again place it at the entrance and will inspect the hole all over again. The wasp can be induced to repeat this behavior dozens of times in succession.[39]

In such situations, where there is no adaptation or learning, it seems inappropriate to attribute intentionality to animals—or to humans, for that matter. Descartes took this kind of situation to be typical of animal behavior rather than recognizing that it is at most a subset of animal behavior. In cases in which animals appear to be behaving in more than merely automatic or instinctive fashion, the question remains whether it is appropriate to attribute intentionality to them. Donald Davidson has argued at length that attributions of intentionality to animals "smack of anthropomorphism."[40] On Davidson's view, thought and linguistic ability are inextricably bound up with one another. In order to have thoughts and form linguistic utterances, one must be a member of a community of interpreters: "A creature cannot have thoughts unless it is an interpreter of the speech of another."[41] To have thoughts in this sense is to have *propositional* beliefs, desires, and intentions.

Davidson does not consider animals to be "blind." He recognizes that animals and small children participate in "a pre-linguistic, pre-cognitive situation" that is "a necessary condition for thought and language, a condition that can exist independent of thought, and can therefore precede it." This pre-cognitive situation "is one that involves two or more creatures simultaneously in interaction with each other and with the world they share; it is what I call *triangulation*. . . . Each creature learns to correlate the reactions of the other with changes or objects in the world in which it also reacts." Davidson suggests that pre-cognitive triangulation occurs when, for example, fish swim in schools or the honey guide lures humans to a bee hive. In the latter case "it is hard—nearly impossible—to tell this story without attributing thoughts to the bird, just as we correctly do to the human hunters. But on reflection we realize that the behavior of the bird, complex and purposeful as it is, cannot be due to propositional beliefs, desires, or intentions, nor does its instructive flight constitute a language."[42]

Davidson recognizes that animals can relate to one another and to their environments in ways that promote their welfare; in a pre-cognitive sense, they can triangulate. Triangulation is "necessary to thought." Yet "it is not sufficient, as shown by the fact that it can exist in animals we do not credit with judgment."[43] The honey guide can lead humans to a beehive, but it cannot make judgments about anything. Judgments, like thoughts, have propositional form:

we predicate a property of a situation or an object. But in order to form judgments we must communicate propositional contents to other agents. Like Rousseau and Wittgenstein before him, Davidson characterizes language as a fundamentally social phenomenon. Rather than being a divine endowment that any isolated agent can possess without contact with other agents, as Descartes and Süßmilch believed, language arises through human interaction in the endeavor to forge and communicate meaning. "Unless the base line of the triangle, the line between the two agents, is strengthened to the point where it can implement the communication of propositional contents, there is no way the agents can make use of the triangular situation to form judgments about the world. Only when language is in place can creatures appreciate the concept of objective truth."[44] Thus, language is the condition for the possibility of knowing that our beliefs and judgments can be true or false, that is, that we may be mistaken in our beliefs and judgments. To the extent that animals lack language, they lack a concept of objective truth and hence cannot properly be said to be able to revise their beliefs in accordance with the receipt of new or conflicting information.

Because they lack language, animals lack the capacity to form beliefs altogether. "One cannot believe something, or doubt it, without knowing that what one believes or doubts may be either true or false, and in particular, that one may be wrong."[45] The formation of beliefs depends on a conception of objectivity, which itself depends on language. Thus, the formation of beliefs, like language, is a social phenomenon. "The intelligibility of [true versus false beliefs] must depend on a background of largely unmentioned and unquestioned true beliefs" that are shared by a community of linguistic interpreters.[46] Since "belief is central to all kinds of thought," and since "a creature cannot have thoughts unless it is an interpreter of the speech of another," animals can be credited neither with beliefs nor with any kind of thought, which Davidson conceives as strictly propositional.[47]

Against the critic who suggests that we need not attribute such elaborate cognitive capacities in animals in order to consider them capable of thought, Davidson argues that propositional attitudes have an all-or-nothing character. "One belief demands many beliefs, and beliefs demand other basic attitudes such as intentions, desires and, if I am right, the gift of tongues. This does not mean that there are not borderline cases. Nevertheless, the intrinsically holistic character of the propositional attitudes makes the distinction between having any and having none dramatic."[48] Davidson is committed to a holism of belief and concepts according to which a dog could believe that a cat went up a particular oak tree only if the dog's belief were part of a larger web of beliefs. "But how about the dog's supposed belief that the cat went up that oak tree? That oak tree, as it happens, is the oldest tree in sight. Does the dog think that the cat went up the oldest tree in sight? Or that the cat went up the same tree it went up the last time the dog chased it? It is hard to make sense of the questions. But then it does not seem possible to distinguish between quite different things the dog might be said to believe." Creatures such as dogs lack the "very complex pattern of behavior [that] must be observed to justify the attribution of a single thought."[49]

Thus, creatures such as dogs are "dumb" animals in the sense that they are "incapable of interpreting or engaging in linguistic communication."[50] Many animals exhibit complex behavior, but an animal's ability to discriminate between different stimuli or "to change its behavior in ways that preserve its life or increase its food intake" does not show "that the creature commands the subjective-objective contrast, as required by belief."[51] But, given that animals can triangulate, they must be something more than mere organic machines. Davidson acknowledges this when he states that "on the issue of how we should treat dumb creatures, I see no reason to be less kind to those without thoughts or language than to those with; on the contrary."[52] Davidson characterizes the problem as one of finding a way to describe behavior that exceeds sheer mechanism but falls short of propositional thought: "We have many vocabularies for describing nature when we regard it as mindless, and we have a mentalistic vocabulary for describing thought and intentional action; what we lack is a way of describing what is in between. This is particularly evident when we speak of the 'intentions' and 'desires' of simple animals; we have no better way to explain what they do."[53]

Davidson frames the problem as one of situating animal behavior squarely between mechanism and thought. Others are willing to make room for forms of thought that fall short of the full apparatus of intentionality. Achim Stephan raises the question "whether there are *other* plausible categories of the 'intentional' that can be located between the *strong* possession of beliefs and concepts on the one hand and a mere capacity to make discriminations on the other, and which thus leave room for rationality in creatures 'lacking language'."[54] Such categories of the (quasi-) intentional would explain the abilities of animals to relate to their environments, without attributing such linguistically based mental phenomena as beliefs and desires to animals.

Norman Malcolm attempts to explore this possibility by making a distinction between thinking that P and having the thought that P; thus the dog can think that the cat went up the tree, but it cannot have the thought that the cat went up the tree. To think that P in this sense is, on Malcolm's view, much like the "thinking" at work when "a friend of mine and I are engrossed in an exciting conversation. We are about to drive off in his car. While holding up his end of the conversation he fumbles in his pocket for the car keys. I, knowing that they are in the glove compartment, say to myself, 'He thinks the keys are in his pocket'. I do not imply that he said to himself, or thought to himself, 'The keys are in my pocket'."[55] Malcolm does not explain why we should assume that any kind of thought is at work in such a situation. He also does not recognize the possibility that I am simply making an observer-relative ascription of intentionality to my friend. Malcolm proposes that not all thought takes propositional form; the kind of thought taking place in the example with the car keys is "nonpropositional." Animals are capable of "a panoply of forms of feeling, of perception, of realization, of recognition, that are, more often than not, nonpropositional in the human case. Their nonpropositional character does not mark them as something less than real forms of consciousness."[56]

The core of Malcolm's view about animals is that they possess consciousness even though they are not linguistic beings. They can be aware that certain things are the case even though they are not capable of forming propositional thoughts about things. This suggests that animals are neither rational nor linguistic, inasmuch as they cannot contemplate individual propositional contents and assess their truth-values. What Malcolm never explains is how a dog can think that the cat is up the tree, which is essentially to believe that the cat is up the tree, without being capable of relating to the propositional content of a thought. In other words, how can a being think that P without at least being capable of having the thought that P? My friend may not explicitly entertain the thought that the car keys are in his pocket when he goes fumbling for them. The only reason I attribute this thought to him is that I know he is capable of entertaining the relevant propositional content. For Malcolm "having the thought that P" simply means to frame what I am thinking in language; he treats "thinking that P" as having-the-thought-that-P-minus-language. In doing so, he fails to recognize McDowell's Kantian insight into the fundamental difference between perception in rational and nonrational beings.

Michael Dummett makes a similar attempt to capture the precognitive nature of animal experience by appealing to the notion of protothought. Protothoughts are sublinguistic mental states that enable a being to make distinctions about objects and events in its environment. Human beings sometimes have protothoughts, and animals always have them. For example, "a car driver or a canoeist may have rapidly to estimate the speed and direction of oncoming cars or boats and their probable trajectory," and a dog can "distinguish between being attacked by one hostile dog and by several."[57] But in neither case is linguistically structured (by which Dummett seems to mean: propositionally structured) thought involved. Protothought differs from "full-fledged thought . . . by its incapacity for detachment from present activity and circumstances." Our thoughts can float free, but protothought "can occur only as integrated with current activity."[58]

Like Malcolm, Dummett fails to make a rigorous distinction between intentionality and pre-linguistic thought. In denying "full-fledged thought" to animals, he implicitly denies animals the ability to form intentional states and the related ability to assess the truth and falsity of beliefs. At the same time, he maintains that protothoughts "are intrinsically connected with the possibility of their being mistaken; *judgement*, in a non-technical sense, is just what the driver and the canoeist need to exercise."[59] Just what judgment "in a non-technical sense" would be Dummett does not say. Nor does he say how such a "non-technical" capacity to make judgments is possible without concepts, which he acknowledges animals do not possess. An animal "does not have any concepts, properly so-called, at all. It does not have any concepts, because it cannot perform the operations upon concepts that a language-user can perform." Thus, a cat can distinguish a long-haired dog from a short-haired one, but it cannot "reflect that some dogs are hairier than others." What facilitates the making of such distinctions is the cat's possession of "proto-concepts,"which make possible "the recognition of something as a dog . . . in the same way as [the cat] can have the recognition of something as rigid or flexible."[60] But to recognize something *as* something—say, a dog as a dog—is to be in possession of mental capacities that transcend the immediacy of the present moment. It is to possess and be able to employ units of meaning that one has abstracted from particular circumstances. And yet this is precisely what Dummett denies is possible in animals.

The attempts of thinkers such as Malcolm and Dummett to attribute some form of subjectivity to animals are laudable inasmuch as they seek to overcome the Cartesian prejudice that animals are physical systems with no inner life. We now know beyond question that animals have complex ways of relating to the world, and it is implausible in the extreme to suppose that these ways of relating lack a core component of subjective awareness. To suggest that most if not all animals lack conscious intelligence is no longer credible. The task is to characterize that intelligence without going to the extreme of attributing to animals more intelligence than they appear to possess. Richard Jeffrey goes to this extreme when he attributes beliefs, desires, and concepts to animals, even though he recognizes that animal subjectivity involves "a dense network [whose] nodes are nonpropositional, and subdoxastic," that is, something less than belief.[61]

McDowell shows us how to avoid this mistake by distinguishing between full-fledged human subjectivity and the mere "proto-subjectivity" of nonlinguistic animals. Subjectivity and protosubjectivity "involve two different modes of orientation to the world, and so two different sorts of content."[62] Only a being possessing language "can emancipate itself into possession of understanding" and "mature into being at home in the space of reasons. . . . The language into which a human being is first initiated stands over against her as a prior embodiment of mindedness, of the possibility of an orientation to the world."[63] Recall McDowell's Kantian viewpoint: To have an orientation to the world is not simply to be able to relate to objects and events; it is to be able to do so in such a manner that we synthesize our different experiences into an overarching unity through the faculty of apperception, which locates an "I" at the center of experience. To be a self in this sense is to recognize that one has a point of view, that this point of view is one among many, and consequently that one can and must reconcile one's beliefs with an objective standard of truth. On McDowell's view, even the distinction between inner and outer worlds is lacking in animals. Nonetheless the protosubjectivity of animals includes such states as pain and fear, although they differ from comparable states in humans in virtue of lacking conceptual, intentional structure. Animals experiencing the world are what Heidegger calls "captivated" (benommen), inasmuch as they cannot break free of the immediacy of present (and perhaps very near-term) stimuli and exigencies.[64]

The advantage of McDowell's distinction between subjectivity and protosubjectivity is that it enables us to avoid attributing to animals capacities that they (or at least all but the most highly intelligent borderline cases) appear to lack, such as a sense of being a self among other selves and a sense of the distant past and future. The possession of intentionality and concepts makes such abstract notions possible. Even though animals relate to their environments in complex ways, they nonetheless appear to lack the capacities for abstraction and predication that lie at the core of full-fledged subjectivity. Hence, even though we are currently at a loss to explain animal behavior in terms that avoid the attribution of concepts and intentionality, the task that lies before us is to do exactly that. To this end, it will be useful to examine some contemporary attempts to attribute linguistic rationality to animals. These attempts show us the types of mistakes that must be avoided in developing a more adequate characterization of animal experience.

# CHAPTER TWO

# Arguments for Rationality in Animals

## WHY ATTRIBUTE RATIONALITY TO ANIMALS?

There is no settled view regarding the precise relationship between intentionality, rationality, and language. To say that animals are "rational" can mean a variety of things. It can mean that animals possess an explicit sense of self and can engage in acts of practical deliberation in an effort to achieve goals they have set for themselves. To attribute rationality to animals in this sense would be to endow them with the ability to engage in acts of abstract reflection, enabling them, for example, to grasp themselves as individual selves among other selves. It might also involve attributing to animals the notion of a goal in general as the background concept in terms of which animals grasp specific goals and distinguish them from other goals. Whether thinking in this sense requires language is a controversial question. It is also unclear whether such intentional states as beliefs and desires require linguistic ability, or even whether such states require the kind of subjective awareness that Nagel attributes to animals.

To say that intentional states are possible in the absence of subjective awareness seems at first blush to be counterintuitive. How could a being have a belief or a desire without being *aware* of having it? How could a being seek to satisfy a desire without being aware of the mental operations it performs in determining the appropriate course of action? One possible answer to these questions, broached in the preceding chapter, is that such a being lacks the "as" or the "as such" that enables linguistic beings to engage in full-fledged practical reason. Perhaps the being—say, a nonhuman animal—does not have a predicatively structured desire but instead has a protodesire, an immediate subjective sense of being drawn to a particular object or action, even though the being does not have a conceptual grasp of objects, actions, or anything else.

> Neither the beaver nor its relatives need a concept of danger—a way of collecting information that regards just danger, *as such*, over time—in order to produce appropriate beaver slaps or respond to them appropriately by diving under. Similarly, an animal's perception of the spatial layout of its immediate environment for purposes of moving about in it, avoiding obstacles, getting through passages, climbing up things or over things and so forth, need not involve any concepts.... There can be mental representation, then, without a grasp of the identity of what is represented, hence without knowing *what* is represented. [1]

Such a picture of mental representation appears to be based on an information-processing model of rationality, according to which that behavior is rational which brings about the appropriate (e.g., adaptive) outcome. James and Carol Gould, prominent apiary ethologists, propose such an explanation for the waggle-dance of the honey bee, arguing that it is entirely possible that the dance language of the bee "requires no conscious grasp of the problem" of directing conspecifics to sources of nectar, etc., inasmuch as "some of the most impressively complex examples of behavior we see are known to be wholly innate."[2]

In what sense is such behavior *rational*? Where do such explanations of behavior leave room for intentional states, such as beliefs, and for capacities, such as self-awareness, which we tend to associate with the notion of rationality? Some philosophers point out that human beings often act on beliefs without entertaining them consciously, as when I brush my teeth in a certain way because my dentist recommended that I do so.[3] Why not suppose that animals have beliefs in the same way? Perhaps animals can be rational even though they lack such capacities as self-awareness or abstract reflection. Perhaps they possess perceptual awareness and the ability to react appropriately to given stimuli, while lacking the higher cognitive functions that would enable them to step back and evaluate the relative merits of different courses of action.

Why should we describe such capacities as rational? Ethologists often describe animal behavior in terms of associations between present stimuli and past experiences rather than in terms of conscious thinking. "On the one hand lie 'rational' explanations of behavior, explanations that advert to norm-governed reasoning involving belief-like representations. On the other side lie non-rational explanations, in terms of 'behaviorist' or (more accurately) associative psychological processes."[4] Explanations of animal behavior in terms of associative mechanisms are "behavioristic" in the sense that they do not acknowledge a dimension of subjective or "inner" awareness but instead appeal exclusively to outward, observable behavior in the language of stimulus and response. On this view, there is no need to appeal to any kind of thinking in order to account for animal behavior. Advocates of such explanations need not explicitly deny that animals possess rationality or subjective states of awareness. They need only maintain that animal behavior can be explained without any recourse to rationality or subjective awareness.

In recent years behaviorism has increasingly fallen out of favor and the discipline of cognitive ethology has begun to gain influence. Cognitive ethology takes as axiomatic the prospect that at least some animals have subjective states of awareness and employ cognitive apparatus similar to those of human beings. Donald Griffin, the ethologist to whom this discipline owes its greatest debt, has argued, on the basis of physiological similarity and evolutionary continuity, that animals can think. For both humans and animals "the most basic and essential aspect of consciousness is thinking about objects and events."[5] Even if linguistic capacity makes human thought more complex than animal thought, it is a mistake to suppose that animals are Cartesian mechanisms with no states of inner awareness. "The customary view of animals as always living in a state comparable to that of human sleepwalkers is a sort of negative dogmatism" inherited from a philosophical tradition determined to proclaim the uniqueness and fundamental superiority of human beings over animals.[6] Following Thomas Natsoulas, Griffin argues that even perceptual consciousness involves "thinking about nonexistent objects or events as well as immediate sensory input. . . . An animal capable of perceptual consciousness must often be aware that a particular companion is eating or fleeing, that is, it must be consciously aware of both the action and of who is performing it." In effect, if an animal has any perceptual awareness, it must possess some degree of reflective consciousness, which means that it "has immediate awareness of [its] own thoughts as distinguished from the objects or activities about which [it] is thinking."[7] Griffin is willing to entertain the possibility that even invertebrates such as bees employ conceptual thought.[8]

Between the two extremes of behaviorism and the attribution of conceptual thought to animals lie a number of more moderate possibilities. Griffin attributes conceptual thought to animals on the grounds that humans and animals share similar neurophysiology, which is the basis of cognition. But one can attribute subjective states of awareness to animals without attributing to them capacities for intentionality and conceptual abstraction. If thinkers such as Griffin have been quick to attribute complex thought to animals, they have done so in reaction to a history of philosophical thinking according to which animals lack the requisite sophisticated cognitive capacities for membership in the moral community. According to this history, all and only linguistic, rational beings are members of the moral sphere; since animals are *aloga*, nonlinguistic and nonrational, they are excluded in principle from the moral community. Thinkers who embrace Griffin's approach implicitly accept the proposition that certain types of cognitive capacities are required for moral status. They argue that animals possess these requisite capacities. These thinkers attribute sophisticated reasoning abilities to animals, such as conceptual understanding in bees, that animals simply do not seem to possess.

As honorable as their underlying intentions are, such thinkers may provide us with a caricature of animal cognition that re-creates animals in our own image. Capacities for reflection and conceptual abstraction enable human beings to perform sophisticated mental operations, such as contemplating the remote past or the distant future or reflecting on the implications of different courses of action, in a way that makes humans capable of moral responsibility. The attention of animals, on the other hand, tends to be confined to immediate practical concerns and perhaps to the recent past and the very near future. Naturally, the degree of an animal's confinement to the present and the immediate past and future depends on the kind of animal in question. Presumably animals with more sophisticated cognitive abilities—such as the higher primates, dolphins, and some birds—are less confined than animals further removed from the dividing line between human and nonhuman animals. As I noted in the preceding chapter, my concern is with animals that are relatively remote from this boundary. It is with regard to such animals that an intermediate position between behaviorism and Griffin's cognitivism is most needed.

Such an intermediate position holds the promise of explaining animal behavior in terms of mental operations and conscious states of awareness that fall short of human rationality but nonetheless do justice to Nagel's observation that there is something irreducibly subjective about animal experience. This does not mean that every form of animal behavior must be explained by recourse to the subjective aspects of animal experience. Even Griffin acknowledges that many types of animal behavior are instinctive, noting that many such behaviors may be accompanied by consciousness even if they are not caused by consciousness.[9] Ruth Millikan distinguishes between "intentional devices generally and a special class of these that I will call 'representations': Sentences and thoughts are representations; bee dances, though they are intentional devices, are not. Representations are distinguished by the fact that when they perform their proper functions their referents are *identified*." To identify "the referent of an intentional device element . . . is the same as *knowing what* one is thinking of or *knowing what* a word represents." Millikan's distinction is between instinctive behavior based on information processing, and predicatively structured states of awareness that enable a being to identify particular objects of thought as such. "Many intentional items—items that are 'about' other things—do their jobs without their interpreters or the organisms that harbor them having any grasp of what they are about. Von Frisch knew what bee dances are about, but it is unlikely that bees do. Bees just react to bee dances appropriately."[10]

But Millikan does not demand that we explain all animal behavior in terms of information processing or instinct. She argues that many higher animals are "Popperian" in the sense of being "capable of thinking hypothetically, of considering possibilities without yet fully believing or intending them," and she speculates that "a certain kind of rationality may occur on the level of perception prior to cognition." Inasmuch as "perception is generally assumed to include object recognition," Millikan takes as "paradigmatic of perception the production of representations suitable for guidance of immediate action, suitable because these represent for the perceiving animal its own present relation to various world affairs as needed for action."[11] Pre-cognitive perceptual rationality would be comparable to the protothought discussed in the preceding chapter, namely, a way of relating to representations that enables a being to act appropriately, where this manner of relating is not purely mechanical.

Colin Allen questions the heuristic value of the sharp distinction between cognition and mechanistic association, stressing that both are involved in many behaviors exhibited by animals. To remain satisfied with a purely associative, and hence deterministic, model of animal behavior is to succumb to "a certain Cartesian residue" that inclines us to "avoid attributing (unsubstantiated) rational thought" to animals.[12] To deny the role of mechanistic or instinctual mechanisms in animals, be they human or nonhuman, is naïve. What is needed is a view that recognizes the compatibility between subjective awareness and "instinctive, genetically programmed" behavior.[13]

Such a view is needed because the Cartesian conception of animals as instinctually driven machines conflicts too wildly with the manifest affinities between the lives of animals and those of human beings. Historically there have been several reasons for denying or ignoring these affinities. One is that to a great extent these affinities are not amenable to scientific proof. Science is capable of proving only matters that can be observed directly. In the case of animal cognition, we have only the outward behavioral effects of cognitive processes to go on. We must draw inferences about the underlying causes of animal behavior, and to some extent these inferences will unavoidably be speculative. The case would be somewhat different if animals shared language in common with us and we could communicate with them about their mental states, as we can with other human beings. We cannot depend entirely on science to discover the truth about the lives of animals, for not everything that is true is scientifically demonstrable.

Another reason why the affinities between human and animal experience have historically been denied is that, from very early on, our culture has expressed a profound anthropocentric prejudice, according to which human beings are fundamentally superior to animals. Aristotle acknowledged that human beings are a type of animal, but he argued that our rationality makes us fundamentally superior to animals. Subsequent philosophers, notably the Stoics, developed this prejudice into a cosmic principle, according to which animals exist for the sake of gratifying human needs. The Stoics argued that because animals lack rationality, they are excluded in principle from the sphere of justice. The Christian philosophers of the Middle Ages accepted this Stoic prejudice virtually unmodified. In the early modern period Descartes advanced the proposition that animals are mechanisms with no capacity for inner states of awareness. Even where subsequent thinkers recognized what Henry More called the "internecine and cutthroat" implications of Descartes's view, they did little if anything to redress the condition of subjection into which this historical prejudice had cast animals.[14] As I demonstrate in chapter 4, Jeremy Bentham recognized that it is not rational capacity but sentience—the ability to experience pleasure and pain—that is the proper basis for making judgments about the moral status of a given being. The key question is not whether a being is rational but whether it can suffer. But Bentham concluded that humans may kill and eat animals on the grounds that death is not as great an evil for animals as it is for humans. Since animals are incapable of contemplating the distant future, we cannot be said to be depriving them of future enjoyments. Animals simply have less to lose than we do.

This line of argumentation points, if only against Bentham's own intention, toward the centrality of cognitive capacities in considerations of moral worth. A being that is sentient relates to the world through complex cognitive operations. However, a being is never merely sentient; sentience is simply one aspect of the inner life of a being that must cope with danger and seek to satisfy vital needs. In this respect, animals are very much like human beings. Even if we should decide that sentience is a sufficient condition for equal moral consideration, as many contemporary thinkers have done, we can work to overcome the anthropocentric prejudice about human superiority by examining and better understanding the cognitive capacities of animals, capacities that in some key respects are not as different from our own as we might like to believe.[15]

## COMMONSENSE ATTRIBUTIONS OF CONCEPTS AND INTENTIONALITY TO ANIMALS

Whatever the precise meaning of rationality, it seems reasonable to treat conceptual ability and intentionality in beings with subjective awareness as rational capacities. Kant took an important step when he maintained that "we can quite correctly infer by analogy, from the similarity between animal behavior [Wirkung] (whose basis we cannot perceive directly) and man's behavior (of whose basis we are conscious directly) . . . that animals too act according to representations [Vorstellungen] (rather than being machines, as Descartes would have it)."[16] Some contemporary cognitive scientists argue that concepts and belief can be understood in purely functional terms, without appealing to inner states of awareness. As Dennett argues about thermostats and Gould and Gould propose about bees, one might construe conceptual and intentional capacities in purely information-processing terms, according to which animals are biological computing machines. Kant's insight—which is somewhat ironic given the fundamentally subordinate status that he ascribes to animals—is that there is a difference in principle between a machine and a living, sentient being. Animals have representations; and even if we should allow the behaviorist or the cognitive scientist to attribute "representations" to machine and animal alike, we must be mindful of a basic difference between the meaning of the term 'representation' in the two cases. As thinkers such as Searle and Dreyfus have argued at length with regard to the difference between computers and human beings, there is nothing intrinsically meaningful in the computer's operations, no sense in which the computer could be said to be following rules or possessing a genuine understanding of what it is doing, whereas human beings subjectively relate to, interpret, and evaluate their representations.[17] Extensive ethological research has made it clear that the same holds, mutatis mutandis, for the differences between animals and computers: Even if some or even many instances of animal (or, for that matter, human) behavior are products of instinct or mechanistic association, in important respects animal behavior is irreducible to such mechanisms and must be conceptualized in terms of subjective mental states that can be understood only by analogy to human mental states. To deny this is to succumb to the Cartesian prejudice that even Kant sought to avoid.

Griffin's ethological work exemplifies a form of commonsense thinking about animals that has increasingly superseded the Cartesian prejudice. Given the evident similarities between human and animal behavior, not to mention a great deal of shared neurophysiology, it seems naïve to suppose that animals lack sophisticated cognitive equipment. Philosophers, too, have increasingly embraced this new form of common sense. In several recent books Martha Nussbaum has discussed the cognitive abilities and moral status of animals. Regarding the former, she takes it as axiomatic that animals are capable "of intentionality, selective attention, and appraisal." Nussbaum's focal point is emotions, which she conceives, along with the Stoic Chrysippus, as involving assent to predicatively structured objects of thought (*lekta*). She maintains that Chrysippus's mistake was to conclude that because emotions have this character, animals, which lack linguistic capacity, could not have emotions.[18]

On Nussbaum's view, emotions are a fundamental part of the lives of sentient beings, who strive to "flourish" in the Aristotelian sense that they seek to actualize the natural potential with which they were born. "All emotions involve a prominent eudaimonistic element, and thus an ineliminable indexical element. . . . The subject is aware that it is *herself* or *himself* who has the goal or attachment in question. So in that sense an awareness of self (and therefore, often, of one's body) is a part of the experience of any emotion."[19] Aristotle uses the term 'eudaimonia' to refer to a life well led, through a process of gradual character formation that involves moral virtue, practical reason, and the regulation of the passions. By associating emotions with the notion of eudaimonia and arguing at length that like humans animals experience emotions, Nussbaum seeks to persuade us that animals possess sophisticated cognitive apparatus that such historical precursors as the Stoics and Descartes reserved for human beings. The Stoics were right to construe emotions as evaluative and hence predicative, but they were wrong to deny that animals experience emotions. "The animal evidence confirms the Stoic view that an emotion is an evaluative appraisal of the world. These ways of seeing will always involve some sort of combination or predication—usually of some thing or person with an idea of salience, urgency, or importance. Moreover, these predications of salience are in turn combined with an assessment of how the goal is faring in the world." Animals need not be reflectively self-conscious in order to be capable of emotional states, but "many if not most animals have something that we may call conscious awareness: that is, there is something the world is like to them."[20]

In sum, "it seems reasonable that, to the extent that animals are capable of general and temporally extended thinking, background emotions of fear, love, and anger will play at least some role in explaining what they do." To be capable of such emotions is to be capable of "combination or predication, and . . . eudaimonistic evaluation." The lack of linguistic ability is no bar whatsoever to the possession of these capacities.[21] Nussbaum neither explains how nor marshals ethological evidence to show that animals can engage in acts of predication without possessing linguistic ability. Indeed, she seems to make the same mistake that Heidegger says the Greeks made about the nature of language: she implicitly treats language as if it were simply syntactically structured strings of words used to make public the contents of thought that is itself already predicatively structured.[22] Nussbaum calls for a theory of "cognitive interpretation as seeing-as" and "a flexible notion of intentionality" that can account for the ways in which animals evaluate and negotiate their environments and pursue their goals.[23] In doing so she attributes to animals the as-structure of interpretation that thinkers such as Heidegger reserve for human beings even while acknowledging that animals possess subjective states of awareness. She also attributes to animals the full apparatus of intentionality, which she construes to be essentially non- or pre-linguistic.

Although Nussbaum briefly discusses some formal studies of animal emotion and appeals to the "adaptive significance" of attributing such states as emotion to animals, the primary basis of her ascription of intentionality to animals appears to be that bane of the scientific researcher, the anecdotal account. "Cognitive psychology has been prone to reductive and inadequate accounts of animal intelligence, accounts that were readily repudiated by people who knew and interacted with animals. This makes us want to hold the scientific accounts up to the best interpretive accounts of behavior, just as we hold scientific accounts of humans up against the rich descriptions we produce from our emotional experience."[24] Even if scientific researchers have offered overly reductive accounts of animal behavior, they have been right to regard anecdotal accounts with some suspicion. There is no settled view of what should count as "the best interpretive accounts of behavior," and the potential for abuse of the anecdotal account need hardly be pointed out.

Nussbaum proposes that a legitimate anecdotal account of animal behavior is one that "avoid[s] the twin pitfalls of reductionism and anthropocentrism." She suggests that "the role of such an account is to invite the reader to mine his or her experience for similar examples."[25] The example that Nussbaum describes is George Pitcher's account of his relationship with a wild dog, Lupa, who took up residence under his tool shed and gave birth to a litter of puppies. Pitcher describes his attempts to gain Lupa's trust and the eventual success of his endeavor. Nussbaum pronounces Pitcher's account of Lupa's behavior to be entirely legitimate. Notwithstanding "Pitcher's own strong emotional response, as the animal's trust unlocked his own ability to give love, which had been compromised by his inability to mourn his mother's death," Pitcher's account is fully credible inasmuch as he "ascribes to Lupa emotions with a definite propositional content, connected with important goals," such as the acquisition of food and the securing of a safe haven for herself and her puppies. Pitcher's descriptions of Lupa's emotions are no less credible than his descriptions of his own emotions. In both cases one can be mistaken, but "we have no reason to suppose the report of Lupa's emotions to be less reliable than Pitcher's own self-report."[26] Pitcher's reminiscences are "convincing accounts of the emotions of two specific dogs [Lupa and her son, Remus], rather than fanciful human projections."[27] Not only is Pitcher's account "consistent with scientific accounts," but its plausibility is increased by the fact that Nussbaum "knew the two dogs in question, and can therefore compare Pitcher's narrative to [her] own experience."[28] "During my own visits in their home, I had no doubt that Lupa felt fear of me, as a menacing outside human who had not gained her trust; that [her son] Remus felt joy when he was asked to go wake me up at 7 a.m. with a bark outside my door, and profound grief, affecting his entire life, when his mother died of old age." Both dogs' emotions were eudaimonistic and, with regard to Pitcher and the other humans they came to know, "much more than instrumental."[29] In other words, one simply cannot make sense of the lives of animals such as Lupa and Remus if one operates with the reductive assumptions of behaviorism, nor is one engaging in mere anthropomorphism in supposing that animals experience eudaimonistic emotional states much like our own.

Searle, too, appeals to common sense and anecdotal accounts to argue for intentionality in animals. (He also offers some specific arguments, which I examine later in this chapter.) "Many species of animals have consciousness, intentionality, and thought processes," which is to say that their minds are "directed at or about objects and states of affairs in the world" and that they experience "temporal sequences of intentional states that are systematically related to each other, where the relationship is constrained by some rational principles."[30] Like Nussbaum, Searle appeals to his personal relationship with a dog to lend credibility to this supposition. His interactions with his dog, Ludwig, make him confident that Ludwig is conscious, just as Ludwig is confident that Searle is conscious. "Any other possibility is out of the question. . . . There is not really any possibility of doubt."[31] Ludwig "is a conscious intentional agent" who "can have such mental representations as beliefs or desires without having any syntactical or symbolic entities at all."[32] Any attempt to deny such capacities in higher mammals seems "breathtakingly irresponsible" and is invariably traceable to the prejudice that "the human possession of language makes human thought possible and the absence of language in animals makes animal thought impossible."[33]

The crux of Nussbaum's and Searle's commonsense attributions of intentionality to animals is the notion that animals are manifestly like humans in the ways in which they interact with their environments and seek to satisfy their needs and desires. This commonsense view gives primacy to the neurophysiological similarities between human beings and animals, the biological basis of intentionality, and the heuristic value of analogy to human experience as a means of conceptualizing animal experience. If only implicitly, this commonsense background guides all the more formal argumentation about animal cognition in the contemporary literature.

## Specific Arguments for Intentionality in Animals

Along with linguistic ability, mathematical ability has long been considered a clear sign of rationality. It has generally been argued that only human beings are capable of mathematical reasoning; the same holds true for complex logical inference. In antiquity some attempts were made to attribute logical or mathematical abilities to animals. The most famous of these is the story of Chrysippus's dog. Sextus Empiricus reports that Chrysippus, a Stoic famous for asserting that no justice relationship exists between human beings and animals, was forced to acknowledge the existence of sophisticated logical abilities in at least some animals:

> According to Chrysippus, who was certainly no friend of non-rational animals, the dog even shares in the celebrated Dialectic. In fact, this author says that the dog uses repeated applications of the fifth-undemonstrated argument-schema, when, arriving at a juncture of three paths, after sniffing at the two down which the quarry did not go, he rushes off on the third without stopping to sniff. For, says this ancient authority, the dog in effect reasons as follows: the animal either went this way or that way or the other; he did not go this way and he did not go that; therefore, he went the other.[34]

Sextus takes this story as proof that the dog must engage in complex inferential reasoning; to head down the third path without even sniffing at it, the dog must be able to infer that the third is the only path the prey could have taken. Plutarch, the most energetic defender among the ancient thinkers of the cognitive abilities of animals, suggests that in this particular case one need not attribute logical inference to the dog to make sense of its conduct, arguing instead that the dog simply perceived (i.e., smelled) its prey down the third path.[35] For his own part, Plutarch sees the purposiveness, preparation, memory, emotion, sociability, deceptive tactics, and courage of animals as clear evidence of their rationality. He suggests that some animals "have cognition of number and can count," and that fish that school in cube formation display a knowledge of geometry.[36]

Notwithstanding the fanciful character of many of Plutarch's stories about the cognitive abilities of animals, it is worth noting that contemporary ethological researchers have sought to confirm some of his intuitions. Irene Pepperberg, who worked with an African gray parrot named Alex for a number of years, has shown that Alex possessed some highly sophisticated abilities. He could correctly answer questions about the color and shape of particular objects and was able to identify which among a set of objects has a certain shape or color. Donald Griffin sees Pepperberg's work with Alex as giving a "strong indication that Alex [thought] about colors, shapes, sameness, and so forth."[37] Pepperberg also conducted experiments designed to explore Alex's comprehension of numerical relations. Alex was able to answer questions about the number of objects present (up to six), and their particular color. Alex's accuracy was "comparable to that of chimpanzees and very young children." Given that "'number sense' requires handling abstract concepts— representations and relations," any subject possessing such a sense "must have a clear representation of quantity that transfers across modalities and applies to any items."[38] Pepperberg concludes that "Alex [used] and comprehend[ed], in appropriate situations, abstract utterances at a representational level" and that he may "have shown a numerical competence not unlike that of humans."[39]

Pepperberg is careful to acknowledge that Alex might simply have been making some kind of elaborate associations between present sense impressions and past experiences, or that he might have been "subitizing," that is, instantaneously recognizing a pattern the way one might recognize a particular die or domino without actually counting the dots. She acknowledges that parrots "might be more advanced perceptually than humans," and that Alex may have been capable of subitizing quantities up to six.[40] But she offers as evidence for the possibility that Alex actually possessed numerical competence the fact that he spontaneously and appropriately employed 'none.' "He had been taught to use 'none' to indicate absence of information in one situation and, without training, transferred its use to another when specifically queried.... In the present study, however, he not only provided the correct response but also set up the question himself."[41] Thus, without any prompting from the researchers Alex employed a notion that is "abstract and relies on violation of an expectation of presence." Pepperberg "cannot claim that Alex understands none or zero in an ordinal sense," inasmuch as even "young children and some apes have some difficulty with ordinal use of zero . . . and understanding the relationship between cardinal and ordinal meaning is a hallmark of abstract numerical sense."[42] But even a little reflection on Alex's numerical abilities suggests that some kind of sophisticated cognitive processes may well have been at work that cannot be accounted for by a mechanistic model of information processing.

Whether the capacity for making complex associations should count as cognition involving subjective awareness and evaluation of content is a highly controversial question. Pepperberg acknowledges the possibility but resists the conclusion that Alex was engaging in mere association because she sees in his conduct signs of subjective awareness and abstract reasoning ability. Although I examine the phenomenon of association in depth in the next chapter, here it is worth noting that researchers tend to see a direct opposition between association and abstract reasoning. Some argue that complex discriminations cannot be performed in the absence of general concepts (e.g., that an animal cannot discriminate blue objects from non-blue ones unless it has some sort of concept of blueness), while others argue that even the highly complex discriminations performed by Richard Herrnstein's pigeons can be accounted for by an associative model of learning.[43]

Lawrence Weiskrantz, who conceives of associative chains as involving sequences of stimulus and response, argues that "rule learning by animals cannot be readily handled in [associative] terms."

Although Weiskrantz acknowledges that "learning categories [e.g., 'same/different'] is not the same as thinking about them," he nevertheless maintains that the ethological evidence points to the likelihood that animals engage in some sorts of thinking.[44]

Weiskrantz does not explicitly define what it would mean for animals to think, but he suggests that it goes beyond the mere identification of object constancy and involves "the mental *manipulation* of images, symbols, words, memories, and the like."[45] Weiskrantz's appeal to the notion of following rules sheds additional light on what it might mean for animals to think. Searle distinguishes between "rule-guided" and "rule-described" behavior. Rule-described behavior is behavior that we might refer to in intentional terms even though the system exhibiting the behavior has no subjective sense of what it is doing, as when we say "the plant wants water" or "the car doesn't want to start." Rule-guided behavior is behavior that is caused by intentional states in the sense that the agent performs a particular action *because* of his or her beliefs or desires, as when I wait a few minutes to try starting the car again because I believe that I have flooded the carburetor. "When I say that I am following a rule I am saying that there is an intrinsic intentional content in me, the semantic content of the rule, that is functioning causally to produce my behavior." Only behavior that is causally influenced by the agent's beliefs and desires is truly intentional. On Searle's view such intentional conduct can be performed by animals that lack language as well as by sleeping human beings.[46] If Weiskrantz is right to attribute rule-following abilities to animals, then Searle would say that Weiskranz is implicitly attributing a subjective grasp of semantic content and such intentional capacities as beliefs and desires to animals, quite apart from the question whether any animals possess linguistic abilities.

Similarly, Allen argues that "the notion of content has a significant role to play in cognitive ethology," and that semantic or representational content is essential to the explanation of "certain facts about the evolution of sophisticated behavioral abilities."[47] Focusing on communicative as well as other abilities in vervets, Allen notes that the flexibility of vervet behavior resists explanation in behavioral terms. He notes that Dorothy Cheney and Robert Seyfarth acknowledge the possibility that vervet learning could be due to simple associative mechanisms and agrees with them that conceptual ability and representations with semantic content would provide vervets with adaptive advantages.[48] But he concludes that "it remains to be seen whether terms such as 'belief', 'knowledge', or 'recognition' are acceptable in descriptions of animal behavior."[49]

Cecilia Heyes and Anthony Dickinson acknowledge the difficulties involved in attributing intentionality to animals, particularly given the seeming impossibility of directly perceiving intentionality in animal behavior. Nevertheless, they see potentially great explanatory value in intentional accounts of animal behavior and, like Allen, offer what they call "a blatantly 'realist' rather than 'instrumentalist' view of intentionality. . . . This means that we regard an intentional account of action as a variety of causal explanation" that can account for "what the animal would have done if its circumstances had been different in certain, specifiable respects from those in which the action actually occurred."[50] If a case for intentionality in animals can be sustained, then it will be the case that animals have beliefs about causal relations, as well as desires and the capacity to make practical inferences.[51]

As noted in the preceding chapter, to attribute intentionality to animals is to endow them with the capacity for mental states with predicative structure. For example, to have a belief is to be committed to the proposition that something is the case. Intentional agents are capable of identifying objects and states of affairs and of attributing particular qualities to them. A primary reason for attributing intentionality to animals is that they exhibit adaptive behavior that arguably would not be possible in the absence of a grasp of certain causal relations. Bernard Rollin has used this reasoning to argue that animals possess concepts and self-awareness. Rollin suggests that historically we have been unwilling to attribute thought to animals because animals lack language. But he argues that the very possibility of language acquisition in humans presupposes pre-linguistic thought. Following Thomas Reid, Rollin proposes that "understanding of reference and meaning requires some non-linguistic comprehension of the linkage between sign and what is signified (such as ostension) prior to the acquisition of language; otherwise the entire process would never get off the ground. In short, language requires a peg of non-linguistic experience on which to be hung."[52]

Moreover, to the extent that "animals have perceptions of objects and causal relations, they must be doing something other than merely sensing. For as Kant himself points out, the senses supply only momentary, ever changing fragments. To experience, to perceive, one must tie these particulars together—'synthesize' them, in Kant's terminology."[53] Rollin's reasoning is of a piece with Griffin's: any being that has perceptual awareness must participate, to some extent, in reflective awareness as well; otherwise there would be no "experience." To the extent that there is experience, there is awareness of objects, events, and who is involved in the action.[54] In appealing to Kant's epistemology to support this claim, Rollin maintains that if humans must employ concepts in synthesizing discrete sensations into a whole experience, then animals must do so as well. And if this holds for concepts, then it must hold even for Kant's transcendental unity of apperception, the unity of self-awareness, which Kant identifies as the core principle of all synthesis and knowledge. "Common sense assumes that animals know the difference between what happens to them and what doesn't. The efforts of animals to protect themselves certainly supports our claim, and if one is willing to admit that animals feel pain, it follows that pain would not be of much use were it not referred to a self."[55]

On its face, Rollin's argument has some serious problems. Chief among them is the fact that Kant presents a very specific conception of experience designed to account for the possibility of absolutely certain ("apodeictic") knowledge in fields such as mathematics and physics. On Kant's view, such knowledge takes the form of predicative judgments that employ pure concepts of the understanding. Moreover, all such judgments are unified into one whole "experience," one unified sense of the world and the subject's relationship to it. Kant never intended to attribute all these capacities to animals. Indeed, it seems absurd to attribute mathematical knowledge to fish regardless of the manner in which they school. Nevertheless,

Rollin makes a very important point: How can an experience, say, of pain *be* an experience of pain unless there is an awareness of the pain as mine? Euan Macphail argues that "a cognitive self is a prerequisite for experience of any kind," and that in particular "pain must be experienced by a self."[56]

Unlike Griffin and Rollin, however, Macphail argues that, "given that there is a case for the claim that language is a prerequisite of the cognitive self, the possibility exists that only language-using humans who have developed sufficiently to have a self are conscious in the sense that they can feel anything, prefer any state to any other—are, in short, sentient beings and proper objects of ethical concern."[57] One consideration that Macphail offers in support of this possibility is that only beings possessing a sense of self seem capable of forming conscious, autobiographical memories. This, together with his claim of a causal link between the development of language and the emergence of a sense of self, leads Macphail to deny a sense of self in animals, even in those animals that outwardly appear to exhibit self-awareness in mirror recognition tests.[58] What animals seem to lack is "the 'aboutness' relation," that is, "the capacity to conceive propositions about this self: an organism cannot become self-conscious without the ability to conceive certain states as being states of itself rather than of some other entity."[59]

The different directions taken by Rollin and Macphail represent two extremes in the conceptualization of animal cognition. Rollin seeks to attribute complex conceptual self-referential abilities to animals to account for their evident capacity to experience states such as pain, whereas Macphail argues that animals, in virtue of lacking linguistic ability, appear to be confined to the formation of associations, which, as I have noted, is typically conceived by ethological researchers in strictly behavioral terms. Neither of these extremes seems appropriate as a characterization of the mental lives of animals for the same core reason: Rollin and Macphail both take the subjective experience of linguistic beings as their model for all experience. Rollin follows Kant, who locates at the center of his notion of experience the capacity for formal judgment and the employment of abstract concepts. On this view, all and only those beings that possess the full apparatus of reason and language are capable of experience in a morally relevant sense. The essential difference between Rollin and Macphail is that the former, like Nussbaum, seems to conceive of language as strings of words employed to communicate pre-linguistic, predicatively structured units of meaning, whereas the latter argues for an essential connection between language and meaning that may leave no room for subjective experience in animals.

The approach taken by Rollin has proved to be more influential than that taken by Macphail. In the wake of Nagel's challenge, it has become increasingly implausible to suppose that animals have no subjective experience whatsoever. In particular, the idea that animals cannot experience states such as pain has lost currency as we have progressively escaped the influence of Cartesianism. David DeGrazia has suggested that it is possible for animals to have conscious experience even if they do not possess self-consciousness. Thus, a being might be "conscious of simpler things than oneself, such as an object ahead," and it appears that "actually existing conscious animals are probably aware," but "consciousness does not *logically entail* self-awareness."[60] If this is the case, then there is no reason to suppose that the ability to experience states such as pain depends on self-consciousness, nor is there any reason to suppose that the capacity to experience states such as "pain, distress, suffering, desires, and many others" depends on complex mental capacities such as the ability to infer the experience of others.[61]

DeGrazia maintains that "for a mental state to have content, it must be intentional; that is, it must be *about* something." DeGrazia takes this to mean that for an animal such as a wolf to be able to "discriminate conditions in which her desire is frustrated (those in which the rabbit gets away) from conditions in which her desire is satisfied (those in which she catches the rabbit)," the wolf must experience intentional states.[62] How can the wolf recognize that her desire has been satisfied (or frustrated) unless she recognizes which states of affairs constitute the satisfaction (or frustration) of that desire? Moreover, how could the wolf be conscious without being conscious *of* certain objects and states of affairs? And if the wolf is conscious of objects and states of affairs and can distinguish different objects from one another, does this not suggest that the wolf possesses concepts on the basis of which she makes such discriminations? DeGrazia believes that, in the case of a dog chasing a cat, "it seems most reasonable to suppose that the dog has some concept that picks out the tree, a concept that picks out the cat, and one that picks out what the cat did."[63] If we refused to attribute intentionality and concepts to animals, "we would lose much explanatory and predictive power regarding animal behavior. But we would also lose much in understanding natural selection."[64]

The problem posed by such accounts of animal consciousness is how to attribute subjective states of awareness to animals sufficient to account for adaptation and innovation, without being forced (à la Rollin) to attribute sophisticated intentional apparatus to animals that they simply do not seem to possess. As I noted earlier, animals do not seem to be able to contemplate the remote past, the distant future, or themselves *as* selves among other selves. In the next chapter I argue that this limitation appears to be due to the inability of animals to engage in acts of genuine abstraction. The most promising work currently being done to solve this problem focuses on the attempt to rethink the notions of belief, desire, and conceptual understanding so that we may attribute them to animals without being forced to attribute full-fledged linguistic abilities to them. A number of thinkers have argued that animals may be capable of grasping concepts that are fundamentally more primitive than the concepts employed by human beings. In *The Case for Animal Rights* Regan argues for a "more or less" view of animal concepts, according to which animals need not grasp every predicate pertaining to a given concept in order to be capable of possessing that concept. Thus, a dog can pick out a bone from among other objects even if it has no conception of a physical object and possesses no specifically osteological notions.[65]

Regan, and DeGrazia after him, treats conceptual ability as part of a larger set of intentional capacities, including beliefs about the conditions for the satisfaction of certain desires. On this view, if animals possess any conceptual ability, then they also possess the capacity for beliefs and desires, and hence can engage in acts of non- or pre-linguistic predication. No adherent of this view has yet explained what such predication would amount to, nor how it would be possible. This in itself does not show this view to be mistaken, but it does give urgency to the question whether a nonlinguistic being can be capable of acts of predication. Just to say that a mental state is "about" something is not to say that it must be predicatively structured. As I previously noted, and as I shall argue in the next chapter, predication seems to involve a specific sense of the "as" that seems unavailable to animals and that is unnecessary as a basis for explaining the adaptive and innovative character of animal behavior.

Fred Dretske offers a tentative analysis of mental operations in animals that adheres to such intentional notions as belief while acknowledging a fundamental difference between the mental states of linguistic and nonlinguistic beings. A key question for Dretske is whether we may legitimately attribute thought to animals. Thought is a necessary condition for agency: "In order to qualify as action, behavior must be explained by *what* we think, by the content or meaning of our thoughts."[66] Action is "behavior controlled by my beliefs and desires," as opposed to being determined by operant conditioning.[67] Thus, if animals are to be agents, as opposed to stimulus-response devices, it must be the case that animals have intentional states such as beliefs. Dretske offers the example of a bird that learns not to eat Monarch butterflies because eating Monarchs makes the bird sick. This bird will also avoid Viceroy butterflies, which closely resemble Monarchs but do not make the bird sick. Dretske's analysis of the bird's avoidance of a Viceroy is that "what it saw was not a nasty tasting bug. No *recognition* took place. There was no knowledge. We need a different word. What is it we (philosophers) call some perceptual state that would be recognition or knowledge if it were true? Belief! So the bird believes the bug it sees tastes bad. This is what it thinks. What it thinks is controlling its behavior."[68] The bird mistook the Viceroy for a Monarch. On Dretske's view, such cases of mistaken identification involve mistaken beliefs.

Although Dretske acknowledges that the bird's reaction involves operant conditioning, he maintains that the bird's "internal representation . . . has both a meaning and a causal role," and that "its meaning explains its causal role."[69] Dretske's account is of a piece with Searle's: when animals act on the basis of internal representations, they are doing something like following rules, whereas machines are simply performing functions that can be *described* as following rules (Searle's "observer-attributed intentionality"). "Meaning is thus explanatorily relevant to why the bird is behaving as it is," whereas meaning plays no intrinsic role in the explanation of the functioning of a machine. The bird's internal representation "means (at least to the bird) that a bug of noxious type is present. . . . It is the meaning of these internal events that explains why these internal events are producing the behavior. In this sense, then, the behavior is being *governed* by meaning. We have a genuine instance of action. In avoiding the butterfly, the bird is an agent."[70]

At the same time, Dretske notes that none of this amounts to a demonstration that an internal representation of this kind really constitutes a thought, which Dretske defines as an "I think that . . ." assertion whose object is a proposition.[71] He thus opens up the possibility of conceiving of a form of internal representation that falls short of thought, with its predicative structure and conceptual determinacy, but which nonetheless has semantic content. Representations of this kind are, "if not thought itself, a plausible antecedent of thought—an internal representation whose meaning or content explains why the system in which it occurs behaves the way it does."[72] Using the example of a pigeon identifying trucks, Dretske proposes the following about such representations:

> It would be misleading to say that a pigeon, though better at identifying trucks than a child, believes what the children believe: *that* they are trucks. Given the bird's impressive performance on discrimination tasks, there must be something in its head that indicates which objects are trucks . . . it would be at best misleading (and at worst simply wrong) to say that it represents these objects *as trucks*. Whatever the pigeon thinks about

these objects, it is probably best expressed, if it can be expressed at all, in some other way. . . . It is this fact, I submit, that makes us want to deny nonlinguistic animals the same concepts, the same beliefs, that we have.[73]

Dretske thus equivocates between attributing intentional states to animals and attributing to them the sorts of protoconcepts and protothoughts discussed in the preceding chapter. On the one hand, he attributes concepts and intentional states such as belief to animals, and, on the other hand, he entertains the possibility that the internal representations of animals ultimately fall short of thought.

Dretske does not address the question how an animal could have a belief, with its semantic content and its causal role in producing behavior, without being capable of conceptually determinate thought. Some preliminary attempts have been made to answer this question. One is to attribute to animals beliefs but not concepts. Following a suggestion made by Donald Davidson, Hans-Johann Glock argues that animals may be capable of having beliefs even if they possess no concepts. Propositional attitudes need not be "relations between a subject and an abstract or mental phenomenon" but are simply "modifications of a person." That-clauses, which lie at the core of intentional states, "no more refer to an object than noun-phrases like 'everything' or 'the past.' "[74] Glock proposes a "modest holism" according to which animals are capable of simple nonlinguistic thought that is confined to "a smaller logical space" than that available to linguistic beings. This model is intended to account for phenomena, such as deceptive behavior in chimpanzees, which on Glock's view demonstrate beliefs about the beliefs of others as well as the ability to recognize mistaken beliefs in others.[75] The difference between belief in linguistic and nonlinguistic beings is one between "holophrastic" (conceptual) and "holodoxastic" (empirical) belief.[76] Glock thus proposes, contra Davidson, a holistic conception of belief that is supposed to account for animal behavior without attributing to animals the capacity to have a concept of belief per se, on the grounds that empirical beliefs need not depend on concepts. Glock's view is similar to that of Millikan, who suggests that "not all intentionality involves concepts" and offers the content of perception as a leading example of nonconceptual intentionality.[77]

Central to the models of animal cognition offered by thinkers such as Glock and Millikan is the attempt to account for the discriminatory abilities of animals in a way that avoids the problem of conceptual holism posed by Davidson, which I examined in the preceding chapter. A related attempt of this kind is offered by Richard Routley, who seeks to refute Davidson's claim that having a belief requires having a concept of belief. Routley maintains that animals could have beliefs without possessing a concept of belief and without grasping the difference between truth and error.[78] All that is required for belief is the capacity to store and retrieve information in a manner that facilitates "a fairly low and undemanding level of discriminatory ability."[79] Like Dretske after him, Routley argues that being mistaken involves having a mistaken belief and that animals can have beliefs even though they lack linguistic ability: *"Awareness of error in belief can be shown by appropriate adjustment or correction of behavior patterns*, and accordingly is attributable to creatures apparently not capable of human linguistic behavior." Thus, animals can experience such states as doubt, hope, and the like without having any linguistic ability.[80] All that is necessary to infer intentionality in animals is "concordance behavior," that is, responding appropriately to given stimuli. "What a creature believes is semantically a matter of what it does, how it behaves and responds in other relevant worlds, i.e. (to phrase it more syntactically) of what it would do, how it would behave."[81]

Routley bases his view of animal belief on the idea that intentional states are essentially independent of language. He proposes that "the ascription of beliefs (even) to linguistically-competent creatures does not require a linguistic model of propositional content, any more than accounting for propositions requires such a model. . . . animals would have beliefs even if there were no linguistically-competent creatures."[82] Routley offers no support for this claim. Indeed, it would be exceedingly difficult (if at all possible) for him to do so. Routley repeats the common error of supposing that propositional competence is independent of linguistic competence, as if a being could be capable of forming and evaluating propositions, which by their nature are predicative, but simply lacked the ability to represent these propositions symbolically. Certainly symbolic representation is an important part of linguistic competence; but so is predication, which lies at the core of any concept of belief that, like Routley's, is founded on what Heidegger calls the as-structure.[83] If, as I shall argue in the next chapter, animals can have representations with semantic content but cannot have representations that involve the "as," then it is necessary to rethink the discriminatory abilities of animals in terms that do not depend on propositional content at all. The resulting model of animal behavior would acknowledge that animals possess some degree of agency, but it would also make sense of some fundamental limitations in the agency of animals.

In the end, it is not clear that a denial of intentionality in animals entails that animals are morally inferior to humans, as Routley avers.[84] Routley's mistake exemplifies contemporary thinking about animal cognition and moral status. The leading tendency in contemporary thought is to suppose that mental life can be understood only in intentionalistic terms, and to suppose that the moral status of animals can be vindicated only by demonstrating that animals possess formal intentional states such as belief and desire. In the remainder of this book I argue that both of these suppositions are mistaken.

# CHAPTER THREE

# An Associationist Model of Animal Cognition

## THE LIMITED RANGE OF ANIMAL CONCERN

The debate examined in the previous two chapters is between what could be called an intellectualist conception and an information-processing conception of animal cognition. In general, proponents of the intellectualist conception maintain that animals employ conceptual abstraction and propositional attitudes. These capacities enable animals to form complex intentions, which account for the ability of animals to engage in such practices as deception and long-term planning. Proponents of the information-processing conception argue that such capacities as self-awareness and predicative intentionality are not needed to account for the abilities of animals to engage in these sorts of practices. In particular, they claim that there is no need to suppose that perceptual awareness presupposes any degree of reflective awareness.

By now it is also clear that there are a variety of positions that fall between these two extremes. These intermediate positions seek to attribute some sort of subjective awareness to animals, without going so far as to attribute the entire apparatus of human intentionality to them. Thus, one might seek to acknowledge that animals genuinely experience states such as pain, while denying that animals can think about these states. Here the task is to explain how animals react appropriately to stimuli they have come to associate with the prospect of pain without attributing to them the capacities for abstract reflection we customarily attribute to ourselves and other human beings. What is essential in this connection is the fact that although animals have mental representations that inform them about potential benefits and harms, there is a fundamental difference between representation in animals and human beings. On the one hand, human beings can step back from their perceptual representations, reflect on them, evaluate them, and form second-order representations about their first-order (i.e., perceptual) representations. Animals, on the other hand, are confined within the scope of their perceptual representations in a way in which mature human beings are not. Ruth Millikan characterizes animal representations as "pushmi-pullyu": "These are representations that are undifferentiated between being indicative and being imperative, between describing and directing." Such representations are perceptual in nature and are "suitable for the guidance of immediate action."[1] Although this sort of representation lacks propositional form, it nonetheless suffices to direct animals' actions appropriately. "For example, bee dances tell at once both where the nectar is and where the watching bees are to go."[2] In characterizing animal representations as "pushmi-pullyu," Millikan seeks to attribute to animals a form of representation that both informs and directs their actions without attributing to them the complex apparatus of propositional attitudes.

Nonetheless, on Millikan's view such representations inform animals *that* something is the case (e.g., the mother hen's food call to its chick informs the chick that food is available now in a certain place). Moreover, such representations often pertain not simply to the present but to events distant both in space and in time. "No matter how simple, most animals have an obvious need to recognize signs of approaching predators and to translate these into appropriate behaviors. . . . The animal for whom a frosty night or the low angle of the sun serves to release winter preparation behaviors is being governed by inner P-Ps whose pushmi faces say that winter is on the way and whose pullyu faces direct what to do about it."[3] A third feature of such representations is that "the purely pushmi-pullyu animal always represents affairs in its world as bearing certain relations to itself. . . . This doesn't require that the animal represent itself explicitly, any more than the bee dance represents nectar, hive, and sun explicitly . . . but the self has to be represented at least implicitly."[4]

As sophisticated as such abilities might sound, Millikan stresses that in animals they are all tied to immediate practical concerns. The sense of self involved in such representations is not the reflective sense of self found in humans. Rather, perceptual or "pushmi-pullyu" representations relate situations, events, and objects to the current, immediate "self" of the animal, as when my cat Pindar discriminates the threat posed to his tail by my careless footstep. This does not mean that Pindar has a sense of self that transcends immediate perceptual situations but simply that at any given moment he can relate a given event to his own body and his bodily integrity. This also does not mean that Pindar has explicit concepts of his body (or of any body, for that matter) but simply that he is able to discriminate particular bodies and perceive properties of those bodies that are relevant to his material welfare. "The pushmi-pullyu animal does not, as it were, *project* its goals. Its behaviors are controlled completely from behind by emerging environmental contingencies. It does not represent its goals as purposed future occurrences or states to which actual accomplishments will be compared." Indeed, on Millikan's view such an animal cannot even "represent its goals in a format that enables it to know whether or when it has reached them."[5]

What is most worth noting in Millikan's characterization of animal representation is that animals, compared to human beings, are *confined* in their perceptual environment in a way that human beings are not. Animals do relate to objects, events, and situations. They even appear to have ways of relating to events distant in space and time. Recall the honey guide (discussed in chapter 1) or the squirrel that begins to make preparations at the first signs of the coming winter. But animals seem not to form *abstract* representations, that is, representations detached from particular perceptual circumstances. When Ajax, one of my cats, used to misbehave, I would threaten him with a water bottle. When he was very young, I had to squirt him a few times to dissuade him from doing things like destroying the furniture; by the time he was a mature cat, I generally had only to brandish the water bottle to get him to desist. Ajax was an indoor cat; had he been an outdoor cat, presumably he would have come to associate my brandishing the garden hose with the prospect of getting wet. But what he would not have been able to do is form an abstract understanding of the *relationship between* the water bottle and the garden hose—an understanding that the same causal factors are at work in both cases. Likewise, although Ajax's representations of situations such as that involving the water bottle related those situations to his current and potential future states, none of them represented Ajax as an individual being as such, without any reference to particular circumstances.

I have stated at the outset that I am not interested in drawing a sharp distinction between human beings and nonhuman animals. Evolutionary continuity and physiological similarity make any such distinction naïve at best. We now know that a variety of animals display sophisticated cognitive abilities, and that not only higher primates but animals such as dolphins and African gray parrots exhibit such abilities. For over two thousand years most philosophers in the European tradition sought to distinguish human beings from animals both cognitively—inasmuch as only human beings possess language and abstract rationality—and morally—inasmuch as only human beings possess the cognitive equipment needed to recognize and respect moral obligations. Occasionally a philosopher in this tradition would proclaim a fundamental continuity between human and animal natures; Pythagoras, Empedocles, Plutarch, Porphyry, Montaigne, and Schopenhauer are conspicuous in this regard. In recent years philosophers, ethologists, and others have sought to overturn the conventional wisdom in favor of a view of animals as being capable of abstract thought. The capacity for such thought would help to account for the apparent ability of many animals to provide for the future and engage in acts of complex reasoning. Moreover, it would help to undermine the traditional conviction that human beings are categorically superior to animals cognitively and hence morally.

As misguided as the tradition has been in supposing that animals lack subjective states of awareness that make their lives meaningful, in our efforts to rethink the cognitive abilities of animals we must not let the pendulum swing from one extreme to the other. Without question, two fundamental prejudices of the tradition need to be challenged: that animals are essentially "dumb" creatures, and that their putatively inferior cognitive abilities confer on them an inferior moral status vis à vis human beings. In its zeal to confer a sense of cognitive and moral uniqueness on human beings, the tradition has too hastily offered reductive accounts of animal cognition that in many respects liken animals to machines. But there is something essentially right in the conventional wisdom concerning the cognitive abilities of animals, and we would be making a grave mistake if we overlooked it in our own zeal to correct the mistakes of the past. The tradition, and even many contemporary thinkers, have tended to see animal cognition as a strict either-or: either animals possess the full apparatus of intentionality or they lack all states of subjective awareness. What is needed is further exploration of the territory that lies between these two extremes. In particular, what is needed is a theory of animal minds that dispenses with appeals to formal intentionality while seeking to acknowledge the richness and sophistication of the inner lives of animals. If the tradition was wrong to deny animals conscious inner states, it was right to deny animals the conceptual and predicative abilities that make possible complex thought, self-reflective awareness, and moral agency.

Here an important distinction must be made between the way a being capable of complex, conceptual thought relates to distant places and times and the way a nonconceptual being relates to them. If we take Millikan's conception of pushmi-pullyu representations as exemplary of animal cognition, then her statement that such representations "can represent affairs that are distal in time as well as distal in space" stands in need of an explanation.[6] If animal representations pertain exclusively to immediate exigencies of action, and if animals do not "project" their goals in the sense of being able to contemplate them as such, then how can an animal have a relationship to anything beyond the immediate present? If Millikan were right to suppose that animal representations take the form *that* something is the case, it would not be difficult to see how an animal represents remote events to itself. For example, the mother hen's food call would produce a representation in the chick that food is available now in that other part of the barnyard. Yet this characterization attributes too much to animals. In effect, it attributes to them the capacity to represent determinate intentional objects, which presupposes that animals are able to produce and employ concepts. But if animals possess all these complex capacities, why can't they make provisions for contingencies that are merely hypothetical or contemplate times about which current circumstances offer no indication (as when I set aside candles for the possibility of a power outage)?

Wittgenstein hints at the problem when he poses the following rhetorical questions: "A dog believes his master is at the door. But can he also believe his master will come the day after tomorrow?—And *what* can he not do here?"[7] It seems right to say that a dog can have a clear sense of his companion human's presence on the other side of the door: the dog perceives familiar sounds and smells and associates these with a particular person and location. But does it make sense to say that the dog *believes that* his favorite human is at the door? Wittgenstein suggests that "one can imagine an animal angry, frightened, unhappy, happy, [or] startled"; but one cannot imagine an animal hopeful, because "only those who have mastered a language" are capable of a state such as hope.[8] Only a being that has been initiated into a "complicated form of life," which includes holistically structured intentional states that enable us to relate to the future as such, can properly be said to entertain a hope about something. Hope can be about the immediate future, but more generally it relates us to events distant in time in a way that seems impossible for animals. The lesson to be learned from Wittgenstein's example of the dog at the door is not that the dog can have beliefs about present states of affairs but not about events in the distant future. Rather, it is that the dog cannot have intentional states, such as belief, at all, inasmuch as such states are bound up with a "complicated form of life" that includes the ability to engage in acts of abstraction that take one far beyond the data of immediate perception. It is one thing to say that an animal begins to make preparations for the winter when it sees the leaves fall off the trees and feels the temperature begin to drop. Yet it is quite another to suppose that an animal could wonder just how much snow we're going to get this winter or represent to itself just how much food it will probably need in the course of the coming months.

Thus, one key revision to Millikan's characterization of animal representations is needed. We must avoid attributing to animals representations with predicative form. Animals do not represent to themselves *that* anything is the case. Their representations are entirely perceptual rather than intentional in nature and (as I argue later in this chapter) are related to goals not by means of conceptual abstraction but rather by means of complex associations. The theory of association that I offer is intended to account for the ability of animals to relate to distant objects—as when the bee dance orients bees on nectar or water in a specific location—while not attributing to animals the sorts of sophisticated conceptual and intentional apparatus that makes possible contemplation of abstract objects, such as the other side of the world, the end of next summer, or the species *Apis mellifera*.

I take Thomas Nagel's challenge to cognitive ethology to be well founded: the perceptual encounters that animals have with the world are so different from our own that we must treat any characterization of animal experience as irreducibly speculative. But this is not to say that our experience has nothing in common with the experience of animals. Another of Wittgenstein's misguided pronouncements about animals is that "if a lion could talk, we could not understand him."[9] Wittgenstein's point is ostensibly that a lion's form of life is so utterly different from our own that we would have nothing in common with the lion—no shared cultural practices or linguistic significations that could serve as the basis for mutual intelligibility. What Wittgenstein and those who endorse his words fail to recognize is that we have a great deal in common with animals. Humans and animals alike participate in the struggle for survival and the enhancement of well-being. Both, as Wittgenstein himself acknowledges, have complex emotional lives, and both actively seek to avoid or ameliorate pain. These are the aspects of animal experience that I take *not* to be speculative. What must forever remain an object of speculation is the inner experience of animals—how, for example, an animal's experience of pain is like and unlike the experience of pain in a being that can think about its pain. In such speculation we must seek to account for the apparent abilities of animals to solve problems and relate to their environment, while not attributing to animals the sorts of cognitive capacities that would facilitate abstract thought. For such thought seems to be beyond the reach of all but the most highly sophisticated animals.

## COGNITIVE DIFFERENCES BETWEEN
## HUMAN BEINGS AND ANIMALS

As I demonstrate in the second half of this book, some of the most influential contemporary arguments for the moral status of animals proceed from the proposition that animals feel pain in a way that confers on them certain moral rights. If the capacity to suffer is the basis for moral status, then there are two alternatives. Either one acknowledges that any animal capable of suffering has a basic right to live its life free of unnecessary pain or one argues that animals simply do not feel pain and hence have no moral status. Descartes advocated the latter when he argued that animals are machines made by the hand of God.[10] As antiquated and regrettable as many contemporary thinkers consider Descartes's views on animals to be, some have adopted a line of thinking that is remarkably close to Descartes's. Peter Harrison invokes the authority of Descartes when he suggests that only beings with rational minds can experience pain.[11] He appeals to C. Lloyd Morgan's Canon, according to which "we should not interpret animal behavior as the outcome of higher mental processes, if it can be fairly explained as due to the operation of those which stand lower in the psychological state of development."[12] On Harrison's view, animals certainly exhibit behavioral responses to stimuli, but there is no reason to suppose that animals are capable of forming beliefs and knowledge, which are requisite for the attribution of pain.[13]

The crux of Harrison's argument is that a being can experience pain only if that being is capable of employing its experience of pain in its *reasoning* about how to react to the pain-causing stimuli. Harrison suggests that animals seem not to exhibit any such reasoning. As evidence Harrison notes that wildebeest exhibit no pain behavior when they are killed by predators, and that animals lack the rational capacity required for moral agency.[14] Although Peter Carruthers takes a somewhat less extreme view of animal cognition, he nonetheless comes to the same conclusion as Harrison. Carruthers argues that many animals—at least mammals—have beliefs and desires and can be conscious of various events in their lives, such as "an acrid smell, a loud noise, or a shove from behind, just as we can."[15] For Carruthers, however, to be conscious of such an event and to have conscious mental states or experiences are two different matters. "A conscious experience is a state whose existence and content are available to be consciously thought about (that is, available for description in acts of thinking that are themselves made available for further acts of thinking)."[16] Conscious mental states or experiences make "perceptual information immediately available to a faculty of reflexive thinking," and are "apt to give rise to spontaneous thoughts."[17] Thus, on Carruthers's view there is no logical connection between perceptual consciousness and reflective consciousness. Although animals can be conscious in the sense of being "aware of the world around them and of the states of their own bodies," they do not have conscious *experiences*, inasmuch as animals are incapable of being *conscious that* they are in the states that they are in.[18] How animals can have beliefs and desires without being able to be conscious *that* . . . Carruthers never explains. He simply advances the view that animals have immediate states of awareness, but that these states do not count as conscious experience since animals cannot think about them.

This leads Carruthers to the same conclusion as Harrison, namely, that animals cannot experience pain. For pain to be conscious, it must be available to conscious thinking. But "if animals are incapable of thinking about their own acts of thinking, then their pains must all be non-conscious ones." And because "there is nothing that it is like to be the subject of non-conscious pain," animal pain does not merit our sympathy.[19] In effect, Carruthers proposes a reversal of the reasoning offered by Rollin and Griffin about animal experience (see chapter 2). Whereas Rollin and Griffin argue that perceptual awareness presupposes reflective awareness, such that individual perceptions are always part of a whole set of experiences had by a single agent, Carruthers accepts the proposition that individual *experiences* presuppose reflective awareness but rejects the idea that an animal can have even one "experience." Again, he never explains how a being that is incapable of experience can have beliefs and desires. He simply avers that the lack of second-order thinking (the ability to reflect on one's experiences) in animals renders them incapable of experience—and hence incapable of subjective states such as pain.

I have advanced the hypothesis that animals neither employ concepts nor have intentional states. One implication of this hypothesis is that animals do not have second-order experiences, that is, they do not reflect on their first-order perceptual experiences. This means that animals do not have a sense of self that endures through the changes in their perceptual experiences and, consequently, that animal experience does not include anything like the "I think" of Kantian apperception that serves in humans as the gathering center of experience. In humans there is always the possibility of adopting the standpoint of apperception and recognizing that all my experiences are tied together in this one stream of experience that is mine and nobody else's. For Kant this capacity is the condition for the possibility of an objective scientific conception of the world as such. John McDowell seizes upon this Kantian idea of having a conception of the world as such when he attributes to humans and denies to animals "a holistically understood conceptual repertoire employed in articulating a world view."[20] He attributes "personal" experience to humans but argues that an animal's encounter with the world is fundamentally "sub-personal."[21] Although he acknowledges that animals certainly feel pain, he argues, on Wittgensteinian grounds, that perceptual states such as pain do not enter into animals' consciousness. To be conscious, to have a worldview, is to be immersed in a network of reasons, which are articulated conceptually and shared publicly. For an animal, which has neither concepts nor reasons, to be conscious of a perceptual state such as pain would require that the animal be capable of relating to a private object.[22]

What, then, can it mean for an animal to feel pain or to be aware of any other sensory phenomena? It seems fair to say that animals lack conceptual capacities and hence the capacities for judgment and self-critical thinking.[23] Even if we grant—which thinkers such as McDowell will not—that animals employ mental representations with causal content in choosing their responses to environmental contingencies, few if any animals seem capable of contemplating individual features of causal chains as such, in a way that enables them to *reason* their way to appropriate choices. In humans, on the other hand, "once language emerges, the representations of such causal connections will be open to *unlimited logical manipulation*, which will vastly enhance the ability of agents to figure out novel behavioral routes to their ends. They will also be able to formulate *complex plans*, perhaps facilitated by an ability to commit themselves to *fixed intentions in advance*."[24] Conceptual, linguistic beings can isolate individual elements of causal chains, contemplate them as such, and bring them into relationships with relevant elements from other causal chains. This is the essence of abstract reasoning in the natural world. According to the hypothesis I am employing, animals are incapable of it.

Animals nevertheless do appear to have inner states of awareness and do not simply respond mechanistically to environmental contingencies. On a view such as McDowell's, to acknowledge that animals feel pain is to grant no more than that animals respond in certain ways to painful stimuli. In denying the possibility of non-conceptual content in experience, McDowell leaves room for no other explanation of what animal pain can mean. It is this sort of reasoning that leads thinkers such as Carruthers to take the position that animal pain is not morally significant: animal pain is nonconscious in principle, and nonconscious experiences "have no phenomenology. So the fact that a creature has sense-organs, and can be observed to display in its behavior sensitivity to the salient features of the surrounding environment, is insufficient to establish that it feels like anything to be that thing."[25]

The task of characterizing animal experience is thus one of acknowledging that animals lack the capacity to think about their perceptual experiences, while also giving an account of the nature and interrelationship between the inner experiential states of animals. Morgan expressed the point in the following way: "Discrimination, localization, and outward projection . . . are the same in kind throughout the whole range of animal life, wherever we are justified in surmising that psychical processes occur." Both humans and (many) animals employ mental constructions; but animal constructions "must be vague and indefinite" and "cannot be particularized in any way."[26] Accordingly, the nature of inference differs in animals and humans. Inference "is of two kinds: first, perceptual inference, or inference from direct experience; secondly, conceptual inference, or inference based on experience, but reached through the exercise of the reasoning faculties. The latter involves the process of analysis or isolation; the former does not. . . . Practical inferences are the outcome of practical experience, but do not go beyond such practical experience. Conceptual inferences are also based on experience, but they predict occurrences never before experienced." Thus, the expectation of a snowstorm when clouds are heavy is a perceptual inference, whereas such an expectation based on falling barometric pressure is a conceptual inference.[27]

This difference in forms of inference corresponds to Morgan's distinction between intelligence and rationality. Inference in general is "the passing of the mind from something immediately given to something not given but suggested through association and experience."[28] Inference can be either perceptual or rational. Perceptual inference can be unconscious or conscious. Morgan defines intelligence as conscious perceptual inference. Whereas perceptual inference "deals with phenomena as wholes," rational inference "analyzes the phenomena and draws conceptual inferences about them."[29] Morgan attributes intelligence to many animals, which means that animals have conscious representations that enable them to deal with "phenomena as wholes." Yet he denies rationality to animals on the grounds that animals lack the capacity to isolate specific properties, contemplate them as such, and draw inferences about them that are detached from any concrete practical situation that the animal has encountered. "There is a great difference between selecting and using a tool for an appropriate purpose, and possessing a conscious knowledge of the relationship between the means employed and the ends attained. I do not think that any conception of means, or end, or relationship is possible to the brute."[30] By the same token, animals have "perceptual volition," that is, they "can choose and [are] probably conscious of choosing." But the human being "not only chooses, and is conscious of choosing, but can *reflect upon his choice*; can see that, under different circumstances, his choice would have been different; can even fancy that, under the same circumstances . . . his choices might have been different. This is conceptual volition."[31]

Morgan's characterization of perceptual inference and volition in animals sheds important light on the mental lives of animals. The key to his characterization is the inability of animals to isolate elements of meaning, contemplate them as such, and make use of them in abstract reflections that go beyond the immediacy of the present and the very near-term future. For an animal to associate falling leaves and dropping temperatures with impending winter does not mean the animal thinks about particular phases of winter or about the spring that will arrive following winter. The capacity to relate to "distal events" is fundamentally different in animals and human beings; the former relate to them only on the basis of immediately given stimuli, whereas the latter can think about them at will, detached from particular contexts of action.

Thus, animals cannot *think about* their perceptual experiences because doing so would require the capacities for conceptual abstraction and the transcendence of immediate circumstances, which are unique to language users. For the same reason, animals cannot have propositional attitudes, such as beliefs and desires. José Luis Bermudez argues that animals do have beliefs and desires on the grounds that "all decision-making involves a selection between different courses of action" and inasmuch as comparing the consequences of one course of action with those of another involves a "sophisticated type of representation that it does not seem possible to understand in terms of noninferential mediate perception at all."[32] On Bermudez's view, animals are not locked within the confines of perceptual experience but are capable of representing and keeping track "of the separable components of the perceived environment and, subsequently, of acting in ways that reflect this capacity. When this is the case the creature's representations of the environment must be structured so as to have separate components that can reappear in, and be extrapolated from, a range of further representations of the environment." In such instances, "the simple perception of analogies and similarities across different environments and situations is not always sufficient for the flexibility of response characteristic of thinking behavior."[33]

I agree with Bermudez that genuine thinking behavior cannot be explained exclusively in terms of analogies and similarities. But I believe that such analogies and similarities are the key feature of what Morgan calls perceptual inference. (In the next section I argue for a view of perceptual inference that can account for all but the most sophisticated animal conduct.) We violate Morgan's Canon and attribute much too much to animals if we follow Bermudez in supposing, for example, that stags employ a primitive form of "expected utility theory" in making choices in red deer roaring contests. In such contests two stags face off against each other in roaring displays and must decide at certain intervals whether to continue roaring or back down. Bermudez suggests that the stags make their choices by means of "instrumental beliefs rather than via complex calculations of preference ordering and utility." Each stag makes "a comparison of contingencies without calculating which course of action in the contrast space of possibilities has the highest likely benefits."[34] This amounts to saying that the stags do not make formal logical inferences—for example, they do not actually draw and analyze decision trees or assign specific expected value coefficients to each possible course of action—but instead make what Bermudez calls "protoinferences" based on representations "that have determinate contents, are compositionally structured, and reflect the mode of presentation under which the creature in question apprehends the immediate environment."[35]

Bermudez's account of "protoinference" in animals is a corollary of his account of "thinking" in animals: it is nonlinguistic and fundamentally more limited than inference in linguistic beings. The key difference between linguistic and nonlinguistic beings, on Bermudez's view, is that the former can *think about* their thoughts whereas the latter cannot. Even though animals cannot think about their thoughts, they can nonetheless engage in the process of belief revision and can "think about the perceptions and desires of other creatures and hence ... can explain and predict behavior in, broadly speaking, psychological terms."[36] Bermudez does not explain how animals can think about the desires of other creatures but not about their own, nor does he clarify how nonlinguistic beings can "explain and predict" the behavior of other beings without being able to explain their own. Indeed, the idea that a nonlinguistic being can explain *anything* seems incoherent.

Bermudez's account of animal cognition has the virtue of being able to account for a wide variety of sophisticated animal behaviors, but this explanatory power comes at the expense of violating Morgan's Canon and failing to acknowledge the insight of Davidson and others into the holistic nature of intentional states. Bermudez adapts Harry Frankfurt's distinction between first- and second-order desires in arguing that animals can have first-order intentional states, such as a belief that a predator is approaching or a desire to drink from this pond, but he maintains that animals cannot have second-order intentional states, such as the belief that some of my first-order beliefs are irrational or the desire that I not have some of the first-order desires that I possess.[37] The problem with this account is that only a being with conceptual abilities can have a belief, and any being that can have a belief can, at least in principle, have beliefs about that belief. This does not presuppose that any being that has beliefs necessarily has a concept of belief as such (as Davidson would have it), although any mature possessor of beliefs probably does have such a concept. But what any being that has beliefs must have is the ability to form second-order beliefs about its first-order beliefs. As Kant's analysis of apperception makes clear, possessors of beliefs are beings whose beliefs cohere in an entire worldview and whose worldview transcendentally has the form "my worldview" or "the worldview of this subject of experience." To say that an animal has beliefs but cannot reflect on them is to misunderstand the nature of belief and the role that it plays in the consciousness of a linguistic being.

In a reflection on the differences between animal and human experience, Seneca suggests that a horse can remember a familiar road when it is brought into sight of the road, but that the horse cannot retrieve a memory of the road at will when it is in its stall.[38] Similarly, Saint Augustine attributes memory of sensory particulars to animals but denies them the capacity to appreciate abstract objects of thought on the grounds that animals are not rational. The capacity of animals to "find their lairs or nests" and to perform the various actions "which are part of their habitual life" crucially depends on memory of sensible particulars ("images of material things"), whereas human beings are capable of a Platonic sort of recollection that enables us to contemplate our own minds, God, and such abstract universals as happiness and beauty.[39] Seneca's and Augustine's reflections on the differences between human and animal cognition point to the conclusion that the horse's memory of the road is not an isolated unit of meaning to which the horse has random access, as it were. Rather, the horse's access to its memory of the road is conditioned by a present perception that gives rise to an *association* with that memory, that is, the present perception causes the horse to recall its memory of the road. Animals such as horses have episodic memory, "a form of memory that 'receives and stores information about temporally dated episodes or events, and temporal-spatial relations among those events,'" but they lack declarative memories, which "have a representational form that allows their content to be deployed flexibly."[40] There is something fundamentally right in Seneca's suggestion that animals can recall situations and events in connection with present stimuli and practical exigencies but lack the flexibility to contemplate individual memories at will, independent of immediate needs or stimuli. Nonetheless, there is some degree of flexibility in an animal's ability to deploy memories in adapting to novel circumstances, a flexibility that is due not to the form of the animal's representations but rather to the nature of the associations the animal is able to make between memories and present perceptions.

## AN ASSOCIATIVE ACCOUNT OF ANIMAL COGNITION

I take it as axiomatic that nonlinguistic beings are unable to make rational inferences, and that the perceptual inferences that animals make are different in kind than rational ones. Rational inferences involve the free manipulation of isolated units of meaning (such as concepts) or of abstract logical symbols and transcend the individual practical contexts in which their results might be applied. Perceptual inferences are always tied to specific contexts of action, and any generalization from a particular context that an animal is able to make is different in kind from the generalizations a linguistic being is able to make. Many of the inferences that human beings make are purely perceptual—what Morgan calls "intelligent"—whereas animals are capable only of "intelligent" (as opposed to rational) inference because they lack the linguistic ability to form and employ concepts.[41] According to some ethologists, even ape communication is always tied to concrete ends and hence is what Morgan would call "intelligent" as opposed to "rational."[42] As Edward Thorndike puts the point, "Animals do not have a stock of independent ideas. . . . The animal's self is not a being 'looking before and after', but a direct practical association of feelings and impulses."[43]

In psychology and ethology, association has for the most part been understood as a mechanistic process. "Much recent thinking about cognition presupposes a sharp dichotomy between computational (propositional, conceptual) cognition...and mechanistic (associationist, non-conceptual) psychology, which involves no representation and hence no [rational] inference as such."[44] But, as David Papineau points out, such a "sharp dichotomy is misconceived.... Representation by no means requires sentence-like vehicles processed as in a digital computer, but will be present as soon as we have the kinds of dispositional architectures produced by associationist learning or analogous processes of natural selection."[45] What we must recognize is that animals have mental representations with nonconceptual content, and that these representations are the basic units for the formation of associations that guide animals in their practical activities.

Earlier I noted a fundamental objection posed by McDowell to the idea of nonconceptual content, namely, that animals cannot be conscious of perceptual states such as pain inasmuch as this view would treat pain as a private object. This sort of reasoning implicitly leads Carruthers to argue that animal pain is not properly an object of our sympathy or moral concern. Both McDowell and Carruthers acknowledge that in some sense animals experience pain, but by denying animals the possibility of conscious awareness of pain they implicitly reduce experiences such as pain to behavioristic reactions to certain types of stimuli. The great advantage of the idea of nonconceptual content is that it avoids this wildly counterintuitive conclusion. The proposition that something enters into conscious awareness only if it becomes part of a holistic practice of reasoning is a remnant of the anthropocentric Cartesian prejudice that only rational, linguistic beings possess any degree of consciousness. The contemporary form of this prejudice is the notion that all conscious states are intentional states, such as beliefs.

As Tim Crane and other proponents of nonconceptual content observe, however, perceptions "are representations of how the world is."[46] Belief is not the first level of experience at which a being can be said to have a conscious sense of how the world is. Rather, "belief conceptualizes the content of perception."[47] Crane characterizes the content of perception as fundamentally "intentional" in the sense that perceptual content is always directed at objects. Intentional states have "aspectual shape," which means that the object is given under certain aspects and not others, and "intentional mode," such as hope or belief.[48] But on Crane's view intentional content need not have propositional form. He conceives of intentional states, such as hope and love, as not possessing propositional content that can be evaluated as true or false.[49] Thus, bodily sensations are "intentional" in the sense that they are always felt in a certain way and felt "to be located at a certain place." A sensation such as ankle pain is intentional on this view: the intentional object is the ankle, and the aspectual shape is that the ankle is "presented to one in a certain way."[50]

This account of sense perception complements Nagel's intuition that there is something it is like to be an animal with perceptual apparatus. On this view "pain is a relation to an intentional content, where the intentional content is the way things seem to a subject. . . . [Pain] is a mental state, because it involves the characteristic mark of the mental: the intentional directedness of the mind upon an object."[51] I do not go as far as Crane in characterizing perceptual states, such as pain, as intentional states. I reserve the term 'intentional' to describe mental states that are not only directed but directed at objects that have been conceptualized and hence brought into relation with other propositional elements. Intentionality involves conceptual content, which requires a grasp of objectivity.[52] Animals lack a sense of objectivity. They do not make judgments about the truth or falsity of propositions, nor do they seek to construct a view of the world as such that serves as the basis for judgments about the truth or falsity of particular propositions. But their perceptions are representations, and these are directed. What needs to be spelled out is the sense in which animal representations of states such as pain are and are not directed, and the ways in which these representations can be associated with other representations to give rise to adaptive behavior.

Animal representations, which are fundamentally perceptual, are directed in the sense that they enable animals to discriminate X's from $Y$'s, for example, to discriminate pain from pleasure. They also enable animals to discriminate one location from another, as when my cat Pindar is aware of pain in his tail as opposed to his right fore-paw. Perceptual representations also enable animals to discriminate between different temporal "locations," as when Pindar is aware of pain in his tail at one moment (right after I inadvertently step on it) and not at another (say, just before or a few minutes after I step on it). But animal representations are not directed in the sense in which they often are in human beings. Pindar never has a representation of his tail or his right forepaw as such, as one object among many whose relations to other objects are thematically grasped. He never has discrete representations of particular moments of time or particular locations as such, that is, in isolation and in explicit contrast to other individual bodily parts, moments, or locations. And he never draws rational inferences on the basis of his representations.

Whether the content of human perception is intentionally structured is a controversial question. Morgan suggests that language informs the basic nature of human perception: "Language is not only involved in our concepts, but also in our percepts, in so far as they are ours."[53] McDowell offers a similar assessment: Because animal perception is fundamentally nonconceptual, it is "blind," whereas human perception is essentially conceptual and hence facilitates reason, freedom, and the capacity to "possess the world."[54] Whether human perception is essentially conceptual is a complicated question whose answer is beyond the scope of this book. For reasons touched upon in chapter 1 in connection with Heidegger's distinction between the apophantic and hermeneutic 'as', I believe that human perception is not essentially conceptual, although the content of human perception can always be (and often is) described in conceptual terms. Human perception has nonconceptual content and thus shares something fundamental with animal perception, namely, that it is directed in a way that enables the perceiver to discriminate between aspects of the environment in the service of satisfying vital needs.

In chapter 1 I noted Allen and Hauser's distinction between having a concept of $X$ and having the ability to discriminate $X$'s from non-X's. To have a concept of X is to "have a representation of X that abstracts away from the perceptual features that enable one to identify X's."[55] To be able to engage in the discriminative activity that is characteristic of much, if not all, animal behavior—not to mention much, although not all, human behavior—a being must have representations that are directed toward particular features of the environment as opposed to others. For example, to be able to discriminate between two potential sources of nectar and choose the better one, a honeybee must have representations in which its focus is directed toward certain locations and not others. Moreover, in order to be able to navigate its way between the hive and a good source of nectar by using a cognitive map, the bee must be able to discriminate particular landmarks in the environment.[56] These and other examples of animal behavior "provide impressive evidence that an animal can form representations of its environment and that such representations often play an essential role in the explanation of animal behavior" even though "the nature of animal representations" remains relatively unclear.[57]

Neither animal representations nor animal conduct depends on an ability to relate to particular features of the environment as determinate objects. Indeed, for reasons developed by phenomenologists such as Heidegger and Merleau-Ponty, even humans do not focus on particular features of the environment as objects unless (a) something has gone wrong or (b) one has deliberately adopted the standpoint of pure, theoretical contemplation. In all other situations, things in the environment function transparently, which is to say that we use things without taking stock of them as such.[58] We typically relate to a whole situation from which we can select particular elements when the need arises. I have a familiarity with tennis rackets and an intuitive, nonconceptual sense of how to use them. Even if I engage in conceptual reflection on my ground strokes in an effort to improve them, the value of this reflection depends on my ability to return to the level of nonconceptual, engaged practice and put my insights to work at the level of intuition or muscle memory. If, while playing, I direct my attention at the racket as a determinate object with isolable properties, this mode of relating to the racket will frustrate my attempts to use the racket appropriately.

Heidegger and Merleau-Ponty go further and question the appropriateness of characterizing preconceptual engaged practice in terms of representation. In the philosophical tradition, the entire language of representation is tied up with a conception of the self as a detached, spectatorial subject viewing an array of determinate objects. Essential to the phenomenological turn is the endeavor to show that engaged practice takes the form of being in the midst of a world that ultimately exceeds the grasp of representation. Taking his cue from Gestalt psychology, Merleau-Ponty states that "I can experience more things than I represent to myself, and my being is not reducible to what expressly appears to me concerning myself. That which is merely lived [as opposed to represented or conceptualized] is ambivalent; there are feelings in me which I do not name."[59] At the level of lived as opposed to theorized experience, we have an immediate relation to our environment, an environment that is "ambivalent" in the sense that it is too rich and complex to be reducible to anything like a determinate representation. We find ourselves enthralled and encompassed by the environment rather than relating to it through the mediation of mental pictures.

One need not resolve the controversy surrounding such a phenomenological account of experience to see its value for understanding the nature of nonconceptual content. Animals find themselves immersed in a world of interrelationships that do not at first present themselves as explicit or determinate. Through experience animals become familiar with various aspects of the environment, but they do not establish a thematic, conceptually informed grasp of them. When confronted with present perceptions that disclose or pertain to certain needs or possibilities, animals relate to these perceptions by making associations between them and prior patterns of behavior that have led to beneficial outcomes. Like humans, animals engage in practices that are directed at beneficial outcomes, but these outcomes are not conceptualized or represented as such—which is to say that they are not depicted in consciousness as explicit intentional objects with conceptually describable relationships to other potential intentional objects. The difficulty in attempting to describe the precise nature of animal directedness is twofold. First, animals cannot tell us what it is like to experience such directedness. Second, our own reflections on engaged, pre-thematic practice are mediated by language to such an extent that we find it difficult simply to characterize our own such practices. Hitting a good ground stroke in tennis is ultimately not a matter of "knowing that . . ." but rather is "a feeling in me which I do not name."

Hume's account of the role played by association in experience has a great deal to offer in the endeavor to understand the nature of animal cognition and action. On Hume's view, both humans and animals form associations between perceptions, and these associations are the basis of our causal inferences and the beliefs that we form about matters of fact. Hume rejects the views of many of his precursors in the philosophical tradition by arguing that the capacity for what Morgan would later call perceptual inference is shared by humans and animals alike. We know by analogy between our own experience and the outward behavior of animals that animals draw inferences. For eample, "From the tone of voice the dog infers his master's anger, and foresees his own punishment. From a certain sensation affecting his smell, he judges his game not to be far distant from him." Judgment here is not to be taken in a formal sense but simply refers to the sort of habitual association that even humans often make. Animals "can never by any arguments form a general conclusion, that those objects, of which they have had no experience, resemble those of which they have. 'Tis therefore by means of custom alone, that experience operates upon them. All this was sufficiently evident with respect to man."[60]

Hume makes a distinction between "relations of ideas" and "matters of fact," with the former pertaining to logical and mathematical reasonings and the latter to perceptual inferences about causal relations. While humans are capable of both sorts of mental operations, animals are capable only of the latter. Even though "the reason of man gives him a great superiority above other animals," the basic associative capacities as well as "the will and direct passions" of animals "are of the same nature, and excited by the same causes as in human creatures."[61] In both humans and animals experience starts with sense impressions, such as bits of color or sound. We are then able to form ideas on the basis of these impressions. These ideas often give rise to what Hume calls impressions of reflection—such as desires, hopes, or fears—as when the idea we form from a sensation of thirst gives rise to a desire to drink.[62] Understanding and volition are guided by the associations we make between our ideas. For example, the dog associates a familiar person's tone of voice with past experiences of being punished by that person upon hearing this particular tone of voice. Hume suggests that animals and humans make their associations on the basis of "RESEMBLANCE, CONTIGUITY in time or place, and CAUSE AND EFFECT. . . . These qualities produce an association among ideas, and upon the appearance of one idea naturally introduce another. . . . Our imagination runs easily from one idea to any other that resembles it, and . . . this quality alone is to the fancy a sufficient bond and association."[63]

On Hume's view, causal inferences made by humans as well as those made by animals are essentially the product of associations we make between given perceptions and past chains of events. Resemblance plays a key role in the formation of associations. For example, in order that the dog associate a certain tone of voice with the prospect of being punished, the tone of voice must resemble a tone of voice that is familiar to the dog and that has customarily been followed by punishment in the past. The more the tone of voice resembles a punishment-related tone of voice in the dog's past experience, the stronger the dog's association between this tone of voice and the prospect of punishment in this instance. It is in this sense that the dog is able to "reason" or "draw inferences" from the presence of a stern tone of voice. Moreover, the association need not simply be between two immediately related units of experience. "Two objects are connected together in the imagination, not only when the one is immediately resembling, contiguous to, or the cause of the other, but also when there is interposed betwixt them a third object, which bears to both of them any of these relations. This may be carried on to great length."[64] Thus, anyone who has seen one domino knock down another domino will not have difficulty envisioning what will happen when the first domino in an appropriately arranged sequence of a thousand dominos is knocked down. A simple inspection of your typical Rube Goldberg contraption will give rise to an inference about the remote consequences of setting the contraption in motion, provided that the viewer has prior experience with causal relations that resemble each of the causal relations involved in the contraption. The greater the resemblance, the greater will be the viewer's sense of confidence about what will happen next.

When Hume states that reason makes human beings superior to animals, he means several things. He means that animals are incapable of mathematics and the like, which depend on relations of ideas. He also means that the inferential capacities of animals are fundamentally more limited than those of human beings. The human being is "a creature, whose thoughts are not limited by any narrow bounds, either of place or time . . . a creature who traces causes and effects to a great length and intricacy; extracts general principles from particular appearances; improves upon his discoveries; corrects his mistakes; and makes his very errors profitable." The animal is "the very reverse of this; limited in its observations and reasonings to a few sensible objects which surround it; without curiosity, without foresight; blindly conducted by instinct, and attaining, in a short time, its utmost perfection, beyond which it is never able to advance a single step."[65] On the basis of this difference between humans and animals, Hume argues that animals do not participate in virtue and vice, and that animals are the property of human beings.[66] Nature "endowed [human beings] with a sublime celestial spirit," whereas "brute-creatures have many of their necessities supplied by nature."[67]

If Hume's views about animals suffer from the limitation of attributing too little cognitive capacity to animals—he maintains that animals act predominantly if not exclusively on blind instinct—his views about the nature of association nonetheless shed a great deal of light on the versatility of animals' responses to environmental contingencies. Much of what Hume says about inference in humans applies more properly to animals. As a strict empiricist, Hume denies even human beings the ability to form genuine abstractions, understood in Allen and Hauser's sense as mental content that is separate from the particulars to which it pertains. Hume never comes to grips with the evident ability of rational beings to form genuine abstractions, instead preferring to attribute to humans a different, more limited capacity for generalization that he borrows from Berkeley.

On Hume's view an abstraction is nothing more than a particular in my experience that serves to remind me of all other particulars of the same kind. Because all our ideas are derived from antecedent impressions, we possess no innate ideas, and we can form no ideas that are completely detached from the particulars from which they are derived. "Every thing, that exists, is particular."[68] By definition a genuine abstraction, such as a concept, would have no particular quality or quantity but would encompass all members of a class regardless of their particular quality and quantity. An abstract concept of a triangle would have no particular shape (e.g., it would not be an isosceles) or size but instead would possess all and only the qualities shared by all triangles. But Hume argues that all our impressions "have a determinate quantity and quality," and that the same must hold for all our ideas inasmuch as they are copies of impressions. Hence it is "absurd to suppose a triangle really existent, which has no precise proportion of sides and angles."[69] What we call abstract notions are, in fact, nothing more than "particular ones, annexed to a certain term, which gives them a more extensive signification, and makes them recall upon occasion other individuals, which are similar to them."[70] When I have an abstract idea of a triangle, I am simply employing the idea of some particular triangle I have experienced to bring to mind all the other objects (triangles) that, to a greater or lesser extent, resemble the triangle I have in mind. This particular idea of a triangle functions in a twofold manner: it retains its particular quality and quantity, but these recede, as it were, into the background while my imagination brings to mind all the other particular ideas I have of similar objects.[71]

As a strict empiricist interested in debunking the metaphysical excesses of such rationalist philosophers as Descartes, Hume seeks to develop a model of the human mind that dispenses with truly abstract cognitive functions as much as possible. Hence he follows

Berkeley in rejecting the possibility of abstract concepts in the sense I have been discussing them. At the same time, he reduces the notion of belief or certainty from a cognitive operation to a kind of feeling. He maintains that reason is not an autonomous faculty but rather "a wonderful and unintelligible instinct in our souls [that] . . . arises from past observation and experience."[72] Even our most solidly grounded beliefs are not grounded in rational reflection but instead are sentiments: "*Belief is more properly an act of the sensitive, than of the cogitative part of our natures.*"[73] To believe something is to feel that it is the case. For example, to believe that yelling will be followed by punishment is to have an irresistible sense that punishment is about to occur because it has typically happened in similar circumstances in the past. Hume even suggests that a (true) belief differs from a fiction only "in the *manner* of its being conceiv'd. . . . An idea assented to *feels* different from a fictitious idea." Compared to a fiction, a true belief has "a superior *force*, or *vivacity*, or *solidity*, or *firmness*, or *steadiness*."[74]

In his haste to offer a comparatively minimalist conception of human mental life, Hume goes too far when he tethers cognitive functions to sensations and passions in the way that he does. Too much in human linguistic abilities speaks against his flat rejection of abstract thought, and he is on extremely thin ice when he tries to explain phenomena such as mathematical reasoning. However, as I previously suggested, we can learn a lot from Hume about the nature of *animal* cognition. The mental operations that Hume attributes to human beings really apply to animals. It is animals, not humans, who are confined in a world of particulars, are incapable of forming genuine abstractions, and are incapable of reasoning about matters of fact that go beyond feelings of conviction grounded in customary regularities in past experience. Even if many of the inferences that human beings make are perceptual rather than rational, *all* the inferences made by animals are perceptual—which is to say that animals form certain feelings based on the similarity of a present perception to perceptions in their past experience, feelings that at the immediate, nonconceptual level in animals often have their human counterpart in intentional states such as hope or belief. In accordance with the language of "protothought" discussed in chapter I, we might call these states of feeling "protobeliefs" to indicate that they function equivalently to beliefs in human beings even though they are not propositionally structured. Although they function equivalently to beliefs in being directed, they are not directed at intentional objects as such. Instead, states of protothought are fundamentally associational. Their directedness is most evident in the way they motivate animals to pursue beneficial outcomes, even though animals do not have representations of the outcomes as such.

Although associative accounts of cognition have tended to assume that "associative responses rest on nothing but blind mechanical response," Papineau and Heyes note that a case can be made for the role of representations, particularly in more complex instances of associative behavior.[75] This would obviate the need to attribute propositional attitudes and concepts to animals. Moreover, it would account for the comparatively limited capacity for inference that animals possess while still attributing to them subjective states of awareness. As the following examples will show, an associative account of animal behavior is also able to account for complex animal behaviors that we might otherwise be inclined to explain by attributing the full apparatus of intentionality to animals. There is something profoundly implausible in Griffin's suggestion that "animals appear to think in 'if, then' terms," and that "when the pigeons are working hard in Skinner boxes to solve these challenging problems, they are thinking something like: 'Pecking this thing gets me food.'"[76]

For its action to be directed in the appropriate sense, an animal must employ "two representations: (1) a representation of the causal nature of the instrumental relationship between an action and its consequence or outcome; and (2) a representation of the current value of the outcome. Mediation by an action-outcome representation with causal content is required if we are to regard the action as *directed* toward the outcome in any sense beyond the purely descriptive."[77] Neither of these sorts of representation necessarily involves rational inference; both can be accommodated within a Humean account of perceptual inference.

Consider the case of the honey guide, which I described at the beginning of chapter 1. The honey guide leads a human being to a remote bee's nest, stopping along the way as needed to wait for the human and sometimes emitting churring sounds as if to encourage the human along the way. It is not difficult to explain such behavior in associative terms. The honey guide has a representation of the instrumental relationship between, say, churring and the human continuing to follow honey guideit. It has experienced the instrumental connection between this kind of action and its outcome in the past, and current circumstances sufficiently resemble those past instances that the honey guide makes an association between the current circumstances and its representation of the outcome, namely, the human continuing to follow it. The honey guide also has representations of discrete parts of the whole journey to the nest, and its ability to associate representations on the basis of resemblance enables it to be flexible in adapting these representations to new circumstances. Thus, the path to this particular nest need not be exactly the same as past particular paths the honey guide has experienced, nor does its churring behavior have to be exactly like it was in past instances. As in human action, the action of the honey guide will presumably become enriched through a process of trial and error. In addition to all these representations, which the honey guide is able to construct into a very long inferential chain (of perceptual rather than rational inference), the honey guide has a representation of the human's action when the human reaches the nest, as well as a representation of the value of the human's action: it yields honeycomb to the honey guide.

If such an account of the honey guide's behavior at first seems implausible, it is worth bearing in mind that many animals appear to possess discriminatory capacities far superior to our own. Richard J. Herrnstein's experiments show that pigeons possess extraordinary capacities for discriminating different sorts of object in their environment; and while Herrnstein believes that "the pigeons display semantic generalization," he notes that "we have no satisfactory theory of generalization."[78] The ability of pigeons to generalize might best be understood in terms of Hume's theory of abstraction rather than in terms of the theory that he and Berkeley criticize. As Herrnstein acknowledges, this would mean that the pigeons may simply be responding to resemblances when they make their discriminations. In this connection, Herrnstein notes the "considerable sensory powers" of pigeons, who notice features of the environment that human beings at first glance tend to miss.[79]

A more complex example is the deceptive behavior of my friend's border collie, Chelsea, which I also discussed in chapter 1. When Chelsea wants a particular spot on the bed and it is already occupied by the other dogs in the house, Chelsea runs to the back door and barks as if an intruder is outside. When the other dogs run to the back door to investigate, Chelsea dashes into the bedroom and takes her favorite spot on the bed. It is tempting to interpret Chelsea's behavior as involving beliefs, including beliefs about the beliefs of the other dogs: I believe that if I make the other dogs believe there is an intruder outside, they will run to the back door and I will have an opportunity to claim my favorite spot on the bed. But a dog is not capable of contemplating the intentional states of other beings any more than she is able, say, to believe that her companion human will come the day after tomorrow. Beings that have a theory of other minds are able to do things that animals, such as dogs, simply are unable to do. Explaining Chelsea's behavior in terms of perceptual associations offers a plausible alternative. Chelsea has a representation of the relationship between noise outside the back door and the action (her own or that of any other dog in the house) of running to the back door. She also has a representation of the relationship between other dogs running from the bed to another location and her favorite spot on the bed becoming available. Perhaps on one occasion Chelsea and the other dogs were lured to the back door by a noise, Chelsea lost interest in the potential intruder before the other dogs did, and she ran back to the bed. Or perhaps she saw one of the other dogs lose interest before the other dogs did and run back to the bed. There is no reason to suppose that Chelsea forms a deliberate, intentionally structured desire that the other dogs be deceived into leaving the bed. One way or another Chelsea's behavior will be the product of associations she makes—in some cases quite complex ones—between current circumstances and past chains of inference to which she has become accustomed.

The examples of the honey guide and Chelsea show what it means for an animal to "think" about distal events. One final example should suffice to demonstrate that we need not attribute rational capacity to animals in such cases but only perceptual representations and associative capacities. It will also serve as a reminder that we must always be on guard against projecting intentional capacities onto animals anthropomorphically. My friend Larry's dog, Higgins, loves to go for walks around the neighborhood. One of Higgins's favorite stops along the way is a yard where several chickens live. Larry is certain that when Higgins is getting ready for a walk while still at home, he has a specific desire to go and see the chickens, who live some distance away. Larry takes this to be a refutation of Seneca's suggestion that a horse in its stall cannot recall a familiar road but must have specific perceptual cues, such as the sight of the road. Higgins can neither see, nor smell, nor hear the chickens, and yet he clearly has a desire to go and see them.

There is no way to tell whether Larry's interpretation of Higgins's mental state is accurate, that is, no way to be sure that the excitement Higgins displays before embarking on the walk has anything to do with representations of the chickens. But let us suppose that it does have to do with the chickens. This situation is no more difficult to explain than either of the other examples I have examined. Higgins has a series of representations that have certain relationships with one another. He hears the jingle of the leash, associates that with embarking on a walk, and associates the beginning of the walk with each of the customary landmarks on the walk, much as bees use cognitive maps to find their way from the hive back to a source of nectar they have discovered. Given the extraordinary perceptual powers of animals such as dogs, particularly in comparison with the perceptual powers of human beings, it is not difficult to imagine Higgins being able to employ a sophisticated array of perceptual representations in the associations he makes. If we are disinclined to believe that dogs or pigeons can make discriminations and associations much more sophisticated than our own, this is because the philosophical tradition has left us with the anthropocentric prejudice that animals are cognitively inferior to human beings.

We would go a long way toward debunking this prejudice if we bear in mind the distinction between perceptual intelligence and conceptual rationality. Animals are intelligent creatures with subjective states of awareness. The more we come to appreciate this fact, the less we will be able to cling to a related anthropocentric prejudice, namely, that animals, being cognitively inferior to humans, are morally inferior as well. It is this kind of thinking that led to the legal classification of animals as property, and to the denial of anything like moral rights to animals. In the remainder of this book I examine this latter prejudice and develop a theory of the moral status of animals that complements the theory of animal cognition just presented.

# CHAPTER FOUR

# Liberal Individualism and the Problem of Animal Rights

## MENTAL LIFE AND MORAL STATUS

In the previous three chapters I examined some important contemporary debates concerning the mental capacities of animals and argued that animals possess perceptual but not conceptual/linguistic intelligence. On my view, animals cannot think in abstract terms. Why, then, has it become more common in recent years for philosophers and ethologists to argue that animals *do* think? There are three principal reasons for this. First, the limitations of behavioral ethology have become increasingly apparent; the proposition that only humans are capable of inner subjective awareness has been losing credibility. Second, the endeavor to attribute complex modes of thinking to animals is part of a strong reaction against a millennia-long tradition of denying thought and language to animals. In effect, the pendulum has swung from one extreme to the other. If the tradition extending from Aristotle to Kant argued that a being must be rational and linguistic to have inherent moral worth and that animals are nonrational and nonlinguistic, too many thinkers today appear to accept the first proposition but deny the second, that is, they tacitly accept the idea that moral worth depends on higher cognitive capacities and argue that animals do, in fact, possess these capacities. Third, because we are forced to argue by way of analogy from our own experience in conceptualizing animal behavior, the problem of anthropomorphizing animal experience looms large; we are virtually at a loss for words when it comes to explaining the nonconceptual and nonverbal experience of animals.

The most influential recent attempts to argue for the moral status of animals have all been based on an appeal to animal capacities. Some have been based on claims about animal intentionality, while others have been based on mere sentience, the ability to feel pleasure and pain. What these approaches all have in common is the notion that individual experience is the proper unit of measure for considering whether a being has moral worth. Nonetheless, thinkers such as Peter Singer end up arguing that animals may be treated as replaceable resources rather than as genuine individuals on the grounds that animals lack the cognitive sophistication to be self-aware. Such thinkers appeal to what Gary Francione calls "similar minds theory," according to which an animal's moral status depends on the degree to which that animal's mental life is sufficiently like the mental life of human beings.

The problem with such appeals is that they run the risk of depriving animals of moral status simply because animals cannot speak, or write, or think symbolically. As Francione points out, such comparisons doom animals to an inferior moral status because of the sorts of capacities that have traditionally been taken to be fundamental. Why focus on, say, the capacity to do calculus rather than on the ability of the Clark's nutcracker to store and retrieve enormous numbers of seeds? Or on the ability to understand and use the syntax of human natural language rather than on the ability to recognize conspecifics by means of smell? Richard Sorabji notes that the question "whether [chimpanzees] can string [linguistic] signs together syntactically . . . is a point of the highest scientific interest, but of absolutely no moral relevance whatsoever."[1] All that matters from a moral standpoint is whether, as Nagel puts it, "there is something it is like" to be the kind of being about whom we raise the question of moral status. Francione, who argues for the abolition of all human uses of animals, points out that "there is no logical relationship between differences in cognitive characteristics and the issue of animal use."[2] If one is going to say that we have the right to use animals for human consumption or for research because animals are "less intelligent" than us, it would seem to follow that more intelligent humans have a right to eat or experiment on less intelligent ones. The only bar to accepting the former while rejecting the latter is the dogmatic speciesist assumption that humans are somehow morally superior to animals simply in virtue of being human.

Surely experiential capacities matter in considerations of moral worth. If they didn't, it would be difficult to explain why we grant moral status to some beings (humans and perhaps at least some animals, such as linguistic apes) while denying it to inanimate objects. The moral status of animals is an urgent question precisely because animals are agents of experience. They strive, suffer, enjoy, and interact with their environments in ways that bear upon their welfare, even if they do not have any conceptual grasp of any of these activities and experiences. They are not indifferent to their lives and their fortunes. In accordance with the language of previous chapters, one might say that life is protomeaningful for animals, which is to say that it is significant for them in ways that we can only try to imagine because our own acquaintance with the phenomenon of significance is mediated through language.

Thus, the issue is not whether capacities are relevant to considerations of moral worth but rather which capacities *are* and *are not* relevant. My view is that perceptual experience (as defined in chapter 3) is sufficient, although perhaps not necessary, for moral status.[3] Any being capable of perceptual experience may be said to have a right to live its life free and unfettered; in particular, it has a right to live its life free of avoidable interference from human beings. For reasons that will become clear in this and the next chapter, I am not entirely comfortable using the language of rights to characterize the moral status of animals because I believe that the entire notion of animal (and perhaps human) rights needs to be grounded in a holistic cosmology.

For the present, however, I will use the language of animal rights as a shorthand for the idea that humans have basic obligations never to use animals for food, clothing, entertainment, or experimentation, even though animals have no corresponding obligations—indeed, no moral obligations whatsoever—toward humans.

I use the language of animal rights provisionally because the discourse of rights has shown the most promise over the past generation in the endeavor to vindicate the moral status of animals, and because the language of rights is intimately bound up with the liberal political tradition that originated in Locke, Rousseau, Kant, and Mill and has as its contemporary proponents thinkers such as John Rawls and Jürgen Habermas. As heirs to this tradition, we tend to find liberal political concepts such as equality, reciprocity, right, and obligation to be intuitively powerful when thinking about the comparative entitlements and duties of different agents of experience. Perhaps not surprisingly, the traditional exponents of liberalism conceptualized the moral status of animals by applying these concepts in the light of what these thinkers considered to be the experiential capacities of animals.

## CLASSICAL LIBERAL APPROACHES TO THE MORAL STATUS OF ANIMALS

The classical model of liberal individualism as envisioned by Locke, Rousseau, and Kant takes the self-reflective awareness and autonomy of the mature individual as an essential precondition for membership in the sphere of right, and hence for participation in a system of reciprocal rights and obligations. Implicitly adhering to the ancient Stoic conception of *oikeíosis* (kinship or belonging), according to which all and only rational, linguistic beings merit membership in the moral and political community, these thinkers exclude animals from the sphere of right on the grounds that animals are *aloga*, that is, fundamentally lacking in language or reason.[4] This exclusion reduces animals to the status of beings lacking inherent moral worth.

Locke, Kant, and a host of other thinkers in the liberal tradition explicitly endorse the proposition that we are justified in treating animals as property, and this is the way animals have long been classified in Anglo-American jurisprudence. Locke infers from their prudential capacities and expressions of emotion that animals can think.[5] But he denies them the capacity for abstraction: "The having of general ideas, is that which puts a perfect distinction betwixt Man and Brutes. . . . For it is evident, we observe no foot-steps in them, of making use of general signs for universal *Ideas*; from which we have reason to imagine, that they have not the faculty of abstracting, or making general *Ideas*, since they have no use of Words, or any other general Signs."[6] Animal thought consists in chains of particular ideas; this confines animals within the present and the immediate future, such that they are incapable of comparing individual ideas "with the reality of Things."[7]

For Locke animals are excluded from the social contract because they are incapable of abstract reasoning. For the same reason they are subject to human dominion. From the first sentence of the *Essay Concerning Human Understanding* Locke links human dominion over animals to our superior understanding: "It is the Understanding which sets Man above the rest of sensible Beings, and gives him all the Advantage and Dominion, which he has over them."[8] Moreover, this dominion over animals is not simply a matter of fact but fundamentally a matter of right. In the *First Treatise of Government* Locke invokes scriptural authority to support his view that God gave humans dominion over all of nature, including "a Right, to make use of the Food and Rayment" that God has given us.[9] We also have a right to "destroy . . . Inferior creatures . . . where need requires it."[10] Locke conceives of human need fundamentally in terms of the protection and cultivation of life, liberty, and property. Accordingly, our treatment of animals is to be consonant with Locke's law of nature, which "teaches all Mankind, who will but consult it, that being all equal and independent, no one ought to harm another in his Life, Health, Liberty, and Possessions."[11] Like any natural resource, animals are essentially property. Originally animals "belong to Mankind in common." They become the property of particular individuals through acts of "appropriation," that is, through the exertion of labor, as when an individual picks apples from a tree that does not already belong to another individual.[12] The law of nature demands that human beings respect each other's life and property, but it imposes no demands on humans as regards animals inasmuch as it classifies animals as mere instruments for the pursuit of human welfare.

In a similar spirit, Kant distinguishes between rational and non-rational beings, arguing that only the former are properly objects of direct moral concern. Kant's basic distinction is between "persons" and "things." A person is a being "whose existence has in itself an absolute worth, something which as an end in itself could be a ground of determinate laws."[13] To be a ground of determinate laws is to be capable of legislating and subjecting oneself to the moral law. Persons are able to recognize the universally binding duty of respect for all rational beings. A person is "something which is not to be used merely as a means and hence there is imposed thereby a limit on all arbitrary use of such beings, which are objects of respect."[14] Things, on the other hand, have "only a relative value as means" or instrumentalities.[15] Animals are essentially things in virtue of their "mechanical ordering," in contrast with humans, who are capable of self-determination.[16] But Kant rejects the Cartesian prejudice according to which animals are mere machines. We may infer "from the similarity between animal behavior [Wirkung] (whose basis we cannot perceive directly) and man's behavior (of whose basis we are conscious directly) . . . that animals too act according to *representations* [*Vorstellungen*] (rather than being machines, as Descartes would have it)." Animals are "living beings" of "the same general kind as human beings."[17]

For Kant animals differ from human beings in being governed by instinct and bodily inclinations. "All animals have the capacity to use their powers according to choice [nach Willkühr]. Yet this choice is not free, but necessitated by incentives and *stimuli* [durch Reitze und stimulos neceßitiert]. Their actions contain *bruta necessitas*."[18] Human beings, in contrast, function "by art," that is, human beings transcend the conditions of natural causation in virtue of their autonomy.[19] Whereas animals are living beings entirely subject to mechanistic principles, "nature gave man reason, and freedom of will based upon reason, and this in itself was a clear indication of nature's intention as regards his endowments. For it showed that man was not meant to be guided by instinct or equipped and instructed by innate knowledge; on the contrary, he was meant to produce everything from out of himself."[20]

Animals "have no free choice, their actions being necessarily determined by sensory impulses."[21] Animals are strictly subject to deterministic laws, whereas human beings are capable of progress in virtue of their rationality. This capacity renders human beings ends in themselves and hence moral beings. For Kant the only possible ultimate end in the world is "man under moral laws."[22] Only "persons," rational beings, are subject to the moral law. Everything else, animals included, is a mere "thing" or instrumentality in the service of man as an end in himself. "Man has, in his own person, an inviolability [eine Unverletzlichkeit]; it is something holy, that has been entrusted to us. All else is subject to man.... That which a man can dispose over, must be a thing. Animals here are regarded as things [Sachen]; but man is no thing."[23] Like Descartes before him, Kant argues that "man is indeed the only being on earth that has understanding and hence an ability to set himself purposes of his own choice, and in this respect he holds the title of lord of nature; and if we regard nature as a teleological system, then it is man's vocation to be the ultimate purpose of nature."[24] In his political writings Kant bases his faith in the infinite perfectibility of human nature on just such a teleological conception of nature. He posits civil society as the final purpose and highest aspiration of rational beings.[25]

In the context of the cosmopolitan ideal that he sketches for humanity, Kant characterizes animal nature as "an instrument for satisfying desires and inclinations [ein Instrument die Begierden und Neygungen zu befriedigen]."[26] Kant envisions civil society as an ideal systematic relationship between rational beings as ends in themselves and animals as living tools to be used in the furtherance of cosmopolitan aims. We have no direct moral duties to animals but only 'indirect duties." This means that any moral duties that we discharge in relation to animals are not for the sake of animals themselves but rather for the sake of rational beings. Like Pythagoras and Aquinas, Kant believes that by treating animals well, we are more likely to treat humanity well. "With regard to the animate but nonrational part of creation, violent and cruel treatment of animals is far more intimately opposed to a human being's duty to himself, and he has a duty to refrain from this; for it dulls his shared feeling of their suffering and so weakens and gradually uproots a natural predisposition that is very serviceable to morality in one's relations with other men."[27] In this sense our duties to animals are indirect rather than direct. "Respect always applies to persons only, never to things. The latter can awaken inclinations, and even love if they are animals (horses, dogs, etc.), or fear, as does the sea, a volcano, or a beast of prey; but they never arouse respect."[28] Any love we feel toward an animal is simply an instance of what Kant calls "pathological" as opposed to genuinely "practical" (i.e., moral) love.[29] At best such feelings ultimately refer not to the animal in question but to humanity. "Even gratitude for the long service of an old horse or dog (just as if they were members of the household) belongs *indirectly* to a human being's duty with regard to [in Ansehung dieser] animals; considered as a *direct* duty, however, it is always only a duty of the human being *to* himself."[30]

Kant's liberalism is focused entirely on relations between rational beings and the prospects for a harmonious human community. Kant adheres to the Stoic principle that all and only rational beings are members of the moral community or sphere of right; animals are categorically excluded from this community on the grounds of their nonrational, instinctual nature. Our only obligations with regard to animals are to treat animals in such a way that we do not compromise our own humanity, our treatment of ourselves and other rational beings. Thus, we may work and even kill animals under certain circumstances. "The human being is authorized to kill animals quickly (without pain) and to put them to work that does not strain them beyond their capacities (such work as he himself must submit to)."[31] Moreover, even though in general animal cruelty violates duties to humanity, such cruelty is permissible if it proves useful to humanity. "When anatomists take living animals to experiment on, that is certainly cruelty, though there it is employed for a good purpose [zu etwas gutem]; because animals are regarded as man's instruments, it is acceptable, though it is never so in sport."[32] On the other hand, "agonizing physical experiments for the sake of mere speculation, when the end could also be achieved without these, are to be abhorred."[33]

The liberal conceptions advanced by Locke and Kant take as axiomatic the notions of personhood, property, equality, reciprocity, and justice. Both thinkers view animals as instrumentalities over which human beings rightfully enjoy dominion. Animals are legally and morally understood as property, and property has no inherent moral worth; its worth is instrumental, and ultimately refers to persons involved in relations of mutual respect. Nonetheless Kant recognizes that animals are sentient beings and that we should not be indifferent to their suffering, even though his reasoning is that the only moral implication of such indifference is that it tends to undermine relations between *human* beings.

At first glance utilitarian thought would seem to hold more promise for overcoming this anthropocentric prejudice of the liberal tradition. Jeremy Bentham, a contemporary of Kant's, argues explicitly that sentience is the basis for recognizing that animals are not mere things, and hence for including animals in our moral calculations. On Bentham's view, the key question in determining the moral worth of animals "is not, Can they *reason*? nor, Can they *talk*? but, Can they *suffer*?"[34] But Bentham also argues that the human practice of killing and eating animals poses no moral problem because animals "have none of those long-protracted anticipations of future misery that we have," and because "the death they suffer in our hands commonly is . . . a speedier, and by that means a less painful one, than that which would await them in the inevitable course of nature. . . . We should be the worse off for their living, and they are never the worse off for being dead."[35] Animals are morally considerable to the extent that they can suffer. But their suffering counts less than human suffering because animals lack the cognitive equipment that would enable them to contemplate the distant future. Thus, death is a greater harm to humans inasmuch as we have a sense of the future opportunities for satisfaction that we lose when we die. Moreover, animals suffer less when we kill them than when they die a "natural" death. Hence we are in effect doing animals a favor by killing them for human consumption. As Francione points out, Bentham never questions the property status of animals.[36]

Bentham introduces a hierarchical sense of moral desert into utilitarianism that is adhered to by subsequent utilitarian thinkers. John Stuart Mill argues in *Utilitarianism* that intellectual and social pleasures are superior in kind to bodily pleasures, concluding that "it is better to be a human being dissatisfied than a pig satisfied; better to be Socrates dissatisfied than a fool satisfied. And if the fool, or the pig, is of a different opinion, it is because they only know their own side of the question. The other party to the comparison knows both sides."[37] Like Bentham, Mill recognizes that sentience confers moral status on animals. But he follows Bentham in asserting a hierarchy of sentient beings, such that those with more highly sophisticated cognitive equipment stand higher in the moral order than those with less sophisticated abilities. In the end, "the ways of Nature are to be conquered, not obeyed. . . . All praise of Civilization, or Art, or Convenience, is so much dispraise of nature; an admission of imperfection, which it is man's business, and merit, to be always endeavoring to correct or mitigate."[38] We may not act with complete indifference toward animals, but the cultivation of civilization directly depends on the subjugation of nature, including animal nature.

In classical liberal political thought from Locke to Mill, a consistent theme is the permissibility of subjugating animals in the service of human interests. The resulting predicament for animals has been well documented. Animals may be subjected to pain and suffering as long as it is considered "necessary" for the furtherance of "important" human interests. Animals have no standing to sue on their own behalf for harms they endure at the hands of human beings.[39] In essence, the legal treatment of animals in the liberal tradition codifies an understanding and evaluation of animals as instrumentalities for the satisfaction of human needs. This modern legal conception of animals echoes Aristotle's view that animals exist expressly for the sake of human beings.[40] The evaluation of animals as instrumentalities lies at the core of legal and moral justifications of animal husbandry, animal experimentation, the killing of animals for human consumption, the use of animals in various forms of entertainment (circuses, rodeos, blood sports, etc.), and the like. The essential thread that links modern and ancient Western justifications of such uses of animals is the belief that animals lack the rationality and linguistic ability required for membership in the sphere of right. This holds even for a utilitarian thinker such as Bentham, who purports that rational and linguistic ability are not the basis of moral status. Like the Stoics before us, we live according to a system of law that refuses to see animals as subjects or individuals and instead sees them as objects or "replaceable" resources.

The subjection of animals in recent centuries has been facilitated by the principles of liberal political theory, according to which animals are excluded from direct moral and legal consideration on the grounds that they do not qualify as autonomous individuals with the capacity for rational self-determination. This raises the question whether a robust sense of the moral status of animals can be established within the framework of liberal theory or whether we must go beyond the boundaries of liberal theory in order to secure the moral status of animals. An examination of modern and contemporary approaches to this problem demonstrates that liberal theory is highly susceptible to anthropocentric prejudice, and that even the best such theory of the moral status of animals implicitly appeals to considerations that stand outside the framework of the liberal approach.

## Contemporary Liberal Approaches to the Moral Status of Animals

Recent efforts have been made to acknowledge the status of animals as subjects within the framework of contemporary liberal legal and moral thought. In *The Case for Animal Rights* Tom Regan offers a modified Kantian approach to the recognition of animal rights. Regan's approach and its limitations are now well known. He argues that animals are best understood as moral "patients," in comparison with rational beings, who are moral agents. A moral patient is a being toward whom we must acknowledge moral obligations even though that being is incapable of taking on reciprocal moral obligations toward others. On Regan's view, infants, the mentally impaired, and certain animals qualify as moral patients. Regan argues that Kant succumbed to anthropocentric prejudice when he limited the sphere of morally considerable beings to rational beings. To be consistent, Kant should have acknowledged that all beings that qualify as "subjects-of-a-life" merit direct moral respect. Regan defines subjects-of-a-life as beings who have inherent value in virtue of having "beliefs and desires; perception, memory, and a sense of the future, including their own future; an emotional life together with feelings of pleasure and pain; preference- and welfare-interests; the ability to initiate action in pursuit of their desires and goals; a psycho-physical identity over time; and an individual welfare."[41]

Regan also argues that all beings with inherent value possess that value equally. Animals "have value apart from human interests," that is, "a value that is not reducible to their utility relative to our interests."[42] As Kant argued, to possess inherent value is to be worthy of respect, and the amount of respect we show to beings possessing inherent worth should not vary with any particular features of those beings' experiences. This also means that we should show equal respect for such beings since their inherent value is absolute rather than relative. Regan adapts this reasoning to argue that animals possess an inherent value equal to that of human beings. Thinkers such as Kant are "arbitrary in the extreme" to affirm the inherent worth of rational agents while denying it to moral patients. Once we acknowledge that animals possess inherent worth, we must also acknowledge that they possess it to exactly the same degree as moral agents.[43]

This would appear to provide the basis for a robust theory of animal rights built upon the foundations of liberal thought. But Regan proceeds to argue for conclusions that clearly privilege human beings over animals. In particular, his resolution of the hypothetical lifeboat case shows the anthropocentrism of his viewpoint. We are asked to imagine four adult humans and one dog in a lifeboat, whose circumstances are such that one of the five must be thrown overboard in order to prevent the boat from sinking and everyone perishing. "No reasonable person would suppose that the dog had a 'right to life' that is equal to the humans' or that the animal should be given an equal chance in the lottery for survival."[44] This is because "the harm that death is, is a function of the opportunities for satisfaction that it forecloses, and no reasonable person would deny that the death of any of the four humans would be a greater prima facie loss, and thus a greater prima facie harm, than would be true in the case of the dog." Indeed, Regan maintains that even a million dogs should be thrown overboard in order to save four humans.[45] The logical extension of Regan's argument is that it would be justifiable to sacrifice every animal on earth in order to save one human being.

This bizarre and, in my judgment, counterintuitive conclusion is a sign that Regan advocates abandoning the principle of equal inherent worth whenever acting on that principle would compromise the welfare of human beings. To do so is to undermine completely the prospect of appealing to a rights-based theory as a basis for protecting the interests of animals. More recently Gary Francione has developed a rights-based theory that avoids this problem and, at the same time, sheds light on a fundamental difficulty in the endeavor to acknowledge the rights of animals. Francione's work proceeds from a distinction between two approaches to considering the moral status of animals: animal welfarism and animal rights. Legal welfarism is the view that "animals, which are the property of people, may be treated solely as means to ends by humans as long as this exploitation does not result in the infliction of 'unnecessary' pain, suffering, or death."[46] Welfarism views animals fundamentally as instrumentalities and seeks to minimize their pain and suffering by prohibiting gratuitous suffering. To the legal welfarist pain and suffering that can be justified as unavoidable in the pursuit of important human goods are permissible. The contradiction of legal welfarism is that it promotes "our almost universal embrace of principles of 'kindness' to animals while we socially tolerate continuing and unequivocally barbarous conduct that almost no one would defend as 'necessary'. . . . What we do tolerate as 'humane' is so unquestionably inhumane that the conduct *could not* be justified morally in the absence of an explanation grounded in the assumptions that animals are property, [and] that property valuation is best done by property owners."[47] If only against the intention of its most staunch advocates, welfarism augments a system of legal sanctions for the exploitation of animals. Indeed, it does so to such an extent "that reforming exploitation through welfarist means will simply facilitate the indefinite perpetuation of such exploitation."[48]

Francione argues that the only way to end the cycle of animal exploitation is to abolish the property status of animals. He grounds his argument in the notion of sentience, according to which to be sentient is to be "an 'I' who has subjective experiences," in particular the capacity to experience feelings of pleasure and pain.[49] As sentient beings, animals have an interest in not suffering, and "a right is a particular way of protecting interests." Thus, animals must be recognized as possessing rights, which "are moral notions that grow out of respect for the individual."[50] The problem with existing legal doctrine in general, and with legal welfarism in particular, is that by treating animals as property we effectively deprive them of legal protection of their interests. "The property status of animals renders completely meaningless any balancing that is supposedly required under the humane treatment principle or animal welfare laws, because what we really balance are the interests of property owners against the interests of their animal property. . . . Such a balance will rarely, if ever, tip in the animal's favor." At bottom "it is *always* necessary to decide against animals in order to protect human property rights in animals."[51]

By classifying animals legally as bearers of rights, we extend to them the principle of equal consideration of interests and thus treat them legally as persons. Once we recognize that animals have an interest in not suffering, we recognize that we have no basis for denying them the right not to suffer. With regard to suffering, at least, animals are on a par with human beings, and we may not privilege humans over animals with regard to the interest in not suffering. We must extend equal consideration to humans and animals with regard to this interest. This does not mean that we must extend equal treatment to animals and humans in all cases. For example, it would not make sense to issue library cards or driver's licenses to animals because they lack the requisite cognitive equipment to establish in them an interest in borrowing books or driving a car. Fundamental to the principle of equal consideration of interests is that "we ought to treat like cases alike unless there is a morally relevant reason not to."[52] One key consequence of this principle is that treating animals as property is no more justifiable morally than is treating (certain) human beings as property. Francione employs Kant's distinction between persons and things, arguing that animals, like humans, have the right not to be treated as things or mere instrumentalities for the satisfaction of human needs.[53] "The principle of equal consideration requires that unless we have a morally sound reason not to do so, we must protect animals from suffering at all from use as human property." This confers on animals the legal and moral status of "persons," that is, individuals who are ends in themselves rather than mere means or instrumentalities.[54] Once we grant legal personhood to animals, we can no longer justify using animals for food, manual servitude, experimentation, entertainment, and the like, any more than we can justify using human beings for such purposes.

An important and innovative feature of Francione's position is the categorical character of its conferral on animals of an interest in not suffering. It is categorical in the sense that it admits of no hierarchies or comparisons among sentient beings; if a being is sentient, then that being has an interest in not suffering and a fortiori an unqualified right not to be property. Although Francione does leave open the possibility that circumstances might arise in which it might be morally justifiable to abrogate this right, he offers no example of such circumstances. It is implicit in his view that a clear and compelling justification would have to be offered for abrogating an animal's—or any sentient being's—right not to be property. More than any previous thinker in the liberal tradition, Francione succeeds in arguing for parity between humans and animals with respect to the right not to suffer.

Regan does not succeed in this regard, nor do contemporary utilitarian thinkers. Singer invokes the classical utilitarian view of a hierarchy in human-animal relations as the basis for his denial that animals have an interest in life. Like Bentham and Mill, he correlates moral worth with the degree of a being's cognitive sophistication. The interests of beings that are more highly aware—and, specifically, those of beings that are *self*-aware—count more in the utilitarian calculus than the interests of beings that lack self-awareness. The logic here is that self-aware beings have an interest in the future that non–self-aware beings lack; hence the former have an interest in *life* that the latter cannot possess.[55] When an animal is killed, "it is not easy to explain why the loss to the animal killed is not, from an impartial point of view, made good by the creation of a new animal who will lead an equally pleasant life."[56] Human beings are, in virtue of our self-consciousness and ability to contemplate the future, individual moral persons, whereas animals are simply replaceable resources. In this respect Singer's position exhibits what Stuart Hampshire has identified as the anthropocentrism characteristic of all utilitarian positions, namely, it "places man at the very center of the universe, with their [*sic*] states of feeling as the source of all value in the world."[57] This anthropocentric prejudice is evident in any theory that ascribes moral superiority to human beings on the grounds that human beings possess more sophisticated cognitive abilities than animals.

## THE LIMITATIONS OF LIBERAL APPROACHES TO THE MORAL STATUS OF ANIMALS

As we have seen, liberal approaches to the moral status of animals, both classical and contemporary, seek to marshal the tools of liberal political theory to vindicate the moral status of animals. In my judgment none of them goes far enough in this endeavor. Their adherence to concepts proper to the sphere of *social* justice imposes limitations on their ability to do justice to the moral status of animals in the *cosmic* sphere. The error or limitation of traditional approaches has been the endeavor to conceptualize the moral status of animals in terms that properly apply only within the narrow scope of social relations between human beings, that is, in terms of what I call social justice. I take the limitations of liberal theory to be signs of a latent anthropocentrism that must be overcome if we are to do complete justice to the moral status of animals. I believe that all attempts to conceptualize the moral status of animals in terms of *social* justice end up, if only unwittingly, subordinating animals to the interests and prerogatives of human beings. What is needed is an approach that inscribes social justice within the larger framework of cosmic justice, which relates human beings to the rest of nonhuman living nature. As I argue in the next chapter, only such an approach promises to give genuine force to moral claims on behalf of animals.

To better understand the inherent limitations of liberal approaches, consider Julian Franklin's arguments. He suggests that the fundamental question with regard to the moral status of animals "is whether [animals] are entities which, by their inherent nature, are to be included in political justice," by which he seems to mean what I mean by "social" justice.[58] To the extent that animals are sentient beings, Franklin believes that they have a fundamental right not to be treated as mere means by human beings.[59] Where Kant argues that all and only autonomous, rational agents have a right not to be treated as mere instrumentalities, Franklin argues that the categorical imperative must be understood as applying not simply to Kantian "persons" but to all sentient beings generally. In doing so, Franklin implicitly follows the reasoning of Regan, who argues that Kant cannot non-arbitrarily deny equal moral consideration to moral patients while extending it to moral agents.[60]

Franklin argues that "concern for the well-being of animals becomes mandatory only when they become participants in a scheme of cooperation instituted by humans."[61] Franklin would dispute my contention that concern for the well-being of animals is mandatory even in situations that do *not* involve schemes of cooperation initiated by humans. I take concern for animals in the context of human activities to be a subset of a larger sphere of concern for animals. While suggesting that we should not be indifferent or gratuitous in our treatment of wild nature, Franklin expresses what I think are several pointedly anthropocentric moral commitments that bear closer scrutiny.

The first is that certain uses of animals, including some forms of experimentation and the use of animals as pets, might be justified on the grounds that the participation of animals in such practices "could perhaps be considered as 'virtually voluntary.'" The conditions for imputing such voluntariness to animals are that we not make the animals "victims of exploitation" and that they "receive equal consideration, relative to their natures, as ends."[62] Thus, we might be able to justify the regime of pet ownership as long as we do not exploit the animals in question and extend equal consideration to animals in all matters that bear upon their inherent capabilities. For example, we need not extend voting rights to pets since animals lack the linguistic and deliberative apparatus requisite for participation in the franchise, but we must extend equal consideration to pets in matters pertaining to their need to enjoy proper types and amounts of physical exercise. Thus a dog's interest in ranging over extensive distances each day, as opposed to simply running around in circles in a small yard, would have to be considered alongside the owner's desire not to be bothered with taking his or her pet dog on extensive daily walks. Provided that we extend equal consideration to such interests, we would guard against the prospect of exploiting pet dogs. On Franklin's account we might be entitled to attribute "virtual voluntariness" to them—which is to say that we could employ the fiction that dogs *want* to be maintained as pets.

Francione's views on pet ownership preclude a priori any such attribution of virtual voluntariness to animals. His demand that we terminate the regime of pet ownership follows directly from his argument that animals have a fundamental right not to be property of any kind.[63] Francione believes that all animal ownership, regardless of our intentions and any precautions we take, fundamentally exploits animals by violating their basic rights. Franklin's belief that we can engage in certain uses of animals without exploiting them follows from his foundational principle: that animals have a fundamental right not to be treated as mere means, *not* that they have a fundamental right not to be property. Thus, we may legitimately use animals as long as we acknowledge their status as ends in themselves.

On such a view, one could justify a wide variety of uses of animals. Nussbaum admonishes us not to buy into the "romantic view of domestic animals" according to which "these animals are being held prisoner by humans" and should be allowed "to live in the wild as nature intended." Given that many domestic species have "evolved over millennia in symbiosis with human beings . . . no plausibly flourishing existence in the wild is possible" for them. Nussbaum proposes that, from a moral standpoint, we should treat such animals "as companions in need of prudent guardianship, but endowed with entitlements that are theirs, even if exercised through guardianship." What does this mean concretely? For Nussbaum it means, for example, that there is nothing wrong in principle with teaching horses "to jump hedges and fences, or to perform dressage, or to race."[64]

As it pertains to horse racing, this chain seems to amount to something like the following. It is in the nature of a horse to run, and perhaps to compete with other horses when running. Domestic horses have been rendered unable to live in the wild. Therefore the institution of horse racing, designed to satisfy human desires, is morally acceptable in principle. If an occasional Barbaro must be "put down" as a consequence of the regime of horse racing, this is unfortunate but does not constitute an infringement on the moral rights of the horses in question, provided that we have endeavored to treat race horses not merely as means but also as ends. It strikes me that such reasoning does not proceed from a consideration of horses as ends but rather from the human desire to use horses as instrumentalities for human entertainment. It considers only as an afterthought the question whether we can find ways to justify such uses as not infringing on the inherent dignity of horses.

Here is another way to approach the problem. Kant repeatedly tells us that there is only one categorical imperative, although he articulates it in at least three or four different ways. These different formulations are meant to bring the ideas of duty and respect for the moral law closer to intuition. Thus, wherever possible we should consider whether a given kind of conduct satisfies not simply one formulation of the categorical imperative but others as well. In the case of horse racing, we might do well to consider whether we can universalize a maxim whereby we use for our entertainment sentient beings whose nature is to run competitively. For there is plenty of evidence that it is in the nature of human beings—and not just of horses—to engage in such activities. Thus we might find a way to justify using human beings in races. Of course, a fundamental difference between humans and horses in this connection is that humans are rational, linguistic beings and can explicitly offer or refuse their consent, whereas horses lack this ability. But why *assume* that horses *want* to be involved in the institution of horse racing, that is, that they participate "virtually voluntarily," when we openly acknowledge that some human beings want to race while others *don't*?

Although Franklin does not address this sort of question explicitly, he does state that in conflicts between animals and human beings regarding the use of nature (e.g., in situations in which the creation of necessary human settlements would displace indigenous species), "there is a rebuttable presumption in favor of the human claim." We still have a duty to avoid animal exploitation, understood in terms of the second formulation of the categorical imperative as neglecting the status of the animals in question as ends; but the real "issue . . . is whether the intended expansion of human activity will enhance or diminish the quality of human life, quite apart from the exploitation of animals as means." Here Franklin relies on Regan's claim that "death is a greater loss to humans than to animals because a human life offers more possibilities of satisfaction."[65]

The basic flaw of liberal approaches to the moral status of animals is that they inevitably invoke the same sort of reasoning, mutatis mutandis, when considering cases of conflict between human beings and animals in which death is *not* on the line as well as in those cases in which it is, and in cases involving conflict between humans and domesticated animals. There is no little irony in the fact that Nussbaum concludes her *Harvard Law Review* article on Steven Wise's *Rattling the Cage* by suggesting that the moral status of animals "is an area in which we will ultimately need good theories to winnow our judgments because our judgments are so flawed and shot through with self-serving inconsistency," given the fact that elsewhere she argues that our scruples against using animals in activities such as horse racing are born of flights of "romantic fantasy."[66]

Francione's approach has the virtue of denying us the opportunity to rationalize practices such as horse racing, by prohibiting any activities that reduce animals to the status of property. To take seriously the proposition that animals have a fundamental right not to be property is, among other things, to be wary of attempts to justify uses of animals on the basis of pressing human need. Rather than positing a rebuttable claim in favor of humans in cases of conflict with animals, we really ought to take as axiomatic *a rebuttable presumption in favor of animals.* Too often in the history of Western philosophy philosophers—Bentham and Schopenhauer are two glaring modern examples—have suggested that we have direct obligations to respect the integrity of animals, only to conclude that practices such as vivisection and killing animals for human consumption are justified by putatively great human need.[67] Both Bentham and Schopenhauer make the familiar claim that death is a greater harm to humans than to animals inasmuch as human beings can contemplate the distant future and have greater opportunities for satisfaction than animals. It is telling that thinkers who make this sort of claim in comparing humans and animals never make a comparable claim in comparing human beings of different levels of intelligence and initiative. There are human beings whose capacities and opportunities for satisfaction are much greater than those of other human beings, and yet we recognize good reasons not to give moral priority to people with such capacities. Our willingness to make such comparisons between human beings and animals but not between different groups of humans is symptomatic of the "self-serving inconsistency" of which Nussbaum speaks.

To render our thinking about the moral status of animals consistent with our thinking about the moral status of human beings is, among other things, to question the conventional wisdom that death is a greater harm to humans than to animals. The magnitude of the harm inflicted on a given being by death is to be determined not in relation to that being's putative intelligence but rather in relation to that being's inherent worth. My cat Pindar does not appear to have the potential to appreciate Schubert's late symphonies, but he appears to have a tremendous capacity to exchange affection with me. For all we know, his capacity for the exchange of immediate, non-reflective affection may be much greater than my own. On what grounds should we suppose that my ability to appreciate Schubert's music, or to engage in philosophical reflection, makes death a greater harm for me, in other words, that I have more to lose by dying? And why *not* conclude from this that Winston Churchill had more to lose by dying than I do? Notwithstanding liberal generalizations to the effect that my potential is no less than Churchill's was, I dare say that his political acumen and tenacity were considerably greater than mine.

The proposition that the death of an animal such as Pindar is no less a harm to him than my death is to me is for many people so counterintuitive that a simple appeal to rational considerations is likely to be inadequate as a means for making it plausible. The reason for this, I think, is that our deepest moral convictions are not simply products of rational reflection but instead rely on a *felt* connection to other members of the moral community. Franklin notes that even Kant makes room in his moral thought for affective regard.[68] Specifically, Kant appeals to what he calls "practical" love, which "resides in the will and not in the propensities of feeling, in principles of action and not in tender sympathy."[69] Kant is careful to distinguish moral love from "pathological" love, by which he means any kind of love attached to sympathy and other forms of personal inclination. Moral love, to the extent that Kant articulates a coherent conception of it, is thus an operation of the will that refers us to humanity generally and makes no particular discriminations between different members of the moral community. If it can be understood to be a form of "feeling" at all, it is different in principle than the sorts of feelings that connect us concretely to others; It is a detached feeling experienced from an abstract standpoint in virtue of which we find ourselves motivated to do our duty and to respect members of the moral community. Kant's goal in distinguishing "moral" and "pathological" feeling is to exclude from the basis of morality all appeals to selfish inclination, which cause us to compromise our respect for humanity and thereby violate the moral law.

Franklin rightly lauds Kant for excluding merely subjective forms of feeling from the basis of morality. He follows Kant in ruling out "feeling and sentiment . . . as the ultimate ground of morals generally."[70] And yet, like Schopenhauer, I can't help wondering whether the endeavor to eliminate feeling altogether from the basis of morality is a mistake. For I believe that a non-anthropocentric form of the moral love mentioned by Kant implicitly plays—or should play—a fundamental role in the establishment of connections to other beings in the moral community. Even in arguments such as Francione's, which purport to base their conclusions on purely rational considerations, I believe that a sense of *felt kinship* with animals plays a fundamental if unspoken role.

If humans are morally superior to animals on the grounds that they are more intelligent—leaving aside for the moment the problem of defining exactly what that means—then by the same reasoning we should conclude that more intelligent human beings are morally superior to less intelligent humans. The amount of intelligence a being possesses has no essential connection with the question of moral status. The ability to draw logical inferences, form abstract concepts, anticipate the distant future or recollect the distant past, engage in acts of linguistic predication—none of these abilities has any bearing on a being's moral status, just as none of them is recognized to have any bearing on a marginal human's moral status.

The question as to which capacities or criteria *are* morally relevant is a difficult one, with several possible answers. Here I shall confine my remarks to the answer offered by Francione, who is the sole thinker to adopt the liberal standpoint and yet avoid the pitfall of anthropocentrism. Francione recognizes the anthropocentric implications of what he calls "similar-minds theory": "Whether nonhumans have minds that are similar or identical to ours may be interesting from a scientific perspective, but it is wholly irrelevant from a moral perspective. If we take nonhuman interests seriously, we have no choice but to acknowledge that only sentience is relevant."[71] As long as we demand that animals possess mental capacities sufficiently similar to our own as a condition for granting animals moral status, animals will inevitably fail to pass the test. Moreover, the only truly relevant capacity for assessing moral status, on Francione's view, is sentience, the capacity to feel pleasure or pain. Bentham was right to identify the capacity to suffer as a sufficient condition for moral status, but he was wrong to make the degree of moral status dependent on cognitive abilities in virtue of which the suffering of humans is supposedly more important than that of animals. Francione argues that sentient beings have an interest in not suffering, and that the principle of equal consideration of interests—to which Regan and Singer both purport to subscribe—demands that we not give preference to the interest of humans over that of animals in not suffering. To the extent that laws are mechanisms for protecting interests, the crux of Francione's argument is that animals have a right not to be the property of humans. As long as animals are classified as property, the law will sanction the exploitation of animals for the gratification of human desires. Thus, the only way to guarantee that the interest of animals in avoiding suffering is protected is to abolish the property status of animals.[72]

That Francione develops his arguments from a liberal standpoint is clear. The operative terms in his analysis are interests, rights, and personhood. To acknowledge that animals have morally significant interests, in particular the interest in not suffering and the interest in continued existence, is to recognize their status as "persons" precisely where Kant argued that animals are mere "things" with no place in the sphere of right.[73] On Francione's view, one cannot consistently acknowledge that animals are sentient and deny that animals have interests, which are the basis of rights. If one accepts Francione's reasoning, then one may conclude that his position obviates the need to question whether only those beings possess rights who are capable of forming beliefs and desires. To attribute interests and hence rights to (some) animals, we need know only that those animals experience pleasure and pain, not whether those animals possess the full apparatus of linguistic intentionality. Thus, we need not know whether animals think in ways comparable to the ways in which human beings think. We need know only that animals are sentient to conclude that they are bearers of a fundamental right, namely, the right not to be the property of human beings.[74]

Francione's position constitutes a major advance over all other liberal approaches to the moral status of animals in that it is invulnerable to the criticism that it privileges human beings over other sentient beings in the legal and moral order of things. Francione's position does not call for equal treatment of humans and animals in all cases. For example, one need not confer the right to vote or the right to obtain a driver's license on animals because animals presumably lack the capacity to vote or drive. In situations of genuine emergency, in which one cannot save both beings, one may save a human being rather than an animal.[75] But what one may *not* do is give preference to the interests of humans over the comparable interests of animals in non-emergency situations, which constitute the bulk of our interactions with animals. To do so would be to disregard the equal inherent worth possessed by humans and animals.[76] Thus, we may not disregard the suffering we cause animals in the name of human pleasure and convenience, nor may we suppose that death is a greater harm to human beings than to animals.[77]

Even if Francione's position is sound—that is, even if it is logically valid and based on all true premises, which I think it is—it is not sufficient on its own to compel the kind of performative assent on the part of human beings that would lead to a thoroughgoing change in the way we value and treat animals in our culture. What is missing is the affective basis that would move human beings who are not predisposed to do so to *acknowledge* the comparability of human and animal situations as regards the problem of suffering and the specter of death. The framework of classical liberalism reproduces the Stoic prejudice that all and only beings who are linguistic and rational merit moral consideration. Liberalism conceives of humans—and only humans—as participants in the sphere of justice and hence as bearers of rights. The most influential contemporary exponent of this conception of liberalism is John Rawls, who argues that only those beings capable of having a sense of justice can be said to be owed justice. We may elect to assert obligations of compassion toward animals, but it is simply incoherent to think of animals as beings with rights.[78] Even Bentham, who acknowledges the capacity of animals to suffer, justifies the use of animals to gratify human desires. Mill places a premium on human over animal feeling, thereby reasserting a hierarchy in which human beings have moral priority over animals.

This anthropocentric prejudice in liberal thought persists because people, by and large, appear unwilling to abandon the belief that our intellectual capacities entitle us to superior moral status vis-à-vis animals. By denying a hierarchy of moral entitlements based on the putative sophistication of a being's capacity to feel pleasure and pain, Francione challenges a basic, if often unexpressed, tenet of the liberal approach. The problem with which Francione leaves us is how to bring about a general acknowledgment of the proposition that beings capable of abstract reflection (and the attendant pleasures that one may experience from exercising such a capacity) merit no greater moral consideration than beings incapable of abstraction—that, for example, the ability to appreciate the sonata form is no more *morally* significant than the ability to enjoy a good nap. The key to solving this problem lies in recognizing that only a change at the affective level can move human beings to accept the key premise of Francione's argument; that only through a felt acknowledgment of our commonality or kinship with animals can one be moved to embrace and enact the program that Francione sets forth.

History has confirmed that the affirmation of this essential kinship with animals cannot be achieved through purely rational argumentation. The affective roots of a robust animal ethic are to be established through the development of a cosmic holism that sees human beings as part of a larger natural environment in which we have fundamental obligations toward other sentient beings. To recognize our place in the totality of nature is to open ourselves to the need to regulate the exercise of our wills with an eye toward the welfare of beings who cannot speak for themselves and hence cannot function as advocates for the promotion of their own interests. It is precisely in acknowledging our responsibilities to beings who cannot assert their own interests and cannot be held morally responsible that we encounter the limits of the liberal model for comprehending the idea of animal rights. We move beyond the realm of *social* justice (i.e., justice among moral and legal agents) and enter the realm of *cosmic* justice, a relation that obtains between moral-legal agents and nonhuman moral-legal patients.

# CHAPTER FIVE

# The Ideal of Cosmic Holism

## A Non-Anthropocentric Conception of Justice

The chief limitation of the liberal perspective as regards the moral status of animals is its anthropocentrism. The liberal perspective is fundamentally concerned with considerations of social justice, and hence with relations between rational human agents. Attempts to vindicate the moral status of animals from within a liberal framework are limited by the anthropocentric vocabulary of individuality, agency, reciprocity, and rights—a vocabulary that, in the absence of a firm grounding in certain non-anthropocentric values, seems ill-suited to fully articulating a possible justice relationship between human beings and nonhuman animals. It is not surprising, for example, that John Rawls categorically denies a justice relationship between humans and animals, arguing that at most we can have duties of humanity or compassion toward animals.[1] For Rawls, 'justice' is a term that, by its very nature, applies only to relations between beings that are capable of having a sense of justice and entering into a social contract.

Two things should be noted here, both of which shed light on liberal approaches generally. The first is that Rawls dismisses as incoherent any notion of justice that purports to apply to relationships between human and nonhuman beings. Thus, nonlinguistic beings are excluded in principle from the sphere of justice, which means, among other things, that nothing we do to animals can be considered an injustice. But why must a being have (or be capable of having) an abstract conception of justice in order to be owed duties of justice? Rawls never answers this question but, like Kant, takes it for granted that only rational agents can be owed direct duties. In doing so Rawls, like Kant, rejects the proposition that animals or any other nonrational beings have inherent worth. As I noted in the preceding chapter, Tom Regan has pointed out the arbitrariness of this view as it applies to sentient nonhuman beings. Moral patients "lack the prerequisites that would enable them to control their own behavior in ways that would make them morally accountable for what they do."[2] Nonetheless, given their subjective states of awareness, moral patients properly qualify as objects of moral concern. "If, in short, we postulate inherent value in the case of moral agents, then we cannot nonarbitrarily deny it of moral patients."[3] Given the characterization of animal subjectivity provided in chapter 4, it is clear that many animals qualify as moral patients, as beings toward whom we have moral obligations even though these animals cannot take on reciprocal responsibilities toward us nor raise moral claims on their own behalf. A key question in this connection is how to awaken acknowledgment in human agents that we have profound moral obligations toward animals. A related question is whether the liberal discourse of rights acknowledges the ultimate basis of our moral obligations toward animals.

This brings me to the other point that should be noted about Rawls's position, namely, that he argues for only limited obligations toward animals. Rawls does not develop his remarks about our obligations toward animals, but a simple reflection on the notions of justice and compassion makes the implications of his remarks clear. Think of the distinction between justice and compassion in relation to the contemporary debate between animal welfarism and abolitionism. The animal welfarist argues that certain uses of animals are perfectly permissible, but that we must be mindful of how we treat animals while we use them. The abolitionist argues that certain uses of animals are categorically impermissible, regardless of how well we treat the animals while we use them. The welfarist implicitly argues for duties of compassion toward animals. We should identify with the animals' suffering and feel a sense of caring regard for them, but this duty of fellow feeling (com-passion, lit. "feeling together with") does not prohibit us from, say, experimenting on them or killing them for human consumption. The abolitionist explicitly argues for duties of justice toward animals. Given that animals have subjective states of awareness that include sentience, we have obligations not to use animals in ways that violate their rights to life and the avoidance of unnecessary suffering. As Gary Francione has put the point on a number of occasions, from the abolitionist standpoint expressing compassion for animals while we use them (e.g., providing animals with comfortable living conditions right up to the instant when we kill them for food) is "like putting color television in a concentration camp."[4]

It is not clear whether the abolitionist criticism of animal welfarism suffices to show that duties of compassion are inadequate in principle in the endeavor to accord animals the moral respect owed them. What is clear is that the notion of compassion can be diluted to provide an implicit sanction for a variety of uses of animals, as when we deplore the treatment of chickens on factory farms and satisfy ourselves that we are doing the right thing by buying only "free range" chickens—even though we are still participating in a regime of animal slaughter, and even though current legal classifications render the term 'free range' all but meaningless inasmuch as the term may be used to describe chickens that may never have seen the light of day. (The term may technically be used as long as the birds have been allotted more than a certain minimum amount of space within which to roam.)

The crucial question as regards the potential of compassion to provide a foundation for cosmic justice is how we are to construe the underling relationship between human givers and animal recipients of compassion. If, like many, if not all, liberal thinkers—Francione is a conspicuous exception—we conceive of the relationship as one between beings that are ultimately unequal, then the corresponding duty of compassion will be weak. Rather than being obligated to change our behavior so as categorically to avoid certain uses of animals, we will consider ourselves obligated simply to feel sorry for animals. We may alter our treatment of animals in certain respects while continuing to use them as instrumentalities for the satisfaction of human desires. The shift in Plutarch's views concerning the moral status of animals is instructive in this connection. In volume 12 of the *Moralia* Plutarch argues that practices such as consuming meat are both "useless and unnecessary" and a transgression against our duties of justice toward animals.[5] At the time he wrote these words Plutarch was an ethical vegetarian. But later in life Plutarch softened his position, arguing that "we know that kindness has a wider scope than justice. Law and justice we naturally apply to men alone; but when it comes to beneficence and charity, these often flow in streams from the gentle heart, like water from a copious spring, even down to dumb animals."[6] Along with this shift in Plutarch's thinking came an abandonment of vegetarianism. The younger Plutarch considered vegetarianism to be part of our obligations of justice toward animals, while the older Plutarch was an early defender of animal welfarism who considered the consumption of meat to be consistent with feelings of kindness toward animals.

What the young Plutarch expresses in his writings on animals in the *Moralia* is a deeply felt sense of kinship with animals. He argues explicitly and at length against the Stoic prejudices that all and only human beings are members of the sphere of justice, and that animals exist for the sake of satisfying human desires.[7] The Stoics construe justice exclusively in social terms, that is, as a relation obtaining only between human beings. Modern liberal thinkers such as Kant and Rawls implicitly follow the Stoics in this characterization of justice. When a liberal thinker such as Francione argues that animals have basic rights, he is in effect arguing that animals are properly members of the sphere of justice. In doing so, Francione takes a subtle but crucial step beyond social justice into the realm of cosmic justice.

Proponents of cosmic justice grasp the underlying relationship between human and at least some nonhuman beings as a relationship between subordinate parts or members of a larger cosmic whole. Those who advocate social justice to the exclusion of any conception of cosmic justice grasp that relationship as one between superiors (humans) and inferiors (nonhumans). It is in this respect that liberal approaches are fundamentally anthropocentric and are ultimately incapable of doing justice to the moral status of animals unless they are rooted in a cosmic perspective that can impose limits on the liberal exercise of individual human autonomy. In effect, liberal individualism needs to be inscribed within the larger framework of cosmic holism in such a way that social justice prevails between human agents and cosmic justice prevails between human and nonhuman beings, particularly animals.[8]

Cosmic holism is what Erazim Kohak has characterized as a "naturalistic" perspective in the sense that it "recognizes the being of humans as integrally linked to the being of nature . . . [and] as fundamentally *at home* in the cosmos, not 'contingently thrown' into it as an alien context and 'ek-sisting' from it in an act of Promethean defiance."[9] The Heideggerian notions of contingent thrownness and ek-sistence emphasize the sense of separation between human consciousness and the natural world from out of which human agency emerges. To say that human beings, unlike other beings, "ek-sist" is to say that we stand apart from the rest of nature in virtue of our ability to contemplate ourselves, our relationships to other beings, and the endeavor to find meaning in existence. Heidegger writes that ek-sistence must be "thought in terms of ecstasis," the notion of being outside of or beyond oneself.[10] Human existence has an ecstatic character in the sense that we are always both in and beyond the present; we always relate to the present both as the present and in relation to the past and future. Thus, on Heidegger's view animals, which are largely confined within the present and have at most a relation to the very near-term future and past, do not "ek-sist" but merely "are," whereas "the 'essence' of the human being . . . lies in his ek-sistence."[11]

And yet Heidegger is at pains to articulate the sort of holistic perspective that motivates Kohak's reflections on the place of human beings in the cosmic scheme of things. In the same text in which he asserts the distinctive ek-static character of human existence Heidegger proposes an understanding of ethics in terms of cosmic dwelling. "If the name 'ethics,' in keeping with the basic meaning of the word ἦθος, should now say that ethics contemplates the abode of the human being, then that thinking which thinks the truth of being as the primordial element of the human being, as one who ek-sists, is in itself primordial ethics."[12] Heidegger conceives of ethics in terms of dwelling or abiding; like Novalis he considers homelessness to be the fundamental ethical problem of modernity if not of philosophy generally.[13] To be ethical is to endeavor to find one's proper place in the larger scheme of things rather than to seek to assert human superiority over the natural world. However, given the ek-static nature of human existence, that is, given the fact that consciousness relates to itself as being separate and at a reflective distance from its objects, human experience fundamentally takes the form of a wanderer in search of a home or proper place in the cosmic scheme of things.

The tension between Heidegger's characterization of human existence as ek-static and his call for ethics as dwelling within a larger cosmic context is a sign that Heidegger never overcame the dualistic influence of Platonic and Christian metaphysics.[14] Heidegger acknowledges that living beings "are in a certain way most closely akin to us." But like the medieval Christian philosophers before him, he considers nonhuman life to be "at the same time separated from our ek-sistent essence by an abyss. . . . Plants and animals are lodged in their respective environments but are never placed freely into the clearing of being which alone is 'world.' "[15] To be "placed freely into the clearing of being" is to be able to relate to oneself, to other beings in the world, and to the phenomenon of meaning *as such*, so that one is able to pose questions about the meaning of self, world, and the relationship between the two. In the first three chapters I argued that the "as such" is the exclusive possession of linguistic beings, that is, beings that employ concepts and intentionality and are able to contemplate life as a whole. Because animals have a limited, non-intentional relationship to their surroundings, "an animal can never be 'evil'. . . .For evil presupposes spirit [Geist]. The animal can never get out of the unity of its determinate rank in nature. . . .The animal is not capable of dealing with principles."[16]

In this sense it can rightly be said that we differ from animals in an important respect. But this does not necessarily imply any moral difference between human beings and animals. As Heidegger notes in a discussion of the confinement of animals within a limited scope of awareness in their local environments, to say that human beings "form" or constitute worldly meaning while animals are comparatively "world-poor" "does not give license to estimations and evaluations of perfection and imperfection. . . . For we encounter the greatest difficulty when we pose the question which are the higher and which are the lower kinds of access to beings. . . . However quick we may be to estimate the human as a higher being than the animal, such an evaluation is questionable, particularly when we consider that the human can sink lower than the animal; an animal can never become corrupted as a human can."[17] Moreover, animals are never homeless wanderers in search of their proper place. Even domesticated animals, which have been forcibly removed from their proper place, do not seek a home because their subjective awareness lacks the ek-static character that would enable them to raise the question of proper place. We have placed domesticated animals in the unfortunate position of lacking a home and having no opportunity to find one.

Even though Kohak's immediate concern is the place of human beings in the natural scheme of things, his reflections shed light on the plight of animals and the prospects for a robust conception of cosmic justice. "What is at issue between naturalism . . . and its denial is not the nature of 'nature' but rather the place of the human in the cosmos: whether we shall conceive of ourselves as integrally continuous with the world about us or as contingently thrown into it as strangers into an alien medium."[18] In the modern age the rise of liberal individualism has occurred hand in glove with the rise of modern science. The fundamental point of linkage is a conception of the human being as a detached spectator and manipulator of nature, a quasi-divine agent operating on a set of instrumentalities with no inherent worth. In his writings on technology Heidegger argues that nature in the modern age has been reduced from a cosmic whole to "standing reserve": "Everywhere everything is ordered to stand by, to be immediately at hand, indeed to stand there just so that it may be on call for a further ordering.... The name 'standing reserve'... designates... the way in which everything comes to presence that is wrought upon by the challenging revealing" of human beings.[19] The human subject looks upon nature not as an integrated whole of which humanity is a part, but as a store of energy waiting to be challenged forth into use. The fundamental relationship between humans and nature is thus a violent and exploitative one. Not only the value of nature but its very being is conceived as power to be used at the whim of human beings. "A tract of land is challenged into the putting out of coal and ore. The earth now reveals itself as a coal mining district, the soil as a mineral deposit."[20] Nature as a whole is no longer a sacred place in which we find our home and measure. Instead it has been reduced to "a gigantic gasoline station, an energy source for modern technology and industry."[21]

It is entirely in keeping with the modern technological conception of nature that animals are treated as delivery devices for food, entertainment, and information. Factory farming is a straightforward instance of treating animals as standing reserve. The technological mode of relating to nature recognizes no limits in the endeavor to manipulate natural beings to satisfy human desires. In 1637 Descartes, the undisputed father of modern technological consciousness, proclaimed that the deployment of modern science in the service of human ends would eventually render human beings "the masters and possessors of nature."[22] Descartes articulated a conception of nature as pure mechanism that has served the aims of technological domination to this day. It is no accident that he advances a conception of animals as pure mechanism, enthusiastically advocates vivisection, and maintains that we may kill and eat animals without moral scruple.[23] Even if we no longer accept the Cartesian view of animals as mere mechanism, as a culture we nonetheless adhere to Descartes's views regarding the use of animals as instrumentalities.

A fundamental change in our moral estimation of animals would require a corresponding change in our conception of our relation to nature as a whole. Kohak notes that such a change would be unnecessary for anyone who sees nature as something essentially divine, for example, "as God's creation, lovingly crafted in His image. . . . [But] once we see the world around ourselves as the arbitrary product of a cosmic accident, we have no guarantee" that people will acknowledge that human beings essentially belong to the cosmos and that this status as a member of a larger totality of being assigns certain responsibilities to us.[24] Indeed, as long as we view ourselves as "the masters and possessors of nature," any such acknowledgment seems impossible in principle. Without a foundation in cosmic holism, liberal individualism seems doomed to failure with regard to the plight of animals. What is lacking is the underlying sense of dwelling alongside animals in a cosmic whole which transcends us and within which we must struggle to find our proper place.

To take seriously the prospect of finding such a sense of place is to accept as ineluctable the need to sacrifice some of our own interests for the sake of animals and perhaps even for the sake of nature generally. From an anthropocentric standpoint, self-limitation makes no sense unless it is in our own interest, as when we accept automobile-emissions restrictions for the sake of ensuring that we and future generations will have clean air to breathe. Thus, even if we acknowledge that animals have moral worth, we will inevitably seek ways to privilege the worth of humans over that of animals. For example, Mary Anne Warren argues that a holistic perspective can be reconciled with an individualistic one provided that we acknowledge that human lives have greater worth than animal lives; human lives "have greater intrinsic value, because they are worth more *to their possessors*."[25] This may be true in a trivial sense: Because human beings alone engage in reflective acts of valuation, only human beings can evaluate their own existence as *having* any worth. Animals, which do not form value judgments, cannot place any value on their own existence. But if (as I have argued in chapter 3) many animals are capable of grasping and valuing their lives and activities at a "proto" or pre-predicative level, then Warren's assertion is highly questionable. As was previously noted, my cat Pindar's life is, at the pre-predicative level, worth every bit as much to him as my life is worth to me. There is simply no non-anthropocentric sense—and certainly no objective sense—in which human life can be said to be more valuable than animal life; we simply *consider* it to be more valuable. As Paul Taylor puts the point, "Whether we are concerned with standards of merit or with the concept of inherent worth, the claim that humans by their very nature are superior to other species is a groundless claim and . . . must be rejected as nothing more than an irrational bias in our own favor."[26]

To accept the need to impose limitations on our conduct for the sake of respecting animals is to recognize that human beings have fundamental obligations to respect lives other than their own. There simply is no reason to suppose, as thinkers such as Rawls suggest, that only those beings capable of grasping the notion of justice can be considered to take part in the sphere of justice. Only if we anthropocentrically limit our conception of justice to include all and only rational agents would such a conclusion follow. If, however, we acknowledge that many animals have rich subjective lives and are involved in life projects—however comparatively "primitive" we might consider those lives and projects to be—the horizon of justice expands to include *at least* all sentient beings. Sentience, the capacity to experience pleasure and pain, is not a stand-alone capacity to be used as an isolated criterion for membership in the moral community. Rather, it is inextricably bound up with other aspects of awareness and behavior that I have explored in previous chapters. Sentience, particularly the capacity to suffer, is perhaps the most conspicuous outward indication of a being's subjective involvement in the struggle for life and well-being. Just as we consider ourselves to be owed duties of non-interference by other human beings in our endeavor to cultivate our own life projects, we must recognize that we owe comparable duties of non-interference to animals, at least sentient ones, as they pursue their life projects. The refusal to recognize these obligations constitutes "human chauvinism . . . a form of group selfishness" pure and simple.[27]

Whether the acknowledgment of such obligations to nonhuman nature must take the form of attributing rights to animals is controversial. There is some force in Holmes Rolston's suggestion that "'rights' is a political word," that the notion of right is "intersubjectively, sociologically real, used to protect values that are inseparably entwined with personality."[28] Rolston warns that we should not "extrapolate criteria from cultural to biotic communities, any more than we extrapolate criteria from biotic to cultural communities." Here he invokes the authority of John Passmore, who "claims that only human communities generate obligations."[29] But Rolston's own arguments show why we should not share his enthusiasm for rejecting the language of rights out of hand. He argues that even if "natural values are not always anthropocentric...they are always anthropogenic (generated by humans)."[30] To say that natural rights are "generated" by humans means that they, like rights and values generally, are construed or identified by human beings, the only living beings capable of the conceptual abstraction necessary for conceiving of rights and values. This does not mean that humans invent or create natural values, except in the trivial sense that values are conceptual tags that we place on phenomena whose significance is *not* generated by us. Even if "value is always and only relational, with humans one of the relata," the proposition that nothing can have significance unless it is assessed by humans to possess significance is an axiom of anthropocentric thinking.[31] In the narrow sense that only human beings reflectively attribute value to things, Protagoras was certainly right to say that "man is the measure of all things."[32] But, as Rolston himself points out, from a biocentric standpoint "animals do not make man the measure of things at all." Indeed, it is difficult to see how we could have an "I-thou" relationship with animals, as Rolston suggests we do, if humans *were* the measure of all things at the cosmic level.[33]

Rolston's readiness to abandon the language of rights with regard to animals appears to be motivated not so much by an abstract reflection on the nature of right as by a commitment to the kind of anthropocentric hierarchical thinking against which Francione warns.[34] When we place animals in a subordinate position in a moral hierarchy, they will inevitably lose. Moreover, if our reasons for placing animals in such a subordinate position are anthropocentric, then the language of rights may be the only way to ensure that animals will be accorded their moral desert. Rolston maintains that "animals with skills that are undeniably more complex than those of lower plants and animals" produce "achievements that are of higher value," and that species higher on the evolutionary scale are more worth saving than those lower on the scale.[35] Beings that are "more conscious" possess greater "natural value" than less conscious ones.[36] Thus, even though "what matters to animals, matters morally," the complexity and sophistication of the human mind "put humans at the apex of it all."[37] Assuming that "if we have to choose between saving a gorilla species and saving a beetle species, we save the gorilla species," it follows that any time we have to choose between saving the human species and any nonhuman animal species, we save humans.[38] Rolston does not address the question of conflicts between human individuals and individual members of nonhuman species, but his reliance on the putative value of complexity points toward the conclusion that we should always save the human individual rather than an individual nonhuman animal, or at least that there is a rebuttable presumption in favor of saving the human being.

What Rolston and like-minded thinkers never explain is why complexity or evolutionary development has *moral* significance. It is easy to say that notions such as right and value are "anthropogenic," but this simply cloaks an anthropocentric interest in stripping animals (and perhaps other living beings) of the prerogatives to live and flourish, or at least in subordinating such interests in animals to the interests of humans. If we seriously consider abandoning the language of rights with regard to animals, then it is difficult to see how we can retain any meaningful notion of justice toward them. Thus we are left in the position of trusting in our capacity for compassion and humanity to protect the interests of animals. It is in this connection that Francione's logic is most powerful: If animals are sentient, then they have interests, including the interest in life (continued existence) and flourishing. Since rights are juridico-moral mechanisms for protecting interests, we are not entitled to deprive animals of certain rights, in particular the basic right not to be property. Implicit in this analysis is the idea that animals possess inherent worth, that this worth must be respected as a matter of justice, and that the language of rights is the best way to ensure just treatment for animals.

Whether or not we ultimately retain the language of rights in seeking to protect the interests of animals, it is vital that we retain some conception of justice. The classical liberal language of individuality, reciprocity, and right, as exemplified by Rawls, presupposes that all and only rational agents are owed duties of justice. Any animal capable of perceptual inference is certainly an individual, but not in the classical liberal sense. Only those beings capable of rational inference can be (or become) moral and legal agents. This is why the liberal conception of justice provides a basis for respecting the prerogatives of animals that is at best tenuous and at worst ineffectual. Any conception of justice that seeks to accommodate animals as well as human beings must proceed from the recognition that the cognitive differences between humans and animals have no moral significance whatsoever, just as more highly intelligent humans do not enjoy greater moral entitlements than less intelligent ones. In both cases, human-animal and human-human, equal consideration of interests is required as a matter of fairness. The same cognitive capacities that enable humans to dominate animals also enable us to recognize and act on the obligations we have not to interfere with the lives of animals. However, this does not mean that we have duties to ameliorate suffering in wild nature, as some thinkers suggest.[39] One could argue on utilitarian grounds that we do have such obligations. In certain cases there might be good reasons to intervene in nature to prevent or reduce suffering—for example, by seeking to control deer overpopulation through contraceptive means rather than by sanctioning hunting or allowing deer to starve to death. But there is tremendous hubris in the proposition that human beings are capable of undertaking a systematic approach to the amelioration of suffering in nature. Such thinking is of a piece with the endeavor to render ourselves "masters and possessors of nature" in that it refuses to recognize both the limits of human capability and the unfortunate, ineluctable fact that life is predicated on suffering and death.

J. Baird Callicott suggests that the way "we human beings could reaffirm our participation in nature" would be to "accept and affirm natural biological laws, principles, and limitations in the human personal and social spheres."[40] But we should not take this to mean, as Callicott does, that equal consideration for animals would render society "ludicrous," nor that animal liberation would inevitably "have ruinous consequences on plants, soils, and waters" and hence would be "utterly unpracticable."[41] This is a little like saying that child prostitution should not be stopped because procurers would lose their livelihood: The "ruinous consequences" that would follow from animal liberation—assuming there were any—would ultimately be the product of factory-farming measures undertaken by human beings to artificially and drastically increase the population of domesticated animals. Thus human beings would have a responsibility to devise measures to prevent or minimize such ruinous consequences. Moreover, it is by no means clear that animal liberation would be attended by such dire consequences. Full recognition of the moral status of animals requires that we cease the practice of domesticating animals altogether. Thinkers such as Callicott implicitly assume that this means that we would simply turn loose billions of domesticated animals. However, as Francione has argued, when we end the activity of domestication, we bear the responsibility to care for the existing domesticated animals until they die out.[42]

The most important reason to challenge thinkers such as Callicott is that their reasoning fails to grasp the fact that animal liberation is required by considerations of *justice*, not utility. In addition to rejecting animal liberation as fanciful, Callicott dismisses the prospect of universal human vegetarianism on the grounds that it would "*probably* [be] ecologically catastrophic." Callicott assumes that universal human vegetarianism would tax the environment in unreasonable ways, concluding that "meat eating . . . may be more *ecologically* responsible than a wholly vegetable diet."[43] Given all the wisdom and technological power that humans purport to possess, it is surprising that Callicott does not even consider the possibility of devising measures to ameliorate the environmental problems that he assumes would follow from the cessation of eating meat. It is also telling that Callicott never once acknowledges that the consumption of meat is a fundamental infringement on the prerogatives of animals to live and flourish. By focusing on biotic community rather than on individuals, Callicott is able to avoid altogether the problem of cosmic justice as it pertains to animals.

But in an important sense, if not in a specifically human one, (most) animals are individuals, and as such they have interests and are due obligations of cosmic justice. To take the principle of equal consideration of interests seriously is to see that death is no less a harm to animals than to humans, and that we quite unnecessarily violate the prerogatives of animals to life and flourishing when we kill and eat them. Callicott alleges that "the hidden agenda of the humane ethic is the imposition of the anti-natural prophylactic ethos of comfort." He advocates "a recrudescence of wilderness and a renaissance of tribal cultural experience" that appears to sanction such practices as hunting and meat eating.[44] In essence, Callicott derides the human endeavor to reduce the amount of suffering and death we impose on animals by suggesting that suffering and death are "natural." He recommends that we dispossess ourselves of such flighty thinking and reaffirm our place in nature as killers and dominators. He deplores factory farming not on the grounds that it causes so much suffering, but because it involves "the monstrous transformation of living things from an organic to a mechanical mode of being."[45] Presumably "a renaissance of tribal cultural experience" means that we still get to use and kill animals to satisfy our desires and do not even have to apologize to them when we do so.

The lives and well-being of the vast majority of human beings do not depend in any fundamental way on the use and consumption of animals. We use and eat animals because it makes our lives easier and more pleasurable. The utilitarian consideration that civilization would not have advanced to its current point of development without the use of animals entirely misses the point that such use is prohibited by considerations of justice. Similarly, one could make a strong argument that the United States could not have achieved its current level of economic prosperity without having relied on the institution of slavery; but this would not justify slavery either in the past or the present. In those few instances in which ethics and survival come into conflict—as, for example, when an indigenous population simply cannot survive without using and perhaps killing animals—the imperative to survive should take precedence. But this is not the situation confronted by most human beings. Given the extensive and enthusiastic use and killing of animals in our society purely for convenience and enjoyment, it is highly doubtful that "a reconciliation, or harmonization, of our relationship to nature" could ever be achieved by "a social theory which envisages the possibility of a transcendence of the requirement for rights and justice."[46] Whether or not we explicitly adhere to the language of rights, what is needed most of all is a recognition that we have duties of justice toward animals, in particular the duty not to interfere with animals' pursuit of life and flourishing.

## KINSHIP AND COSMOPOLITANISM

The prospects for acknowledging our duties of justice to animals depend on affirming our natural continuity and kinship with them. While the philosophical tradition extending from the ancient Greeks to the postmoderns has overwhelmingly asserted the underlying differences between humans and animals as a basis for proclaiming the moral superiority and prerogatives of humans, philosophers have occasionally asserted a fundamental kinship as the basis for recognizing the moral status of animals.[47] The most influential of such thinkers take an explicit stand against the Stoics, who argue for a theory of kinship bounded by species membership. In the remainder of this chapter I propose a revision of the Stoic theory of *oikeiosis* (kinship or belonging) that provides the affective basis for affirming our obligations of justice toward animals.

The Stoics inherit from Aristotle a conception of our proper place in the cosmos according to which human beings stand between divinity and animality. Aristotle characterizes the highest form of human life, the "happy" or eudaimon life, as an activity of the soul that is crucially dependent on rational contemplation, which Aristotle characterizes as a divine activity. The highest kind of life for human beings would be one of pure contemplation, but due to "our composite nature" (i.e., the fact that we have an irrational as well as a rational part) such a life is not possible for us.[48] Thus the highest life achievable by a human being is one in which we engage in as much rational contemplation as the practical necessities of life permit. The lowest kind of life for humans would be one in which we succumb to our passions and let them govern us, in the same way that passion governs the lives of animals. According to Aristotle animals are capable of volition but not deliberate choice, the difference between the two being that choice involves rational deliberation, whereas volition consists simply in acting immediately on impulses of pleasure and pain.[49] Because human beings are rational and linguistic whereas animals act merely on impulses of pleasure and pain, Aristotle categorically excludes animals from the sphere of justice.[50]

Aristotle envisions human life as a struggle to regulate passion with reason. The more we employ reason to guide our actions, the more we are like the gods. The more we succumb to passion and the prospects for pleasure (or the avoidance of pain), as in the case of vicious or incontinent people, the more we render ourselves like mere animals. The Stoics follow Aristotle in conceiving of the ideal human life as one that employs reason to subjugate passion. They advance a cosmopolitan ideal that reaffirms the Aristotelian desire to render human beings as much as possible like the gods and as little as possible like animals. The possession of reason enables human beings to adopt a standpoint detached from the immediacy of experience, from which they can contemplate "the universal law" evident in nature.[51] This capacity places human beings in intimate company with the gods. The "cosmopolis" envisioned by the Stoics is a rational community in which gods and humans contemplate the divine logos, in which a human being who has overcome the influence of passion and the lure of worldly goods can become "a citizen of the world."[52]

To be a citizen of the world in this sense is to stand above animals, which exist for the sake of satisfying human needs. "With the exception of the world everything else was made for the sake of other things: for example, the crops and fruits which the earth brings forth were made for the sake of animals, and the animals which it brings forth were made for the sake of men. . . . Man himself has come to be in order to contemplate and imitate the world."[53] World citizenship is membership in a special kind of community, a rational community (koinoía).[54] It "involves the idea that the world is providentially organized to be the proper habitation of human beings, whose possession of divine rationality, construed as the prescriptions of *correct* reasoning, makes them participants with God in a shared law and therefore a shared community, irrespective of their local nationalities and interests."[55]

The logic underlying this cosmopolitan ideal is that because only human beings are rational, only they can take on the universal standpoint from which alone it is possible to contemplate the universe as such. The Stoics believe that all and only those beings capable of such a universal standpoint merit inclusion in the sphere of justice. What we refer to today as moral patients have no place in community in the highest, cosmopolitan sense; hence nothing we do to animals can be considered an injustice. A related Stoic commitment that reinforces and seeks to explain this fundamental distinction more fully is the doctrine of *oikeiosis*. The term signifies belonging or relatedness, which on the Stoic view manifests itself in increasingly large spheres of inclusiveness depending on the cognitive abilities of the beings in question. The most immediate level of *oikeiosis* is the sense each living being has of being at one with its own body. "Immediately upon birth . . . a living creature feels an attachment for itself, and an impulse to preserve itself and to feel affection for its own constitution and for those things which tend to preserve that constitution; while on the other hand it feels an antipathy to destruction and to those things which appear to threaten destruction."[56]

Each individual animal has a sense of being at one with its own body and the pursuit of its own welfare that is more intimate than the sense it has of being related to anything else.

Subsequent stages of *oikeiosis* broaden the scope of belonging or relatedness to include other living beings. At the second stage of *oikeiosis*, living beings express regard for members of their immediate families, particularly their offspring. "Nature creates in parents an affection for their children. . . . It could not be consistent that nature should at once intend offspring to be born and make no provision for that offspring when born to be loved and cherished. Even in the lower animals nature's operation can be clearly discerned; when we observe the labour that they spend on bearing and rearing their young, we seem to be listening to the actual voice of nature."[57] At this level of *oikeiosis* "the actual voice of nature" speaks equally to animals and humans, investing both with a sense of felt kinship and loving regard for their progeny. We may even take the regard that animals exhibit for their offspring as an indication of the way we ought to feel toward our own. "A sheep does not abandon its own offspring, nor a wolf; and yet does a man abandon his?"[58]

At this point, however, the Stoics argue that the similarities between human beings and animals come to an abrupt end. Because animals lack rationality, they are not able to expand the scope of *oikeiosis* beyond filial bonds and perhaps a sense of connection with the immediate group of animals of their own kind, of which they find themselves a part. Human beings, in virtue of their rationality, are able to extend the range of *oikeiosis* to include all rational beings. Unlike animals, human beings are able to form a communal bond with all others of their own kind. Nature bestows on humans a "sense of mutual attraction which unites human beings as such."[59] Some animals, such as bees and ants, exhibit a conspicuous social sense, but in human beings the "bond of mutual aid is far more intimate," such that we are able to recognize our kinship even with human strangers. "The outermost and largest circle [of *oikeiosis*], which encompasses all the rest, is that of the whole human race. . . . It is the task of the well-tempered man, in his proper treatment of each group, to draw the circles together somehow towards the centre."[60]

The basis of our responsibility to humanity as a whole is a felt sense of kinship conferred on us by nature. "The mere fact of their humanity requires that one man should feel another man to be akin to him."[61] Nature has conferred on us two roles or personae: "One of these is universal, from the fact that we share in reason and that status which raises us above the beasts; this is the source of all rectitude and propriety, and the basis of the rational discovery of our proper functions. The second role [persona] is the one which has been specifically assigned to individuals."[62] Animals are unable to recognize any natural kinship with members of their own kind beyond their immediate conspecifics. Humans, in virtue of reason, are able to feel their natural connection with the rest of humanity and are able to recognize and act in accordance with principles of "rectitude and propriety." Humans are also able to enact the persona of the individual, presumably on the basis of the rational capacity that enables them to conceptualize themselves as individual beings within a community of similar individuals.

The Stoics prefigure modern liberal thinkers such as Kant and Rawls in conceiving of membership in this largest sphere of *oikeiosis*, the sphere of right, as an all-or-nothing proposition: any being lacking rationality, and hence lacking the ability to function as an agent, is categorically excluded from membership in the sphere of right. The Stoics maintain that "there can be no question of right [*dikaion*] as between man and the lower animals, because of their unlikeness."[63] Due to our lack of kinship with animals, "men can make use of beasts for their own purposes without injustice."[64]

This proclamation follows from a straightforwardly speciesist conception of the highest level of *oikeiosis*. To "draw the circles together toward the center," as Hierocles proposes, can be understood in a number of ways. The Stoics conceive of it specifically in terms of drawing humanity together into a unified community that *excludes* all other species rather than include them, the goal being to assimilate human beings to the gods and distinguish them from animals. Even though they recognize that human beings are "natural" beings in some of the same basic ways in which animals are natural, the Stoics nonetheless consider the emergence of rationality to constitute a breaking point with the prior—the Stoics would say with the "lower"—circles of *oikeiosis*. In key respects our struggle for life and flourishing are closely allied with the life struggle of animals. The Stoics are arbitrary in *morally* distinguishing humans from animals, just as thinkers such as Kant and Rawls are arbitrary in doing so. The underlying motivation seems to be a desire to characterize human beings as unique and central in the cosmic scheme of things. In short, the Stoic view is motivated by arch-anthropocentrism.

There is another, more "natural" way to understand drawing the circles together toward the center. All beings that struggle for survival and well being, at the very least those that do so through subjective states of awareness, share a basic bond of kinship. All humans and at least some animals are capable of *feeling* this kinship toward others—and not just with others of their own species. Abstract reflection can help humans to awaken this felt sense of kinship with animals, but sooner or later it must be felt rather than thought in order for it to exercise an authoritative influence over our conduct. Millennia of thinking have done little to alter the fortunes of animals at the hands of human beings in our society. We must learn to identify with animals, to see ourselves in them and them in ourselves, in order to appreciate their plight and their prospects in a world that has been dominated by human beings simply because human beings *can* dominate the world—not because we have a right to do so.

Rethinking and re-feeling kinship along these lines would hold the promise of a comparable revisioning of the cosmopolitan ideal. Rather than seeking to attribute to ourselves quasi-divine status and prerogatives by distinguishing ourselves from the rest of nature, we would acknowledge our mortality and the fundamental limitations that we share with animals. In an age that has witnessed the putative death of God, we would seek to understand ourselves in relation not to the divine but rather to animals, the earthly beings most like us. Our enmity toward animals and our abhorrent treatment of them will cease as soon as we overcome the hubris of viewing ourselves as superior to animals. This is the hubris of the Stoics, who considered animals to exist expressly for the sake of human beings, and of most modern European philosophers, who have followed Descartes and Kant in supposing that human beings are rightfully "the masters and possessors of nature."

To accept our mortality is to recognize our shared kinship with animals. It is to open ourselves to what Karl Löwith calls a "cosmopolitical" perspective that freely acknowledges the priority of our belonging to nature over our belonging to a human social whole. The "pre- and supra-human world of heaven and earth, which stands and maintains itself utterly on its own, infinitely eclipses the world that stands and falls with human beings."[65] Löwith counsels a sense of resignation about our mortality and the prospects for bringing about genuine change in the world. "What is 'interesting' in history is what is seemingly uninteresting, namely that which is constant and repeats itself in all change, because humans are as they always already were and always will be."[66] Ultimately humans are subject to the ineluctable cycles of "struggle and suffering, short glories and long miseries, wars and intermittent periods of peace."[67] Little if any revision would be necessary to render these statements equally applicable to animals, who are just as subject to death and the struggle for existence as human beings.

In this respect animals share common cause with human beings. Human beings have capitalized on the silence of animals, just as certain human beings have historically imposed silence on certain other human beings by denying slaves the right to literacy, denying women the right to own property, and denying both the right to vote. In each case silence has been exploited as a means of maintaining dominance. The emancipation of disenfranchised humans has been due to the fact that women and slaves were able to find their own voices, assert their moral rights, and help to awaken in free men the natural sense of kinship that prevails among all human beings. Whereas women and slaves had the benefit not only of their own voices but also of an already existing sense of kinship in the hearts of some free men, animals are at a dramatic disadvantage. Not only are animals unable to avail themselves of language to assert their own rights, but many fewer humans have a clear sense of kinship with animals than have a clear sense of kinship with other humans.

Among beings with subjective states of awareness, animals are the untouchable caste, those whom human others would rather not acknowledge, let alone render assistance.

Given this perception of animals on the part of the vast majority of humanity, it is hardly reasonable to suppose that simply conferring rights on animals will solve the problem of animal exploitation. What is needed more than anything else is a living, affective acknowledgment that the inability of animals to use language and reason distinguishes us from them cognitively, but that this difference has no logical connection with moral status. We humans assert a higher moral status for ourselves simply because we can. An authentic recognition that animals merit equal moral consideration with humans is utterly inconsistent with long-standing cultural prejudices; this is no basis for concluding that such a recognition is without foundation.

Even some contemporary writers whose goal is to argue for a conception of cosmic justice advocate exactly the kind of moral hierarchies against which Francione rightly warns. Gary Varner seeks to articulate an environmentalist ethics yet advocates an "axiological anthropocentrism" that acknowledges direct moral standing in animals but "favor[s] at least some human interests when these conflict with the interests of nonhumans."[68] Varner also asserts a hierarchy of moral desert among animals, giving preference to mammals on the grounds that only they among animals seem to have desires.[69]

Peter Wenz argues for a "concentric circle perspective" very similar to the Stoic doctrine of *oikeiosis*, according to which "the closer our relationship the stronger our obligations in that relationship." The sense of closeness here "is not formally tied to emotional attachments or to subjective feelings of closeness" but rather to "commonly respected justifications."[70] Given the priority Wenz ascribes to "commonly respected justifications" rather than any natural sense of felt kinship or any kind of rigorous argumentation, it is not surprising that he believes that "special consideration [should be] made for human beings." As long as we "try to avoid degrading ecosystems and causing the extinction of species," we are fulfilling our obligations to living nature.[71] Moreover, "the negative rights of nonhuman subjects-of-a-life may sometimes be overridden in circumstances that would not justify overriding the negative rights of a human being. Thus, when a direct choice between them must be made, and all other things are equal, the negative right of a human being overrides the negative right of an animal."[72]

The crux of Wenz's reasoning is that because humans lie in a closer concentric circle to other humans than do animals, our obligations to humans are greater. What Wenz, like the Stoics before him, never questions—presumably because it is a comfortable "commonly respected justification"—is whether the human and animal circles truly merit different levels of moral consideration. It is permissible, as Francione suggests, to give preference to a human over a dog in a situation in which we can save only one—not because the human is morally more deserving but "simply because I better understand what is at stake for the human than I do for the dog. But this is a matter of my own cognitive limitation and how that plays out in these extreme circumstances in which *my decision will necessarily be arbitrary to some degree* and in which no decision will be perfectly satisfactory."[73] The doctrine of *oikeiosis* makes it clear why most people would save their own child rather than a beloved animal or, for that matter, anyone else's child: the second level of *oikeiosis* has a more immediate and profound hold on us than does the third level, which relates us to humanity generally. At the same time, it should be noted that we are capable of reversing the order of priority among levels of kinship, as in instances of self-sacrifice for the sake of another human being. In such cases we give preference to another human over ourselves, even though the most immediate level of *oikeiosis* is self-regard. By the same token, we should be prepared to reverse the order of priority in our felt obligations toward humans and animals when circumstances demand that we do so.

Such reversals constitute precisely the sort of self-sacrifice or self-limitation for the sake of animals that I have suggested is required when we take our kinship with animals seriously. Given the dominance we have exercised over animals for millennia, there is no way we can do justice to animals without incurring a great deal of inconvenience for ourselves. Our natural tendency to regard ourselves first—a tendency that is not always justified—influences our judgments about what is "reasonable" or morally just from the ground up. Pursuing the procedure of reflective equilibrium with regard to human-animal relations, as Wenz does, projects a veneer of legitimacy onto what are really long-standing anthropocentric prejudices.[74] Thus, some thinkers find it possible to make the following type of assertion with utter confidence: "An imagined society in which all animals capable of sensibility received equal consideration or held rights to equal consideration would be so ludicrous that it might be more appropriately and effectively treated in satire than in philosophical discussion."[75]

The key to overcoming such extreme anthropocentric prejudice toward animals (and perhaps other living beings) is to cultivate "a sense of kinship with them as fellow members of the Earth's community of life," a community in which each animal, like each human being, is "a teleological center of life striving to realize its own good in its own unique way."[76] The way beings appear to us is determined by our underlying motivations in relating to those beings in the first place. If our motivation is to dominate other beings, then we will relate to those beings as objects of domination. The Stoics related to animals as beings that were created expressly to satisfy human needs. Descartes related to animals as biological mechanisms destined to be mastered by human beings. However much we purport to care about animal welfare, this is the legacy we have inherited. The only way to overcome this regime of animal exploitation is to bring about a fundamental change in the way we relate to animals.

Heidegger recognizes the perils of imposing preconceptions on beings in the endeavor to dominate them. He suggests a way of overcoming the distorting force of such impositions that is as simple as it is at odds with prevailing ways of relating to beings. We must learn to "let beings be," to "engage [ourselves] with beings" in such a way that we permit "beings as a whole [to] reveal themselves as φύσις," as nature in the ancient sense of that which emerges from out of an unknown and ultimately unknowable origin.[77] Only by recognizing that nature transcends us and opens itself up to us as an irreducible mystery can we find the modesty needed for relating to other beings as fellow members of a community of which we are neither the origin nor the sovereign.[78] In doing so we assert, as Schopenhauer did against Descartes and Kant, our fundamental continuity with animals and the common cause we share with them. Once we recognize "that animals *are in all essential respects identical with us* and that the difference lies merely in the degree of intelligence," we will acknowledge that "we owe to the animal not mercy but justice."[79]

# CHAPTER SIX

# "Cosmo-Politics"

## Grounding Liberal Individualism in Cosmic Holism

### THE CONFLICT BETWEEN HOLISM AND
### LIBERAL INDIVIDUALISM

To be a cosmic holist in the sense I articulated in the preceding chapter is to be committed to the moral parity of all sentient beings. The ideal of cosmic holism acknowledges human duties of justice toward animals on the grounds that animals are teleological centers of life and that many animals are sentient beings whose lives matter to them. In calling for a "cosmo-politics," Karl Löwith affirms the Stoic ideal of living in accordance with nature (*kata physin*). To live in accordance with our own nature as political beings is to take our bearings from the totality of nature. "The shared life of human beings in a polis cannot be in order if that life is not established in accordance with the cosmos. As one whose life is humanly ordered, one who is magnanimous is in tune with the cosmos. In this respect, Greek philosophers and the Eastern way think very similarly, i.e., cosmo-politically in the literal sense."[1]

To attempt to order human life without taking our bearings from the cosmos as a whole is to give absolute primacy and centrality to human needs, desires, and values in the scheme of things. Such an anthropocentric orientation fundamentally distorts our relation to the cosmos and hence is incapable of illuminating the sense of order or measure required for a more adequate sense of dwelling. Even the Heidegger of *Being and Time* is subject to this criticism. "Ever since *Being and Time*, we speak in many ways of Dasein [human being] as 'Being-in-the-world'; but the world of this Dasein is not the ordered cosmos but rather our immediate and mediate social world and environment, which has a kind of order only to the extent that it is centered on human dealings and concerns. The three hyphens of Being-in-the-world are not capable of making clear the world as the one and independent totality of natural beings."[2]

Liberal individual concerns—equality, reciprocity, fairness, and rational autonomy—are by their very nature oriented on exclusively human dealings and concerns—specifically, on the coordination of human actions in a just polity. Whether and to what extent these liberal conceptions can be adapted so as to encompass our dealings with animals is a controversial matter. A key consideration in addressing this question is how human actions are to be regulated, with an eye toward giving proper respect to animals, without infringing unfairly on the prerogatives of individual human beings to exercise their wills as they see fit. From the liberal individualistic perspective, the central issues are what constitutes "fair" infringement on the prerogatives of human individuals and which political mechanisms can be devised to ensure that the freedom of the individual is protected as much as possible. From the cosmic holistic perspective, the central issue is how the hegemony of human willing can be mitigated so as to "order" human action in accordance with nature.

On its face the conflict seems insuperable. The holist outwardly appears to demand a radical subjugation of human individuality and freedom for the sake of animals and perhaps for the sake of nature as a whole, while the liberal individualist tends to see nature primarily in instrumental terms, or at least in terms that exclude it in principle from the sphere of justice. This would appear to be an irreducible conflict between anthropocentric and non-anthropocentric conceptions of the good. And while the prospects for a resolution of the conflict between individualism and holism do require an abrogation of human prerogatives, a closer examination of the terms of the debate between the two shows that the inscription of liberal individualism within a cosmic framework need not have the totalitarian implications often alleged against holistic environmentalism.

## THE LIBERAL CRITIQUE OF COSMIC HOLISM

A surprisingly common liberal criticism lodged against environmental or cosmic holism is that holists are neo-Nazis. Tom Regan offers a muted form of this criticism when he notes "the difficulties [in] reconciling the *individualistic* nature of moral rights with the more *holistic* view of nature emphasized by many of the leading environmental thinkers."[3] A view such as Aldo Leopold's, according to which "a thing is right when it tends to preserve the integrity, stability, and beauty of the biotic community [and] is wrong when it tends otherwise," brings with it "the clear prospect that the individual may be sacrificed for the greater biotic good, in the name of 'the integrity, stability, and beauty of the biotic community.'"[4] The sort of holistic perspective advocated by thinkers such as Leopold, "emotive connotations to one side, might be fairly dubbed 'environmental fascism.'"[5]

Regan implies that a holistic environmental perspective could be characterized as fascism to the extent that it entails the imposition of totalitarian principles of rule on human individuals. Terence Ball makes the charge of environmental fascism even clearer: "Environmentalism . . . can take, and in several significant instances has taken, authoritarian and anti-democratic forms." In particular, "one of the most murderous regimes of the twentieth century extolled environmental values. Hitler and the German Nazi party were strongly supportive of environmental protection and condemned cruelty to animals. . . . Admirable as these acts might have been, they were promulgated by a regime that was anti-democratic and totalitarian to its core."[6]

Luc Ferry makes an even more pointed claim, namely, that *any* viewpoint that would reject anthropocentric values in favor of cosmic holism is "a bit khaki in its green."[7] Environmental holism expresses a "love of the native soil," just as the Nazis did, and hence a "hatred of humanity."[8] Ferry asserts a "radical opposition" between the recognition of inherent value in nature and "the legal humanism that dominates the modern universe."[9] The essential conflict is between the Kantian autonomy of the human individual (the prerogative of self-determination) and the subordination of individual human interests to the putative inherent value of anything nonhuman. Noting the extensive environmental legislation enacted by the Nazis in the 1930s, Ferry concludes that "some of deep ecology's roots lie in Nazism."[10] On his view, the connection between Nazism and environmental concern is no accident. Nazism subordinates the human individual to the whole and conceives of the whole in terms that value nature more highly than the rule of law and individual autonomy.

Thus, it is not uncommon for proponents of liberal democracy to warn us of the dangers posed by "an environmental gestapo" that would require the sacrifice of individual autonomy as part of a cosmo-political *Gleichschaltung*.[11] Even though the facile assimilation of cosmic holism to Nazism is repugnant—the choice between democracy and environmentalism is not the strict either-or that it is often portrayed to be—it nonetheless contains a kernel of truth, namely, that extreme environmentalism has the potential to impose on human individuals a substantive conception of the good that they do not endorse. To make such an imposition is to violate a basic tenet of liberal individualism. Liberal theories of justice concern not specific substantive conceptions of the good but rather rules designed to ensure procedural fairness in society. By their nature such theories attempt to remain neutral regarding different first-order conceptions of the good. They seek to provide the conditions for citizens to develop and pursue their individual conceptions of the good to the extent that doing so is consistent with rules of procedural fairness. Brian Barry characterizes the beneficiaries of social justice as "people who are well informed, concerned to further their own interests and conceptions of the good, but capable of recognizing reasonable objections on the part of others." All parties enjoy "equal footing" in the sense that they "have their interests and perspectives expressed with equal force and effectiveness. [The decision-making process] is fair to the extent that it aims at consensus where possible, and where consensus is not possible it treats everybody equally (e.g., by giving everybody one vote)."[12]

The focus on rules of fairness is intended to ensure equal opportunity among the citizenry to express and pursue vital interests, while remaining neutral with respect to competing substantive conceptions of the good. By design, "the rules endorsed by impartial justice . . . leave a great deal of scope for people to live within them according to their own moral ideas. . . . Justice as impartiality is not designed to tell us how to live."[13] The liberal ideal does have a conception of the good, but it is a second- rather than a first-order conception. First-order conceptions of the good specify core or ultimate substantive goods (e.g., the inherent value of nonhuman sentient beings), while second-order conceptions of the good specify which sorts of procedures, mechanisms, or conceptions are best designed to facilitate fairness in the determination of first-order goods. Thus, the liberal conception of autonomy "is a second-order conception of the good in that it does not specify what the good actually consists in" but instead holds the key to ensuring the kind of equal footing required by justice.

Liberal thinkers such as Barry argue that by its very nature social justice must remain neutral with respect to particular substantive conceptions of the good because the liberal conception of justice is simply a "framework for social cooperation" and because "no [first-order] conception of the good can justifiably be held with a degree of certainty that warrants its imposition on those who reject it."[14] Within the framework of social cooperation, individuals must be free to pursue their own substantive conceptions of the good. Autonomy is a second-order good that facilitates such a free pursuit. "We may thus contrast autonomy as a conception of the good with a substantive conception, for example, a religiously based conception, of the good."[15] A religiously based conception of the good is a first-order conception and as such may not legitimately be imposed on any individual in a liberal society. Here Barry implicitly follows Kant, who argues that autonomy is so fundamental that we must never irrevocably subscribe to any substantive conception of the good:

> But should not a society of clergymen . . . be entitled to commit itself by oath to a certain set of inalterable doctrines, in order to secure for all time a constant guardianship over each of its members, and through them over the people? I reply that this is quite impossible. A contract of this kind, concluded with a view to preventing all further enlightenment of mankind for ever, is absolutely null and void, even if it is ratified by the supreme power, by Imperial Diets and the most solemn peace treaties. Our age cannot enter into an alliance on oath to put the next age in a position where it would be impossible for it to extend and correct its knowledge, particularly on such important matters, or to make any progress whatever in enlightenment. This would be a crime against human nature, whose original destiny lies precisely in such progress.[16]

On Kant's view, we must never sacrifice our powers of rational scrutiny in the name of principles or conceptions of the good that derive from anything other than autonomous reason. To do so would be to commit heteronomy, the subjection of one's will to a source of guidance other than one's own reason.[17] Although he asserts that he "found it necessary to deny knowledge, in order to make room for faith," Kant ultimately subjects even religious notions to the authority of each individual's rational autonomy.[18]

To accept Kant's principle of autonomy is thus to accept the privatization of substantive conceptions of the good. As Barry observes, just as "religiously based conceptions of the good" must be left to the discretion of individuals, so must judgments about an ecocentric ethic. "I do not see how [the claims of ecocentrism] can be presented in such a way as to show that it would be unreasonable to adopt a different view."[19] If individuals cannot reasonably be expected to accept ecocentrism as an indisputable good, then the imposition of an ecocentric conception of the good on society would constitute a totalitarian abrogation of individual autonomy.

The terms of Barry's discussion suggest that the same would hold for the imposition of a zoocentric conception of the good. One aspect of the neutrality or impartiality of the liberal conception of justice, as Barry conceives it, is its putative neutrality regarding the choice among anthropocentrism, zoocentrism, and ecocentrism. The liberal conception of justice neither mandates nor forbids concern for animals and the environment. "An impartialist theory does not have to confine its concern to the interests and concerns of human beings."[20] In principle such a theory leaves room for concern for all sentient beings (zoocentrism) and for all living beings (ecocentrism). For example, principles of justice could be adapted to ensure "an equal weighting for the interests of all sentient beings." However, Barry cautions that such an equal weighting "turns out to mean only that *arbitrary* distinctions are ruled out, which leaves us with an ill-defined problem comparing the interests of cockroaches and cats to those of human beings."[21] Because the liberal conception of justice remains neutral with respect to specific substantive conceptions of the good, there can be no definitive solution to the problem posed by comparisons of the interests of animals or natural systems with those of human beings. There will inevitably be "disagreements arising from" the different substantive conceptions of the good held by anthropocentrists, zoocentrists, and ecocentrists.[22]

The liberal conception of justice sketched by Barry allows for disagreements regarding the moral status of animals. In particular, it leaves ample room for giving fundamental preference to the interests of human beings over those of animals. Simply put, Barry's conception of justice as impartiality remains neutral regarding the acceptability (i.e., the first-order goodness) of speciesism. But his conception does not tolerate sexism or racism. Laws that are impartial "do not mandate or permit differential treatment of people who are in other respects similar ... but differ in race, gender, or some other characteristic, where that characteristic should not be regarded as relevant."[23] Thus, the liberal conception of justice is not really neutral as regards the choice between anthropocentrism, zoocentrism, and ecocentrism but is essentially anthropocentric. It ensures second-order impartiality in relations between human beings. And even though it does not involve any conception of first-order impartiality—for example, it permits "special regard for one's own interests, situation, and relations with others"—the liberal conception manages, by means of second-order impartiality, to ensure a sense of fairness among human beings that is patently lacking in relations between human beings and animals.[24] In this respect the notions of democracy and liberalism are, "if nothing else, anthropocentric."[25]

This limitation has led some thinkers to propose either the wholesale rejection of liberal democratic theory (e.g., in favor of some form of socialism) or a revision of liberalism so that "it [accepts] limits to neutrality and [rids] itself of its anthropocentric bias."[26] But is a limitation of neutrality compatible with the fundamental tenets of liberalism? And does socialism hold the promise of liberating animals while preserving the individual autonomy that Kant recognized to be essential to our humanity? Friedrich Hayek's *Road to Serfdom* gives us reason to doubt whether either of these questions can be answered in the affirmative. Hayek's focus is the inherent dangers of centralized planning, which involves the sacrifice of individual choice in economic matters. Writing during the Second World War, Hayek offered a diagnosis of the totalitarian character of Soviet Communism and German National Socialism. The key question in any economy is whether "it is better that the holder of coercive power should confine himself in general to creating conditions under which the knowledge and initiative of individuals are given the best scope so that *they* can plan most successfully; or whether a rational utilization of our resources requires *central* direction and organization of all our activities according to some consciously constructed 'blueprint.'"[27] The Soviets and the Nazis opted for the latter course, giving primacy to systematic coercion rather than to individual judgment and initiative, all in the name of satisfying material needs.

Collectivist economies seek freedom from material want at the expense of freedom of individual choice. "The various kinds of collectivism, communism, fascism, etc., differ among themselves in the nature of the goal toward which they want to direct the efforts of society. But they all differ from liberalism and individualism in wanting to organize the whole of society and all its resources for this unitary end and in refusing to recognize autonomous spheres in which the ends of the individuals are supreme. In short, they are totalitarian in the true sense."[28] A society in which an elite of planners makes choices on behalf of individuals is fundamentally coercive inasmuch as central planning can work only by abrogating individual judgment. In a centrally planned economy "control cannot be made dependent on a majority's being able to agree; it will often be necessary that the will of a small minority be imposed upon the people, because this minority will be the largest group able to agree among themselves on the question at issue."[29] Even where the intentions of the planners are as noble as can be, collectivism is ineluctably totalitarian because collective planning leaves no room for individual dissent.

Against collectivism Hayek argues that free-market capitalism is the only form of economic organization that is compatible with the exercise of individual moral conscience. Only in capitalism "is democracy possible," where the latter is "essentially a means, a utilitarian device for safeguarding internal peace and individual freedom." Even though democracy does not preclude oppression and dictatorship, "planning leads to dictatorship because dictatorship is the most effective instrument of coercion and the enforcement of ideals and, as such, essential if central planning on a large scale is to be possible. The clash between planning and democracy arises simply from the fact that the latter is an obstacle to the suppression of freedom which the direction of economic activity requires."[30] Centralized planning involves the "intellectual hubris" of supposing that the social process can be comprehensively directed, whereas individualism is "an attitude of humility before this social process and of tolerance to other opinions."[31]

Hayek's criticism of central economic planning holds, mutatis mutandis, for the coercive imposition of environmental principles on society. The imposition of an ecocentric or zoocentric ethic on society would amount to "environmental fascism" in the sense that it would force a kind of first-order impartiality, and hence a first-order conception of the good, on individuals without their consent. In a zoocentric regime individuals would be required to extend equal consideration to animals even if they did not consider such consideration to be reasonable. Individuals would no longer be granted the autonomy to decide for themselves whether zoocentrism (or ecocentrism) is more reasonable than anthropocentrism. In his discussion of an environmentalist ethic, Hans Jonas extols the virtues of "centralized power." In particular, such power affords "the advantages of autocracy as such. . . . The decisions from the top, which can be made without prior assent from below, meet with no resistance (except perhaps passive) in the social body and, given a reasonable dependability of the lower echelons, are assured of implementation. . . . Such measures are precisely what the threatening future now demands and will increasingly demand as we go on."[32] Jonas considers such autocratic methods to be necessary on the grounds that "the Baconian program by itself, that is, under its own management, has at the height of its triumph revealed its insufficiency in the lack of control over itself, thus the impotence of its power to save not only man from himself but nature from man. Both need protection now because of the very magnitude of the power man has reached in the pursuit of technological progress."[33] On Jonas's view, the Cartesian-Baconian program to render human beings the masters and possessors of nature has unleashed such power, with such unpredictable consequences, that it is naïve to suppose that this program can be regulated through the efforts of autonomous individuals. "Only an elite can assume, ethically and intellectually, the kind of responsibility for the future" that is needed in the face of our unprecedented power to destroy nature and ourselves.[34]

Although Jonas's primary concern is ethical obligations toward humanity, he leaves open the possibility of obligations toward any being that "is alive, in its constitutive indigence and fragility."[35] Thus, Jonas gestures toward the prospect of an ecocentric ethics that is implemented through recourse to centralized planning and authority. Centralized planning and autocratic decision making could be implemented within the framework of ecocentrism or zoocentrism, with an eye toward redressing the grievous wrongs done to the environment or to animals, respectively. Ferry flatly rejects such an approach on two interrelated grounds. Jonas employs a "heuristics of fear" that takes worst-case scenarios as foregone conclusions. He tries to scare the reader into accepting totalitarian coercion by sketching an unduly dark picture of our technological future and placing too little faith in the power of individual autonomy and judgment.[36] Moreover, Jonas subscribes to a conception of humanity's place in nature that overvalues the latter and is driven by "blatantly nationalist and communalist sensibilities."[37] On Ferry's view the distinctive feature of autonomy is that it enables each individual to engage in a moment of *separation* from nature and inherited values.[38] This separation enables each individual to subject all inherited beliefs and values to rational scrutiny. To succumb to the "communalist sensibilities" at work in Jonas's thought is to capitulate to precisely the forces of tradition and prejudice against which Descartes and Kant warned us. It is to sacrifice one's judgment for the sake of some romantically conceived vision of "the whole." This is tantamount to a Nazi "love of the native soil," which expresses a "hatred of modernity."[39]

To this extent, if only against its own intention, holistic environmentalism runs the risk of being "a bit khaki in its green." Concern for nature, whether it takes the form of ecocentrism or zoocentrism, entails totalitarianism if it sacrifices individual autonomy and judgment for the sake of the putative interests of someone or something outside the human community. As Ferry and Hayek would have it, the choice is a strict either-or between liberal individualism and arch-totalitarianism.

## THE HOLISTIC CRITIQUE OF LIBERAL INDIVIDUALISM

This critique of concern for animals and/or natural systems raises two questions. The first is whether liberal individualism is a plausible basis for ensuring that animals will be treated justly. In the preceding two chapters I suggested that this depends on whether the human individuals engaged in deliberative democratic practices have affirmed their felt kinship with nonhuman animals. If they have not done so, then, as Rawls and Barry make clear, there is nothing *requiring* members of a liberal polity to affirm duties of justice toward animals. Indeed, individuals might not even be required to affirm duties of compassion toward animals. I am thinking here of Peter Carruthers's lapidary assertion that animal pain has no moral significance.[40] The problem is that as long as liberal theory lacks a grounding in a holistic sense of kinship with animals, it remains neutral *by definition* with regard to such matters as the moral status of animals. The problem is not simply that democratic deliberations about animals would be "messy and time-consuming" but that robust measures on behalf of animals would necessitate an appeal to a substantive conception of the good that is not mandated by the liberal (or what I have called the social) conception of justice.[41] The second question with which the liberal critique of holism leaves us is whether the choice that confronts us is really a strict either-or between liberalism and totalitarianism. I examine this latter question in the remainder of this chapter.

As regards the moral status of animals, liberal critiques of cosmic holism address a narrow but vital procedural question: How are we to ensure that the values disclosed by the holistic viewpoint will be embraced through legitimate means by human society—in other words, that the citizenry will voluntarily affirm these values rather than being subjected to them by dint of force? This question applies equally to zoocentric and ecocentric conceptions of the good. Whether one conceives of holism in terms of regard for individual animals, species, or natural systems, the problem is how to bring about a change in the behavior of human agents whose values are pointedly anthropocentric. I will focus here on individual animals and leave aside species and natural systems because, as I argued in chapter 3, many animals possess sufficient cognitive equipment to qualify as individuals even if they do not qualify as rational individuals; the immediate moral question with regard to animals is how to do justice to them *as individuals*. (Among other things, I leave aside the question whether duties of cosmic justice are owed to nonsentient living beings.) One important consideration in connection with this focus on sentient beings is that holistic concern for individual animals does not ineluctably entail the romantic-totalitarian consequences that thinkers such as Ferry allege against ecocentric holism. What is at stake is not love of the native soil or a totalizing concern for nature in the abstract but rather moral concern for sentient individuals whose lives matter to them just as much as our lives matter to us.

Nonetheless the question remains: How we are to preserve the achievements of liberal individualism while acknowleding the inherent worth of all sentient beings? There is no little truth in Hayek's defense of democracy: the freedom of self-determination is vital to a just society. The single greatest task in the endeavor to secure justice for animals is how to balance the rightful claims of social justice and the human individual against those of cosmic justice and sentient beings generally.

Jonas challenges the conventional liberal wisdom that we are faced here with a strict either-or:

> The disruption between man and total reality is at the bottom of nihilism. The illogicality of this rupture, that is, of a dualism without metaphysics, makes its fact no less real, nor its seeming alternatives any more acceptable: the stare at isolated selfhood, to which it condemns man, may wish to exchange itself for a monistic naturalism that, along with the rupture, would abolish also the idea of man as man. Between that Scylla and this her twin Charybdis, the modern mind hovers. Whether a third road is open to it—one by which the dualistic rift can be avoided and yet enough of the dualistic insight saved to uphold the humanity of man—philosophy must find out.[42]

Whereas thinkers such as Ferry celebrate the moment of separation between self and world afforded by our capacity for rational reflection, arguing that it liberates us from what would otherwise be blind obedience to tradition, Jonas offers a considerably more subtle analysis. He recognizes that this capacity to establish critical distance from inherited values and beliefs partly defines our humanity and, as such, must not be sacrificed for the sake of immersing ourselves in some romantically conceived "monistic naturalism." But he also recognizes the destructive power of this moment of separation, which constantly and insistently uproots us from any established sense of value and is responsible for the nihilism of modernity. With no abiding sense of meaning at the core of its being, modern humanity is fundamentally homeless and lost. In this respect Novalis was right to suggest that "philosophy is really homesickness, the urge to be at home everywhere in the world."[43]

Ferry sees only one horn of this dilemma. He deplores the totalitarian implications of any monism that would submerge humanity in the anonymity of nature. Opting instead for the utter divorce of the human mind from nature, he thereby lauds, if only unwittingly, the nihilistic homelessness of modernity. Jonas challenges the conventional wisdom that we are confronted with a strict either-or and gestures toward a third possibility: the incorporation of the rational individual within a sense of the larger cosmos. The ideal of a cosmo-politics demands not only that we overcome the hubris of supposing that human beings are morally superior to other beings but also that we affirm the rational autonomy that enables us to fulfill our moral obligations toward sentient beings, both human and nonhuman alike. To be a cosmopolitan in this sense is, more than anything else, to exhibit a sense of humility. It is to acknowledge that our closest (and perhaps true) kin in the cosmos are not gods but rather animals.

## TOWARD A RESOLUTION OF THE CONFLICT BETWEEN HOLISM AND INDIVIDUALISM

One need not embrace a position as extreme as Ferry's to see that there is a fundamental problem with the attempt to affirm cosmic holism while preserving the achievements of liberal democracy. There appears to be an unresolvable contradiction between the freedom of the human individual and the acknowledgment that we are each subordinate to the cosmic order. But, as Hegel knew, not all contradictions are truly unresolvable. The seeming contradiction between cosmic holism and liberal individualism is one that we must confront and overcome. In Hegel's words, we must "sublate" it by seeing how these two terms are mediated by a higher dialectical term. Hegel's own dialectical analysis of human individuality provides a clue to the resolution of this problem. Hegel conceives of true individuality not as the raw power to do whatever one wants but rather as a mature state in which one *willingly* restricts one's own choices for the sake of the whole.[44] His conception of the individual serves as the mediating term between selfish desire and the recognition that each self is just one among many. Properly reconceived, this dialectical sense of "individuality" holds the key to understanding our relation to the universe of (not just human) subjects of which we are a part. This understanding is the precondition for a sense of *community* with nonhuman subjects that does not sacrifice the achievements of Western liberalism.

Charles Taylor sees in "Hegel's philosophy of history and politics . . . an attempt to resolve in the sphere of politics . . . the basic dilemma of this generation, how to combine the fullness of moral autonomy, with the recovery of that community, whose public life was expressive of its members and whose paradigm realization in history was the Greek polis."[45] For Hegel the political goal of modernity is to resolve the manifest tension between the autonomy of the individual, asserted by Descartes and elaborated by Kant, with the sense of unified community that characterized the Greek polis. Dialectically understood, the goal of resolving this tension cannot take the form of a naïve return to the Greek form of political order because the Greeks had not yet grasped the significance of freedom.[46] Following Kant, Hegel sees freedom not as the subjective Hobbesian ability to act in accordance with one's desires but rather as obedience to the law. For Kant this is willing obedience to the moral law that one legislates from out of one's own reason. For Hegel it is the individual's voluntary subjection to the objectivity of a freedom that can be realized only at the level of the state, which Hegel (like Aristotle) considers to be the only self-sufficient unit of measure for ethics. We freely acknowledge the law as such, and in doing so we voluntarily subject ourselves to it. We subordinate our subjective preferences and our traditional values to the demands of universal reason. We see ourselves as parts of a larger whole that, on Hegel's view, is a rational, increasingly self-conscious, and ultimately anthropocentric whole.

Hegel's vision of the realization of absolute spirit, which he identifies with the increasing actualization of self-consciousness and freedom, takes as axiomatic the moment of separation discussed by Ferry. However, for Hegel this moment of separation contains within it the prospect of an eventual unification. Hegel ultimately lauds not the moment of separation but the moment of edified unification that it makes possible.

> Spirit is initially divided from itself, and has yet to return to itself. If man is to rise to the point where he can be the vehicle of this return, he has to be transformed, to undergo a long cultivation or formation (Bildung).... The form of life which man must attain in order to be an adequate vehicle of Spirit ... must be a social form.... In order to realize God's (Spirit's) fulfillment, man has to come to a vision of himself as part of a larger life. The state is the real expression of that universal life which is the necessary embodiment ... for the vision of the absolute."[47]

Hegel seeks "to unite somehow the radical moral autonomy of Kant and the expressive unity of the Greek polis ... [to unite] the ultra-modern aspiration to autonomy, and a renewed vision of cosmic order as the foundation of society.... This synthesis he saw as the goal of history."[48]

Hegel's clearest indication of the form such a synthesis is to take is found in the dialectic of the individual in *The Philosophy of Right*. There Hegel displays the dialectical opposition between the will or freedom as finite with the will or freedom as infinite. The first moment of this dialectic is the abstract ego, which constitutes freedom in the negative sense that the ego is not related to any specific content. Here the ego is not tied to any particular objects or events. It represents "the element of pure indeterminacy or that pure reflection of the ego into itself which involves the dissipation of every restriction and every content either immediately presented by nature, by needs, desires, and impulses, or given and determined by any means whatsoever. This is the unrestricted infinity of absolute abstraction or universality, the pure thought of oneself."[49] This moment of the will constitutes "the annihilation of particularity" in the sense that abstract reflection fundamentally transcends the limitation or specificity of any and all finite objects of thought or desire, toward the sheer self-awareness of the Cartesian ego.[50] In abstract reflection I always see particular objects of desire or thought as situated within a context of limitless other such objects. It is in this spirit that Sartre later observes that bad faith consists in the false self-restriction of the ego to particular roles or ways of being, when in fact the identification with any particular role is an act of freedom that in principle presupposes the transcendence of that role toward a multitude of possible other roles. In this sense the ego is consciousness of possibility, without any essential limitation.

This negative moment of freedom finds its dialectical opposite in a moment that is "positive" in the literal sense that it posits "a determinacy as a content and an object.... Through this positing of itself as something determinate, the ego steps in principle into determinate existence. This is ... the finitude or particularization of the ego."[51] This "natural will" is determined by "impulses, desires, [and] inclinations." It possesses a content that "has the general character of being mine" in the sense that it asserts the primacy of my particular, selfish desires and inclinations.[52] This natural will "finds itself determined" by its inclinations rather than settling on them rationally. Thus, the dialectical opposition between the positive and negative moments of the will or freedom is the conflict between selfish desire and the recognition that one's personal preferences are one set of preferences among many such sets. It is the conflict between what each of us wants subjectively without regard to the needs or desires of others, and the recognition that we exist alongside other subjective wills and that the desires of these many wills cannot be satisfied simultaneously.

This dialectical opposition finds its resolution in concrete individuality. "It is the *self*-determination of the ego, which means that at one and the same time the ego posits itself as its own negative, i.e., as restricted and determinate, and yet remains by itself, i.e., in its self-identity and universality."[53] The positive and negative moments of the will "taken independently ... are false." Only in their resolution in the concept of individuality do they achieve truth.[54] Only in individuality does the negative moment of Cartesian subjectivity obtain concrete content and hence cease to be mere form. Only in individuality does the positive moment of selfish desire become mediated by the recognition that one is always in community with other wills whose value is equal to one's own. Only here does the will achieve unity of content and form.[55]

This sublation or resolution (Aufhebung) of the conflict between the negative and positive moments of the will renders the will capable of entry into the sphere of right as "the embodiment of the absolute concept or of self-conscious freedom."[56] Here subjective freedom becomes conscious of itself as existing in relation to other free agents, which prepares the will for the establishment and voluntary acceptance of reciprocal rights and obligations. Here the will takes on the capacity to be responsible to itself, to others, and to the community as a whole. But for Hegel, as for Kant, self, other, and community are all essentially rational, self-conscious beings. Implicitly following the Stoic tradition, according to which all and only rational beings belong to the sphere of right, Hegel's conception of right excludes nonrational, nonlinguistic beings, which in effect means that it excludes all non*human* beings. In the *Encyclopedia Logic* Hegel restates the traditional conviction that thought separates us from animals, and in *The Philosophy of Right* he states that humanity is "degraded" by any viewpoint that subordinates it to animality.[57] Because animals lack thought, they are incapable of true freedom. Hence they are incapable of entering into the sphere of reciprocal rights and obligations.

It would appear that Hegel's dialectic of the individual provides no resources for the resolution of the conflict between cosmic holism and liberal individualism. But it is possible to overcome this limitation of Hegel's outlook if we can think past the anthropocentric confines of his conception of community. The confrontation between Hegel and Schopenhauer contains clues to such a rethinking. For Hegel the real is rational; hence greater rationality is a clear sign of superior status in the cosmic order of things. For Schopenhauer, on the other hand, the real is precisely *not* rational; it is instead the endless striving of a universal world will that has no essential meaning, rational or otherwise.[58] Where Hegel sees humanity and no other being as the agent of Spirit, Schopenhauer sees humanity as differing from animals not in kind but merely in degree. Schopenhauer states that animals lack concepts and self-reflective awareness (Besonnenheit), but at the same time he stresses the shared capacities of humans and animals, notably understanding (which renders animals subjects of experience) and the capacity for suffering.[59] To understand is to possess an immediate acquaintance with chains of cause and effect in nature. Whatever possesses eyes—even an insect—is in this sense a subject of knowledge and experience.[60] To understand or possess knowledge, which for Schopenhauer is non- or preconceptual, is also to be involved in a process of striving based on motives.[61]

Schopenhauer's thought starts from a postulate of metaphysical continuity between human beings and the rest of nature that enables us to rethink the notion of community in terms of cosmic rather than merely human community. Even though humans differ from animals in possessing abstract knowledge, "the principal thing in the animal and man is the same . . . . The inner nature . . . in both alike [is] the *will* of the individual."[62] Animals and humans are identical in possessing immediate, pre-reflective understanding and desire. Both are identical in experiencing the suffering that is inseparable from the activity of willing. Both are individuals, even if the capacity to contemplate one's individuality and live outside of the immediacy of the present is exclusive to human beings.[63]

To conceive of animals as individuals is to open the possibility of including them in a modified dialectic of the will or freedom. Even if animals lack the capacity for conceptual abstraction required for the negative or Cartesian moment of the dialectic, they nonetheless possess the capacities requisite for the positive moment. The fact that animals cannot enact the second moment of the dialectic need not exclude them from the sphere of right, any more than this inability need exclude human moral patients. Fully rational agents are able to perform the dialectical operations involved in generating a sphere of right not only for themselves but for these others as well. Schopenhauer reminds us that we share an intimate kinship not only with our fellow human beings but with other subjects of experience as well. Some of the subjective wills involved in the positive moment of the will are rational, while others are not. The fact that these others cannot recognize their objective relation to others is no basis for excluding them from the sphere of rights and obligations. These nonrational individuals are beings toward whom we have obligations, even though they are not capable of having reciprocal obligations toward us. The resulting community is thus not restricted to fully rational beings but is instead broad enough to embrace all beings that share in our subjective struggle for life and well-being. It is a community in which we continue to observe reciprocal rights and obligations among fully rational beings, and in which we also voluntarily restrict our wills where we see the need to do so in order to respect the needs of subjective wills in the community who are unable to demand their own rights. It is a community in which, above all, we affirm our kinship with other subjective wills without regard to differences in cognitive abilities.

The burden of historical prejudice about animals, particularly the influence of the Stoics, weighs heavily upon us. We are heirs to a historical tradition that has represented human beings as cognitively and hence morally superior to animals. Already in antiquity, however, there were philosophers who pointed out the fundamental injustice of our treatment of animals. In particular, Porphyry decried the injustice of killing and eating animals. "Justice lies in restraint and harmlessness towards everything that does not do harm. . . . Someone who does not restrict harmlessness to human beings, but extends it also to the other animals, is more like the god" than one who, like the Stoics, denies justice to animals.[64] Animals, like humans, are beloved of the gods. Thus, to take on anything like a cosmopolitan standpoint is to affirm our affinities with, rather than our differences from, animals. Porphyry argues for cosmic rather than merely social justice and grounds his prohibition of meat eating in a sense of kinship with animals.[65] But if our kinship with animals is so basic, then why have we overwhelmingly tended to disregard it? "Injustice is very clever at persuading itself and at corrupting those subject to it, because its association with its nurslings is accompanied by pleasure. . . . Those who advocate meat-eating . . . are really motivated by lack of control and licentiousness."[66]

The goal of cosmic holism as I have articulated it is to reveal the licentiousness of meat eating and other forms of violence toward animals for what they are—injustices that we seek to rationalize by means of specious arguments about the emptiness of animal experience and the moral superiority of human beings. Cosmic justice demands nonviolence toward animals, just as social justice demands nonviolence toward human beings. In both cases there will be instances in which violence may be unavoidable, as when we defend ourselves against deadly human or animal adversaries. Leaving such situations aside, there is absolutely no justification for using animals to satisfy human desires. There is considerable controversy concerning what sorts of guidelines and calculations should be employed in unavoidable trade-offs between humans and animals. Much work remains to be done in this connection.[67] What is absolutely clear is that cosmic justice demands universal veganism, the refusal to consume animal products of any kind.[68] The more inured we are to anthropocentric values, the more unreasonable, burdensome, and impracticable this proposal will seem. The better we understand the nature of animal experience and recognize the ways in which it is like our own, the more we will appreciate the sense in which we truncate the notion of justice by restricting it to the human sphere. To affirm cosmic justice is to abandon our fantasy of being "the masters and possessors of nature." It is to let animal beings be in such a way that we no longer project upon them a diminished reflection of our own image but instead value their mortality as we value our own.

NOTES

PREFACE

1. Arthur Schopenhauer, *The World as Will and Representation*, vol. 1, trans. E. F. J. Payne (Indian Hills, Colo.: Falcon's Wing Press, 1958), sec. 8, p. 36.

2. Throughout this book I take it for granted that human beings are animals. When I refer to humans or human beings, I mean human animals; when I refer to animals, I mean nonhuman animals.

3. Gary Steiner, *Anthropocentrism and Its Discontents: The Moral Status of Animals in the History of Western Philosophy* (Pittsburgh, Pa.: University of Pittsburgh Press, 2005).

1. ARGUMENTS AGAINST RATIONALITY IN ANIMALS

1. See Herbert Friedmann, "The Honey-guides," *U.S. National Museum Bulletin* 208 (1955): 1–292.

2. Friedmann, "The Honey-guides," p. 163.

3. Carolyn A. Ristau, "Aspects of the Cognitive Ethology of an Injury-Feigning Bird," in *Readings in Cognitive Ethology*, ed. Marc Bekoff and Dale Jamieson (Cambridge, Mass.: MIT Press, 1996), p. 88.

4. Colin Allen and Marc Bekoff, "Intentionality, Social Play, and Definition," in *Readings in Cognitive Ethology*, ed. Marc Bekoff and Dale Jamieson (Cambridge, Mass.: MIT Press, 1996), p. 234.

5. Donald Griffin, a pioneer in cognitive ethology, suggests that this sense of limitation "may tell us something about the limited imaginations of scientists.... At early stages in the development of any branch of science

it is often necessary to do the best one can with fragmentary evidence and hypotheses that cannot be neatly formulated into crisp alternatives for the very reason that the subject is poorly understood." Donald R. Griffin, *Animal Minds* (Chicago: University of Chicago Press, 1992), p. 23. Griffin never spells out how science could ever find evidence that would demonstrate the precise nature of animal minds.

6. See, e.g., Griffin, *Animal Minds*, p. 119; James L. Gould and Carol Grant Gould, "Invertebrate Intelligence," in *Animal Intelligence: Insights into the Animal Mind*, ed. R. J. Hoage and Larry Goldman (Washington, D.C.: Smithsonian Institution Press, 1986), pp. 24, 28.

7. I have examined this history at length in my book *Anthropocentrism and Its Discontents: The Moral Status of Animals in the History of Western Philosophy* (Pittsburgh, Pa.: University of Pittsburgh Press, 2005).

8. See, e.g., David DeGrazia, *Taking Animals Seriously: Mental Life and Moral Status* (Cambridge: Cambridge University, 1996), p. 83.

9. Douglas Keith Candland, *Feral Children and Clever Animals: Reflections on Human Nature* (New York: Oxford University Press, 1993), p. 369.

10. Martin Heidegger, *Being and Time*, trans. John Macquarrie and Edward Robinson (New York: Harper and Row, 1962), Div. I, chap. 3.

11. Hans-Georg Gadamer, *Wahrheit und Methode: Grundzüge einer philosophischen Hermeneutik* (Tübingen: J.C.B. Mohr (Paul Siebeck), 1975), pp. 420–21. All translations are my own unless otherwise indicated.

12. Heidegger, *Being and Time*, p. 201. See also Martin Heidegger, *Logik: Die Frage nach der Wahrheit*, vol. 21 of *Gesamtausgabe* (Frankfurt: Klostermann, 1975), pp. 135–61.

13. Martin Heidegger, *Die Grundbegriffe der Metaphysik: Welt-Endlichkeit-Einsamkeit*, vol. 29/30 of *Gesamtausgabe* (Frankfurt: Klostermann, 1983), pp. 285, 360.

14. John McDowell, *Mind and World* (Cambridge, Mass.: Harvard University Press, 1994), p. 119.

15. Thomas Nagel, "What Is It Like to Be a Bat?" in *Mortal Questions* (Cambridge: Cambridge University Press, 1979), pp. 166, 170.

16. See, e.g., Griffin, *Animal Minds*, pp. 237, 260.

17. John Searle, *Intentionality: An Essay in the Philosophy of Mind* (Cambridge: Cambridge University Press, 1983), pp. 40–41.

18. Immanuel Kant, *Critique of Pure Reason*, trans. Norman Kemp Smith (New York: Humanities Press, 1950), at A51/B75.

19. Kant, *Critique of Pure Reason* at A106.

20. McDowell, *Mind and World*, p. 46.

21. Ibid., pp. 114–15.

22. Ibid., p. 122.

23. See Donald Davidson, "The Emergence of Thought," *Erkenntnis* 51 (1999): Thought in the sense of intentionality involves "predicat[ing] properties of objects and events" (p. 17). In advocating this view, I am taking sides in a heated philosophical controversy. Thinkers such as Hans-Johann Glock have argued that having a propositional attitude does not require having a relationship to an object or a proposition, and that beliefs need not involve concepts. See "Animals, Thoughts and Concepts," *Synthese* 123 (2000): 42, 44. See also K. V. Wilkes, "Talking to Cats, Rats and Bats," in *Thought and Language*, Royal Institute of Philosophy Supplement 42, ed. John Preston (Cambridge: Cambridge University Press, 1997), p. 179.

24. Christopher Peacocke, *A Study of Concepts* (Cambridge, Mass.: MIT Press, 1992), p. 126.

25. Colin Allen, "Animal Concepts Revisited: The Use of Self-Monitoring as an Empirical Approach," *Erkenntnis* 51 (1999): 34. According to Allen, it is reasonable to attribute conceptual ability to a being when that being "systematically discriminates some $X$'s from some non-$X$'s . . . is capable of detecting some of its own discrimination errors . . . [and] is capable of learning to better discriminate $X$'s from non-$X$'s" (p. 37).

26. Colin Allen and Marc Hauser, "Concept Attribution in Nonhuman Animals: Theoretical and Methodological Problems in Ascribing Complex Mental Processes," *Philosophy of Science* 58 (1991): 227.

27. See Gottlob Frege, *Die Grundlagen der Arithmetik: Eine logisch mathematische Untersuchung über den Begriff der Zahl / The Foundations of Arithmetic: A Logico-Mathematical Enquiry into the Concept of Number*, 2nd rev. ed., German with English trans. by J. L. Austin (Evanston, Ill.: Northwestern University Press, 1968): "If for example, in considering a white cat and a black cat, I disregard the properties which serve to distinguish them, then I get presumably the concept 'cat'" (p. 45).

28. Frege, *Die Grundlagen der Arithmetik/The Foundations of Arithmetic*, pp. 41–42.

29. See Michael Martin, "Perception, Concepts, and Memory," in *Essays on Nonconceptual Content*, ed. York H. Gunther (Cambridge, Mass.: MIT Press, 2003): "Taking beliefs to be conceptual is to see them as arising out of . . . a web of conceptual abilities, reflected in the particular thoughts and beliefs one has" (238). See also Gregory L. Murphy, *The Big Book of Concepts*

(Cambridge, Mass.: MIT Press, 2002): concepts are always "part of a broader knowledge-representation scheme" (p. 488).

30. John Searle, "Minds, Brains and Programs," *Behavioral and Brain Sciences* 3 (1980): 451.

31. John R. Searle, "The Explanation of Cognition," in *Thought and Language*, Royal Institute of Philosophy Supplement 42, ed. John Preston (Cambridge: Cambridge University Press, 1997), p. 123. "In the case of thermostats we have rigged up physical systems to behave as if they were following computational rules. But the intentional, rule-following computation of the thermostat is entirely observer-relative" (p. 124).

32. See Daniel Dennett, "Conditions of Personhood," in *Brainstorms: Philosophical Essays on Mind and Psychology* (Cambridge, Mass.: MIT Press, Bradford Books, 1978), p. 277; Dennett,"Intentional Systems in Cognitive Ethology: The 'Panglossian Paradigm' Defended," *Behavioral and Brain Sciences* 6 (1983): 344, 351; Dennett, "Do Animals Have Beliefs?" *Comparative Approaches to Cognitive Ethology*, ed. Herbert L. Roitblat and Jean-Arcady Meyer (Cambridge, Mass.: MIT Press, 1995): "Chess computers and amoebae have beliefs" (117–18).

33. Daniel Dennett, "Reply to Arbib and Gunderson," *Brainstorms*, p. 30.

34. For a detailed discussion of this point, see chapter 6 of my book *Anthropocentrism and Its Discontents*.

35. Bernard Williams, *Problems of the Self* (Cambridge: Cambridge University Press, 1973), pp. 138–39.

36. Dennett, "Intentional Systems in Cognitive Ethology," pp. 350–51.

37. Allen, "Animal Concepts Revisited," p. 36.

38. See Robert Huber et al., "Serotonin and Aggressive Motivation in Crustaceans: Altering the Decision to Retreat," *Proceedings of the National Academy of Science* 94 (1997): 5939–42. The researchers found that increased serotonin levels led to a reduced likelihood of retreat and increased duration of fighting encounters.

39. Gerardus Pieter Baerends, "Fortpflanzungsverhalten und Orientierung der Grabwespe *Ammophila campestris*," *Tijdschrift voor Entomologie* 84 (1941): 68–275.

40. Donald Davidson, "Thought and Talk," in *Mind and Language*, Wolfson College Lectures 1974, ed. Samuel Guttenplan (Oxford: Clarendon Press, 1975), p. 7.

41. Ibid., p. 9.

42. Davidson, "The Emergence of Thought," p. 12.

43. Ibid., p. 13.

44. Ibid., p. 14. See also p. 13: "The point is not that consensus defines the concept of truth, but that it creates the space for its application. If this is right, then not only language, but thought itself, is necessarily social."

45. Ibid., p. 12.

46. Davidson, "Thought and Talk," p. 21.

47. Ibid., pp. 8–9. Moreover, "in order to have a belief, it is necessary to have the concept of belief," which in turn depends on having language. To attribute this or any other belief to animals is wholly implausible, on Davidson's view, because "to have the concept of belief is . . . to have the concept of objective truth." Donald Davidson, "Rational Animals," in *Actions and Events: Perspectives on the Philosophy of Donald Davidson*, ed. Ernest LePore and Brian McLaughlin (Oxford: Basil Blackwell, 1985), pp. 478, 479–80.

48. Davidson, "Rational Animals," p. 473.

49. Ibid., pp. 474, 476. On the holism of concepts and its relation to the holism of belief, see Davidson, "The Emergence of Thought," pp. 8–9. Steven P. Stich offers an argument very similar to Davidson's about the holism of belief; see *From Folk Psychology to Cognitive Science: The Case Against Belief* (Cambridge, Mass.: MIT Press, 1983), p. 104–5; Davidson, "Do Animals Have Beliefs?" *Australasian Journal of Philosophy* 57 (1979): 17–18.

50. Davidson, "Rational Animals," p. 477.

51. Ibid., p. 480.

52. Ibid., p. 474 n. 1.

53. Davidson, "The Emergence of Thought," p. 11.

54. Achim Stephan, "Sind Tiere 'schwer vom Begriff'?" *Deutsche Zeitschrift für Philosophie* 52 (2004): 576.

55. Norman Malcolm, "Thoughtless Brutes," *Proceedings and Addresses of the American Philosophical Association* 46 (1973): 14.

56. Ibid., p. 16.

57. Michael Dummett, *Origins of Analytical Philosophy* (Cambridge, Mass.: Harvard University Press, 1994), p. 122.

58. Ibid., p. 123.

59. Ibid., p. 122.

60. Ibid., p. 125.

61. Richard Jeffrey, "Animal Interpretation," in *Actions and Events: Perspectives on the Philosophy of Donald Davidson*, ed. Ernest LePore and Brian McLaughlin (Oxford: Basil Blackwell, 1985), pp. 485–86.

62. McDowell, *Mind and World*, p. 122.

63. Ibid., p. 125.

64. Heidegger, *Die Grundbegriffe der Metaphysik*, pp. 390–91. McDowell calls this captivation "enslavement to immediate biological imperatives" (*Mind and World*, p. 117).

## 2. ARGUMENTS FOR RATIONALITY IN ANIMALS

1. Ruth Garrett Millikan, *On Clear and Confused Ideas: An Essay about Substance Concepts* (Cambridge: Cambridge University Press, 2000), p. 199.

2. James L. Gould and Carol Grant Gould, "Invertebrate Intelligence," in *Animal Intelligence: Insights into the Animal Mind*, ed. R. J. Hoage and Larry Goldman (Washington, D.C.: Smithsonian Institution Press, 1986), p. 24.

3. See Ruth Garrett Millikan, *Language, Thought, and Other Biological Categories: New Foundations for Realism* (Cambridge, Mass.: MIT Press, 1984), p. 65.

4. David Papineau and Cecilia Heyes, "Rational or Associative? Imitation in Japanese Quail," in *Rational Animals?* ed. Susan Hurley and Matthew Nudds (Oxford: Oxford University Press, 2006), p. 188.

5. Donald R. Griffin, *Animal Minds* (Chicago: University of Chicago Press, 1992), p. 3.

6. Ibid., p. 5.

7. Ibid., pp. 10–13.

8. Ibid., p. 140.

9. Ibid., pp. 256–57.

10. Millikan, *Language, Thought, and Other Biological Categories: New Foundations for Realism*, pp. 12–13. Here Millikan defines "representation" differently than she does later in *On Clear and Confused Ideas*. There she seems to classify intentional devices such as the bee dance as a form of representation in which the animal having the representation does not grasp "the identity of what is represented," whereas in *Language, Thought and Other Biological Categories* she defined representations as thoughts or sentences "whose referents are identified." The important point is that many animals have mental states that guide their behavior, even though the animals experiencing the mental states cannot explicitly grasp the referents of those states.

11. Ruth Garrett Millikan, "Styles of Rationality," in *Rational Animals?*, pp. 118–19.

12. Colin Allen, "Transitive Inference in Animals: Reasoning or Conditioned Associations?," in *Rational Animals?* p. 181.

13. Griffin, *Animal Minds*, p. 256.

14. Henry More, letter to Descartes, December 11, 1648, in *Oeuvres de Descartes*, 12 vols., ed. Charles Adam and Paul Tannery (Paris: Vrin, 1964–74), 5:243.

15. On sentience as sufficient for equal moral consideration, see Gary L. Francione, *Introduction to Animal Rights: Your Child or the Dog?* (Philadelphia, Pa.: Temple University Press, 2000), p. 174. See also DeGrazia, *Taking Animals Seriously*, p. 93. Tom Regan argues that being "subject-of-a-life," which includes intentional capacities as well as sentience, is sufficient for equal moral consideration; see *The Case for Animal Rights* (Berkeley: University of California Press, 1983), pp. 243, 245–46.

16. Immanuel Kant, *Critique of Judgment*, trans. Werner S. Pluhar (Indianapolis, Ind.: Hackett, 1987), sec. 90, p. 356 n. 64 (Ak. 464) (translation altered).

17. See, e.g., John Searle, "Minds, Brains, and Computers," *Behavioral and Brain Sciences* 3 (1980): 417–57; Hubert L. Dreyfus, Stuart E. Dreyfus, and Tom Athanasiou, *Mind Over Machine: The Power of Intuition and Expertise in the Era of the Computer* (New York: Free Press, 1986).

18. Martha C. Nussbaum, *Upheavals of Thought: The Intelligence of Emotions* (Cambridge: Cambridge University Press, 2001), p. 91. On the Stoic view, see Richard Sorabji, *Animal Minds and Human Morals: The Origins of the Western Debate* (Ithaca, N.Y.: Cornell University Press, 1993), pp. 40–44, 58–59; and Steiner, *Anthropocentrism and Its Discontents*, pp. 77–92.

19. Nussbaum, *Upheavals of Thought*, pp. 118–19.

20. Ibid., pp. 125–26.

21. Ibid., pp. 127–28.

22. See Martin Heidegger, *Being and Time*, trans. John Macquarrie and Edward Robinson (New York: Harper and Row, 1961), p. 201. I discuss Heidegger's critique of this conception of language in chapter 3.

23. Nussbaum, *Upheavals of Thought*, p. 129.

24. Ibid., pp. 119–20.

25. Ibid., pp. 120, 118. Here Nussbaum seems to mean anthropomorphism, not anthropocentrism.

26. Ibid., p. 122.

27. Ibid., p. 120.

28. Ibid., pp. 92, 121.

29. Ibid., p. 123.

30. John R. Searle, "Animal Minds," in *Consciousness and Language* (Cambridge: Cambridge University Press, 2002), p. 61.

31. Ibid., p. 62.

32. John R. Searle, "The Explanation of Cognition," in *Consciousness and Language*, pp. 122, 117–18.

33. Searle, "Animal Minds," p. 64.

34. Sextus Empiricus, *Outlines of Pyrrhonism* I.69, in *The Skeptic Way: Sextus Empiricus's "Outlines of Pyrrhonism,"* trans. Benson Mates (New York: Oxford University Press, 1996), p. 98.

35. Plutarch, *The Cleverness of Animals* 969C–D, in *Moralia*, vol. 12, trans. Harold Cherniss and William C. Helmbold (Cambridge, Mass.: Harvard University Press, 1995), p. 379.

36. Plutarch, *The Cleverness of Animals* 974D–E, 979E–F, pp. 411, 443.

37. Griffin, *Animal Minds*, p. 174. See also William A. Hillix and Duane Rumbaugh, *Animal Bodies, Human Minds: Ape, Dolphin, and Parrot Language Skills* (New York: Kluwer Academic/Plenum, 2004).

38. Irene M. Pepperberg, "Number Comprehension by a Grey Parrot (*Psittacus erithacus*), Including a Zero-Like Concept," *Journal of Comparative Psychology* 119, no. 2 (2005): 197.

39. Ibid., p. 204.

40. Ibid., pp. 197–98, 206.

41. Ibid., p. 202.

42. Ibid., p. 203.

43. See, e.g., Nicholas J. Mackintosh, "Abstraction and Discrimination," in *The Evolution of Cognition*, ed. Cecilia Heyes and Ludwig Huber (Cambridge, Mass.: MIT Press, Bradford Books, 2000), pp. 128, 125, 135. For a summary of Herrnstein's research with pigeons, see Griffin, *Animal Minds*, pp. 128–32.

44. L. Weiskrantz, "Thought without Language: Thought without Awareness?" in *Thought and Language*, Royal Institute of Philosophy Supplement 42, ed. John Preston (Cambridge: Cambridge University Press, 1999), pp. 136–37, 146.

45. Ibid., p. 144.

46. Searle, "The Explanation of Cognition," pp. 111–12, 114, 117. On the parallel distinction between intrinsic intentionality and observer-relative ascriptions of intentionality, see Searle, "Minds, Brains, and Programs," p. 451.

47. Colin Allen, "Mental Content and Evolutionary Explanation," *Biology and Philosophy* 7 (1992): 1, 3.

48. Ibid., pp. 5–6, 8–9.

49. Ibid., p. 10. See also Colin Allen, "Mental Content," *British Journal for the Philosophy of Science* 43 (1992): 552.

50. Cecilia Heyes and Anthony Dickinson, "The Intentionality of Animal Action," *Mind and Language* 5, no. 1 (1990): 88. Cf. Allen, who explains that "a realist attitude toward mental representations" is one according to which "certain organisms really do have mental representations" ("Mental Content and Evolutionary Explanation," p. 9). Elsewhere he adds: "By a 'realist understanding', I mean the view that mental states and their contents are ontologically respectable for scientific explanations of behavior" ("Mental Content," p. 537).

51. Heyes and Dickinson, "The Intentionality of Animal Action," pp. 88–89.

52. Bernard Rollin, "Thought without Language," in *Animal Rights and Human Obligations*, ed. Tom Regan and Peter Singer (Upper Saddle River, N.J.: Prentice Hall, 1989), p. 45.

53. Ibid., p. 46.

54. See Griffin, *Animal Minds*, pp. 10–13.

55. Rollin, "Thought without Language," pp. 46–47.

56. Euan M. Macphail, "The Search for a Mental Rubicon," in *The Evolution of Cognition*, p. 268.

57. Ibid., p. 268.

58. Ibid., p. 264.

59. Ibid., p. 267.

60. DeGrazia, *Taking Animals Seriously*, pp. 94, 175.

61. Ibid., p. 94.

62. Ibid., pp. 137–38.

63. Ibid., pp. 155–56.

64. Ibid., p. 157. DeGrazia suggests that the lack of a successful alternative framework for explaining animal behavior "counts as excellent behavioral evidence for asserting that animals do, in fact, have beliefs and desires" (pp. 147–48).

65. Regan, *The Case for Animal Rights*, pp. 54–56.

66. Fred I. Dretske, "Machines, Plants and Animals: The Origins of Agency," *Erkenntnis* 51 (1999): 22.

67. Ibid., p. 27.

68. Ibid., p. 28.

69. Ibid., p. 29.

70. Ibid., p. 30.

71. Ibid., p. 30 n. 2.

72. Ibid., p. 30.

73. Fred Dretske, *Explaining Behavior: Reasons in a World of Causes* (Cambridge, Mass.: MIT Press, 1998), p. 154.

74. Hans-Johann Glock, "Animals, Thoughts and Concepts," *Synthese* 123 (2000): 42.

75. Ibid., pp. 59–60.

76. Ibid., pp. 42, 53.

77. Millikan, *On Clear and Confused Ideas*, p. 196.

78. John Bishop makes a similar argument; see "More Thought on Thought and Talk," *Mind* 89 (1980): 1–16.

79. Richard Routley, "Alleged Problems in Attributing Beliefs, and Intentionality, to Animals," *Inquiry* 24 (1981): 390; see also p. 403.

80. Ibid., p. 400.

81. Ibid., pp. 405, 408.

82. Ibid., p. 412.

83. Cf. Routley's assertion that "belief that *p* is the belief that the world is that way, as *p*" ("Alleged Problems in Attributing Beliefs, and Intentionality, to Animals," p. 408).

84. Ibid., p. 387.

### 3. An Associationist Model of Animal Cognition

1. Ruth Garrett Millikan, "Styles of Rationality," in *Rational Animals?* ed. Susan Hurley and Matthew Nudds (Oxford: Oxford University Press, 2006), pp. 119–20.

2. Ruth Garrett Millikan, *Varieties of Meaning*, 2002 Jean Nicod Lectures (Cambridge, Mass.: MIT Press, 2004), p. 81.

3. Ibid., p. 163.

4. Ibid., p. 168.

5. Ibid., pp. 168–69.

6. Ibid., p. 163.

7. Ludwig Wittgenstein, *Philosophical Investigations*, trans. G.. E. M. Anscombe (New York: Macmillan, 1968), p. 174.

8. Ibid., p. 174.

9. Ibid., p. 223.

10. See chapter 6 of my book *Anthropocentrism and Its Discontents*.

11. Peter Harrison, "Do Animals Feel Pain?" *Philosophy* 66 (1991): 37–38.

12. C. Lloyd Morgan, *Animal Behavior* (London: Edward Arnold, 1900), p. 270; cf. Harrison, "Do Animals Feel Pain?" p. 34.

13. Ibid., p. 33.

14. Ibid., pp. 38, 36.

15. Peter Carruthers, *The Animals Issue: Moral Theory in Practice* (Cambridge: Cambridge University Press, 1992), p. 184.

16. Ibid., p. 181.

17. Ibid., p. 183.

18. Ibid., p. 182; see also p. 184.

19. Ibid., pp. 189–90.

20. John McDowell, "Reply to Commentators," *Philosophy and Phenomenological Research* 58 (1998): 428.

21. John McDowell, "The Content of Perceptual Experience," *Philosophical Quarterly* 44 (1994): 195.

22. McDowell, "Reply to Commentators," p. 429.

23. Ibid., p. 410.

24. David Papineau, "Human Minds," in *Minds and Persons*, Royal Institute of Philosophy Supplement 53, ed. Anthony O'Hear (Cambridge: Cambridge University Press, 2003), p. 179; see also p. 165.

25. Carruthers, *The Animals Issue*, p. 171.

26. C. Lloyd Morgan, *Animal Life and Intelligence* (Boston: Ginn, 1891), pp. 338–39.

27. Ibid., p. 328.

28. Ibid., p. 362.

29. Ibid., p. 366.

30. Ibid., p. 371.

31. Ibid., p. 460.

32. José Luis Bermudez, *Thinking without Words* (Oxford: Oxford University Press, 2003), p. 55.

33. Ibid., p. 57.

34. Ibid., p. 137. For further details of the red deer roaring contests, see pp. 135–36.

35. Ibid., pp. 187–88. See also page 147, where Bermudez attributes "protocausal understanding" to nonlinguistic beings.

36. Ibid., p. 188.

37. See Harry Frankfurt, "Freedom of the Will and the Concept of a Person," *Philosophical Review* 68 (1972): 5–20.

38. Seneca, *Ad Lucilium Epistulae Morales*, vol. 3, Latin with English trans. by Richard M. Gummere (London: Heinemann / New York: G. P. Putnam's Sons, 1925), 124.16–18, p. 445.

39. Saint Augustine, *Confessions*, trans. R. S. Pine-Coffin (London: Penguin, 1961), X.17, p. 224; X.20–21, pp. 226–27.; X.24, pp. 230–31.

40. Nicola Clayton, Nathan Emery, and Anthony Dickinson, "The Rationality of Animal Memory: Complex Caching Strategies of Western Scrub Jays," in *Rational Animals?*, pp. 206–7 (citing Endel Tulving's definition of episodic memory). In this essay the authors argue for several conclusions with which I disagree: that scrub jays have beliefs (p. 203) and declarative memories (p. 207), and that they are capable of "mental attribution or 'mind reading'" (p. 213).

41. See Morgan: "Nine-tenths at least of the actions of average men are intelligent and not rational" (*Animal Life and Intelligence*, pp. 376–77).

42. See H. S. Terrace, "Animal Cognition: Thinking without Language," *Philosophical Transactions of the Royal Society of London* B 308 (1985): 119.

43. Edward L. Thorndike, *Animal Intelligence: Experimental Studies* (New Brunswick, N.J.: Transaction Publishers, 2000), p. 142.

44. Papineau, "Human Minds," p. 180.

45. Ibid.

46. Tim Crane, "The Nonconceptual Content of Experience," in *The Contents of Experience: Essays on Perception*, ed. Tim Crane (Cambridge: Cambridge University Press, 1992), p. 151.

47. Ibid., p. 155.

48. Tim Crane, "The Intentional Structure of Consciousness," in *Consciousness: New Philosophical Perspectives*, ed. Quentin Smith and Aleksandar Jokic (Oxford: Clarendon Press, 2003), p. 38.

49. Ibid., p. 40.

50. Ibid., p. 44.

51. Ibid., pp. 54–55.

52. See Christopher Peacocke, "Does Perception Have a Nonconceptual Content?" *Journal of Philosophy* 98 (2001): 263–64.

53. Morgan, *Animal Life and Intelligence*, p. 375.

54. John McDowell, *Mind and World* (Cambridge, Mass.: Harvard University Press, 1994), pp. 54, 116–18. See also chapter 1 in the present study.

55. Colin Allen and Marc Hauser, "Concept Attribution in Nonhuman Animals: Theoretical and Methodological Problems in Ascribing Complex Mental Processes," *Philosophy of Science* 58 (1991): 227.

56. On the use of cognitive maps by honeybees, see Steiner, *Anthropocentrism and Its Discontents*, pp. 247–48.

57. H. S. Terrace, "Animal Cognition," in *Animal Cognition*, ed. H. L. Roitblat, T. G. Bever, and H. S. Terrace (Hillsdale, N.J.: Lawrence Earlbaum, 1984), p. 19.

58. See Martin Heidegger, *Being and Time*, trans. John Macquarrie and Edward Robinson (New York: Harper and Row, 1962), pp. 95–107.

59. Maurice Merleau-Ponty, *Phenomenology of Perception*, trans. Colin Smith (London: Routledge and Kegan Paul/Atlantic Highlands, N.J.: Humanities Press International, 1978), p. 296.

60. David Hume, *A Treatise of Human Nature*, 2nd ed., ed. P. H. Nidditch (Oxford: Clarendon Press, 1981), pp. 176, 178.

61. David Hume, "Of the Immortality of the Soul," in *Essays Moral, Political, and Literary*, rev. ed., ed. Eugene F. Miller (Indianapolis, Ind.: Liberty Fund, 1987), p. 593; *A Treatise of Human Nature*, p. 448.

62. Hume, *A Treatise of Human Nature*, pp. 7–8.

63. Ibid., p. 11.

64. Ibid.

65. David Hume, "Of the Dignity or Meanness of Human Nature," in *Essays Moral, Political, and Literary*, p. 82.

66. Hume, *A Treatise of Human Nature*, pp. 326, 428, 509. I find completely implausible Deborah Boyle's suggestion that Hume's account leaves room for the possibility that animals could participate in virtue and vice. See "Hume on Animal Reason," *Hume Studies* 29 (2003): pp. 22–23. As Antony Pitson notes, on Hume's view a "comparative inferiority of reason . . . renders [animals] incapable of taking the general point of view required for the operation of the moral sense" ("The Nature of Humean Animals," *Hume Studies* 19 [1993]: 301, 316).

67. David Hume, "The Stoic," in *Essays Moral, Political, and Literary*, p. 146.

68. Hume, *A Treatise of Human Nature*, p. 658.

69. Ibid., p. 19.

70. Ibid., p. 17.

71. As Berkeley puts the point, "An idea . . . becomes general, by being made to represent or stand for all other particular ideas of the same sort." George Berkeley, *A Treatise Concerning the Principles of Human Knowledge*, ed. Jonathan Dancy (Oxford: Oxford University Press, 1998), p. 94.

72. Hume, *A Treatise of Human Nature*, p. 179.

73. Ibid., p. 183.

74. Ibid., pp. 628–29.

75. Papineau and Heyes, "Rational or Associative? Imitation in Japanese Quail," p. 193.

76. Donald R. Griffin, *Animal Minds* (Chicago: University of Chicago Press, 1992), pp. 122, 131.

77. Anthony Dickinson and Bernard W. Balleine, "Causal Cognition and Goal-Directed Action," in *The Evolution of Cognition*, ed. Cecilia Heyes and Ludwig Huber (Cambridge, Mass.: MIT Press, Bradford Books, 2000), p. 186.

78. R. J. Herrnstein, Donald H. Loveland, and Cynthia Cable, "Natural Concepts in Pigeons," *Journal of Experimental Psychology: Animal Behavior Processes* 2 (1976): 299.

79. R. J. Herrnstein, "Riddles of Natural Categorization," *Philosophical Transactions of the Royal Society of London* B 308 (1985): 132.

## 4. LIBERAL INDIVIDUALISM AND THE PROBLEM OF ANIMAL RIGHTS

1. Richard Sorabji, *Animal Minds and Human Morals: The Origins of the Western Debate* (Ithaca, N.Y.: Cornell University Press, 1993), p. 216.

2. Gary L. Francione, "Introduction: The Abolition of Animal Use vs. the Regulation of Animal Treatment," in *Animals as Persons: Essays on the Abolition of Animal Exploitation* (New York: Columbia University Press, 2007), p. 12.

3. I plan to explore the possibility that nonsentient living nature has moral status in subsequent work. On such a view, perceptual experience would be sufficient but not necessary for moral worth.

4. On the Stoic conception of *oikeiosis* (belonging) and its influence on subsequent philosophical thought regarding the moral status of animals, see Steiner, *Anthropocentrism and Its Discontents*.

5. John Locke, *An Essay Concerning Human Understanding*, ed. Peter H. Nidditch (Oxford: Clarendon, 1990), bk. 2, chap. 1, sec. 19, p. 116.

6. Ibid., bk. 2, chap. 11, sec. 10, p. 159f.

7. Ibid., bk. 2, chap. 11, sec. 11, p. 160; bk. 4, chap. 4, sec. 18, p. 573.

8. Ibid.,, bk. 1, chap. 1, sec. 1, p. 43.

9. John Locke, *First Treatise of Government*, in *Two Treatises of Government*, ed. Peter Laslett (Cambridge: Cambridge University Press, 1988), chap. 4, secs. 39–41, pp. 167–69; see also secs. 28–30, pp. 160–62.

10. Ibid., chap. 9, sec. 92, p. 209.

11. Locke, *Second Treatise of Government*, in *Two Treatises of Government*, chap. 2, sec. 6, p. 271.

12. Ibid., chap. 4, secs. 26–27, pp. 286–88.

13. Immanuel Kant, *Grounding for the Metaphysics of Morals*, trans. James W. Ellington (Indianapolis, Ind.: Hackett, 1981), p. 35 (Ak. 428).

14. Ibid., p. 36 (Ak. 428).

15. Ibid., pp. 35–36 (Ak. 428).

16. Immanuel Kant, "Idea for a Universal History with a Cosmopolitan Purpose," in *Political Writings*, ed. H. S. Reiss (Cambridge: Cambridge University Press, 1991), p. 43.

17. Immanuel Kant, *Critique of Judgment*, trans. Werner S. Pluhar (Indianapolis, Ind.: Hackett, 1987), sec. 90, pp. 356–57 nn. 64, 66 (translation altered).

18. Immanuel Kant, *Lectures on Ethics*, ed. Peter Heath and J. B. Schneewind, trans. Peter Heath (Cambridge: Cambridge University Press, 1997), p. 125.

19. Ibid., p. 218.

20. Kant, "Idea for a Universal History with Cosmopolitan Purpose," p. 43.

21. Kant, *Lectures on Ethics*, p. 234.

22. Kant, *Critique of Judgment*, sec. 86, p. 334 (Ak. 445).

23. Kant, *Lectures on Ethics*, p. 147 (translation altered).

24. Kant, *Critique of Judgment*, sec. 83, p. 318 (Ak. 431).

25. Ibid., sec. 83, pp. 318 (Ak. 431), 320 (Ak. 432); see also sec. 86.

26. Kant, *Lectures on Ethics*, p. 156.

27. Immanuel Kant, "The Doctrine of Virtue," in *The Metaphysics of Morals*, ed. Mary Gregor (Cambridge: Cambridge University Press, 1996), sec. 17, pp. 192–93. (Ak. 443); see also *Lectures on Ethics*, p. 212.

28. Immanuel Kant, *Critique of Practical Reason*, 3rd ed., trans. Lewis White Beck (Upper Saddle River, N.J.: Library of Liberal Arts, 1993), pt. 1, bk. 1, chap. 3, p. 80.

29. Kant, *Grounding for the Metaphysics of Morals*, p. 12 (Ak. 399).

30. Kant, "The Doctrine of Virtue," sec. 17, p. 193 (Ak. 443).

31. Ibid., sec. 17, pp. 192–93 (Ak. 443).

32. Kant, *Lectures on Ethics*, p. 213.

33. Kant, "The Doctrine of Virtue," sec. 17, p. 193 (Ak. 443).

34. Jeremy Bentham, *Introduction to the Principles of Morals and Legislation* (New York: Hafner, 1948), pp. 310–11 n. 1.

35. Ibid.

36. Gary L. Francione, *Introduction to Animal Rights: Your Child or the Dog?* (Philadelphia, Pa.: Temple University Press, 2000), p. 133.

37. John Stuart Mill, *Utilitarianism*, in *On Liberty and Other Essays*, ed. John Gray (Oxford: Oxford University Press, 1998), p. 140. Mill elaborates: "Human beings have faculties more elevated than the animal appetites, and when once made conscious of them, do not regard anything as happiness which does not include their gratification.... Pleasures of the intellect, of the feelings and imagination, and of the moral sentiments [have] a much higher value than [do] those of mere sensation" (p. 138).

38. John Stuart Mill, "Nature," in *Three Essays on Religion* (New York: Henry Holt, 1878), pp. 20–21. Gary Francione offers a different analysis of Bentham and Mill. Rather than introducing a hierarchy of moral desert, these thinkers were simply taking the position that "as an empirical matter, animals lack characteristics beyond sentience" that would make them candidates for personhood, and that this difference between animals and humans justifies differential moral treatment. Bentham and Mill believed that they were "accommodating animal interests within a liberal perspective (but adjusting for empirical differences)" (private communication). See also Francione, "Taking Sentience Seriously," *Journal of Animal Law and Ethics* 1 (2006): 3–5. My own sense is that this may well be what Bentham and Mill thought they were doing, but that they were in effect creating a hierarchy by granting privileged status to human beings over "merely sentient" animals.

39. See, e.g., Joseph Mendelson III, "Should Animals Have Standing? A Review of Standing Under the Animal Welfare Act," *Boston College Environmental Affairs Law Review* 24 (1997): 795–820. See also Cass R. Sunstein, "Standing for Animals (with Notes on Animal Rights)," *UCLA Law Review* 47 (2000): 1333–68.

40. Aristotle, *Politics* I.8 at 1256b15–22, I.5 at 1254b20–25.

41. Tom Regan, *The Case for Animal Rights* (Berkeley: University of California Press, 1983), p. 243. Regan considers at least "normal mammalian animals aged one or more" to qualify as subjects-of-a-life (p. 81), leaving open the question which other animals also qualify as subjects-of-a-life. See also page 349, where Regan entertains the possibility that poultry should be considered subjects-of-a-life.

42. Ibid., p. 356.

43. Ibid., pp. 240, 279.

44. Ibid., pp. 285–86.

45. Ibid., pp. 324–25. Regan goes on to maintain that in order to argue otherwise, we would have to appeal to utilitarian considerations, which would conflict with his rights-based approach.

46. Gary L. Francione, *Animals, Property, and the Law* (Philadelphia, Pa.: Temple University Press, 1995), p. 18. According to Francione, "necessary" suffering refers to what is morally necessary (p. 22).

47. Ibid., p. 115.

48. Ibid., p. 257.

49. Francione, *Introduction to Animal Rights*, p. 6.

50. Ibid., pp. xxvi–xxvii.

51. Ibid., pp. xxiv–xxv. In *Animals, Property, and the Law* Francione states that "even the recent *Model Penal Code* maintains that the purpose of anticruelty statutes is to improve human character and not to protect animals" (p. 132).

52. Francione, *Introduction to Animal Rights*, p. 84.

53. Ibid., pp. 94–95. Cf. Kant, *Grounding for the Metaphysics of Morals*, pp. 35ff. (Ak. 428ff.).

54. Francione, *Introduction to Animal Rights*, pp. 100, 95.

55. Francione has succinctly diagnosed the fundamental problems with Singer's views. See "Taking Sentience Seriously," pp. 14–15, and *Introduction to Animal Rights*, pp. 135–48.

56. Peter Singer, *Animal Liberation*, 2nd ed. (New York: New York Review of Books, 1990), p. 229.

57. Stuart Hampshire, "Morality and Pessimism," in *Public and Private Morality*, ed. Stuart Hampshire et al. (Cambridge: Cambridge University Press, 1978), p. 2.

58. Julian Franklin, *Animal Rights and Moral Philosophy* (New York: Columbia University Press, 2005), p. 58.

59. Ibid., p. 60.

60. See Regan, *The Case for Animal Rights*, pp. 178, 239.

61. Franklin, *Animal Rights and Moral Philosophy*, p. 62.

62. Ibid., pp. 62–63.

63. Francione, *Introduction to Animal Rights*, p. 170. Francione does not call for an immediate end to pet ownership but instead argues that no more pet animals should be brought into existence, and that we have an obligation to care for all existing pet animals.

64. Martha C. Nussbaum, *Frontiers of Justice: Disability, Nationality, Species Membership* (Cambridge, Mass.: Harvard University Press, Belknap Press, 2006), pp. 376–77.

65. Franklin, *Animal Rights and Moral Theory*, pp. 90–91.

66. Martha C. Nussbaum, "Animal Rights: The Need for a Theoretical Basis," *Harvard Law Review* 114 (2001): 1548. See also her *Frontiers of Justice: Disability, Nationality, Species Membership*, p. 377.

67. See Bentham, *Introduction to the Principles of Morals and Legislation*, pp. 310–311 n; Arthur Schopenhauer, "On Religion," in *Parerga and Paralipomena*, 2 vols., trans. E. F. J. Payne (Oxford: Clarendon Press, 2000), 2:373–74.

68. Franklin, *Animal Rights and Moral Theory*, p. 85.

69. Kant, *Grounding for the Metaphysics of Morals*, p. 12 (Ak. 399).

70. Franklin, *Animal Rights and Moral Theory*, p. 85.

71. Francione, "Taking Sentience Seriously," p. 17.

72. See Francione, *Introduction to Animal Rights*, pp. 75, 174.

73. Ibid., p. 100.

74. According to Francione, sentience is necessary and sufficient for the possession of interests, which is the basis for possessing moral status (*Introduction to Animal Rights*, pp. 174–75). Francione argues that animals possess self-awareness (p. 114). If a being is sentient, then "there is an 'I' who has subjective experiences" (p. 6).

75. Francione acknowledges that the preference one expresses here is "arbitrary and not particularly amenable to satisfying general principles of conduct. . . . I may . . . in these true emergency situations . . . choose the human simply because I better understand what is at stake for the human than I do for the dog" (*Introduction to Animal Rights*, p. 159).

76. Ibid., p. 128.

77. Ibid., p. 159.

78. John Rawls, *A Theory of Justice*, rev. ed. (Cambridge, Mass.: Harvard University Press, 1999), p. 448.

## 5. The Ideal of Cosmic Holism

1. John Rawls, *A Theory of Justice*, rev. ed. (Cambridge, Mass.: Harvard University Press, Belknap Press, 1999), pp. 15, 441, 448; see also John Rawls, *Political Liberalism*, rev. ed. (New York: Columbia University Press, 2005), p. 246.

2. Tom Regan, *The Case for Animal Rights* (Berkeley: University of California Press, 1983), p. 152.

3. Ibid., p. 240.

4. For Francione's criticisms of animal welfarism, see *Rain Without Thunder: The Ideology of the Animal Rights Movement* (Philadelphia, Pa.: Temple University Press, 2004). See also "Reflections on *Animals, Property, and the Law* and *Rain Without Thunder*," in *Animals as Persons: Essays on the Abolition of Animal Exploitation* (New York: Columbia University Press, 2007, pp. 72–96).

5. Plutarch, *On the Cleverness of Animals* 999A, in *Moralia*, vol. 12, Greek with English trans. by Harold Cherniss and William C. Helmbold (Cambridge, Mass.: Harvard University Press, 1995), p. 579.

6. Plutarch, *Life of Marcus Cato* 5.2, in *Plutarch's Lives*, vol. 2, Greek with English trans. by Bernadotte Perrin (Cambridge, Mass.: Harvard University Press / London: William Heinemann, 1985), p. 317.

7. For a detailed discussion of the Stoics and Plutarch, see chapters 3 and 4 of Steiner, *Anthropocentrism and Its Discontents*.

8. Here I defer the question whether cosmic justice imposes moral obligations on humans vis-à-vis nonsentient nature and focus exclusively on the question of human-animal relations.

9. Erazim Kohak, *The Embers and the Stars: A Philosophical Inquiry into the Moral Sense of Nature* (Chicago: University of Chicago Press, 1984), p. 8.

10. Martin Heidegger, "Letter on 'Humanism,'" in *Pathmarks*, ed. William McNeill (Cambridge: Cambridge University Press, 1998), p. 249. See also Heidegger's *Being and Time*, trans. John Macquarrie and Edward Robinson (New York: Harper and Row, 1962), p. 377.

11. Martin Heidegger, "Introduction to 'What Is Metaphysics?'" in *Pathmarks*, p. 284; "Letter on 'Humanism,'" p. 247.

12. Heidegger, "Letter on 'Humanism,'" p. 271 (translation altered).

13. Ibid., p. 258; cf. Novalis, "The Universal Brouillon: Materials for an Encyclopedia," sec. 857, in *The Early Political Writings of the German Romantics*, ed. Frederick C. Beiser (Cambridge: Cambridge University Press, 1996), p. 90.

14. See Karl Löwith, "Der Weltbegriff der neuzeitlichen Philosophie," *Sitzungsberichte der Heidelberger Akademie der Wissenschaften, Philosophisch-historischer Klasse* 44 (1960): 7, 19.

15. Heidegger, "Letter on 'Humanism,'" p. 248.

16. Martin Heidegger, *Schellings Abhandlung über das Wesen der menschlichen Freiheit (1809)*, ed. Hildegard Feick (Tübingen: Niemeyer, 1971), pp. 173–74.

17. Martin Heidegger, *Die Grundbegriffe der Metaphysik: Welt—Endlichkeit—Einsamkeit*, vol. 29/30 of *Gesamtausgabe* (Frankfurt: Klostermann, 1983), pp. 286–87.

18. Kohak, *The Embers and the Stars*, p. 8.

19. Martin Heidegger, "The Question Concerning Technology," in *The Question Concerning Technology and Other Essays*, trans. William Lovitt (New York: Harper Torchbooks, 1977), p. 17 (translation altered).

20. Heidegger, "The Question Concerning Technology," p. 14.

21. Martin Heidegger, "Memorial Address," in *Discourse on Thinking*, trans. John M. Anderson and E. Hans Freund (New York: Harper Torchbooks, 1969), p. 50.

22. René Descartes, *Discourse on Method*, pt. 6, in *The Philosophical Writings of Descartes*, vol. 1, trans. John Cottingham, Robert Stoothoff, and Dugald Murdoch (Cambridge: Cambridge University Press, 1985), pp. 142–43. (translation altered).

23. For a detailed discussion of Descartes's technological conception of nature, see chapter 4 of Steiner, *Descartes as a Moral Thinker: Christianity, Technology, Nihilism* (Amherst, N.Y.: Prometheus/Humanity Books, 2004). For a discussion of Descartes's views concerning the moral status of animals, see chapter 6 of Steiner, *Anthropocentrism and Its Discontents*.

24. Kohak, *The Embers and the Stars*, p. 50.

25. Mary Anne Warren, "The Rights of the Nonhuman World," in *The Animal Rights / Environmental Ethics Debate: The Environmental Perspective*, ed. Eugene C. Hargrove (Albany, N.Y.: SUNY Press, 1992), p. 192.

26. Paul W. Taylor, "The Ethics of Respect for Nature," in *The Animal Rights/Environmental Ethics Debate*, pp. 105–6.

27. R. Routley and V. Routley, "Against the Inevitability of Human Chauvinism," in *Ethics and Problems of the 21st Century*, ed. K. E. Goodpaster and K. M. Sayre (Notre Dame, Ind.: University of Notre Dame Press, 1979), p. 45.

28. Holmes Rolston III, *Conserving Natural Value* (New York: Columbia University Press, 1994), pp. 106, 108.

29. Ibid., pp. 81–82.

30. Ibid., p. 158.

31. Ibid.

32. Aristotle, *Metaphysics*, bk. 11, chap. 6 at 1062b13, in *The Complete Works of Aristotle*, 2 vols., ed. Jonathan Barnes (Princeton, N.J.: Princeton University Press, Bollingen, 1995), 2:1678.

33. Rolston, *Conserving Natural Value*, p. 101.

34. See the section entitled "The Limitations of Liberal Approaches to the Moral Status of Animals" in chapter 4 of the present study.

35. Rolston, *Conserving Natural Value*, pp. 42–43, 63.

36. Ibid., p. 103.

37. Ibid., pp. 102, 138.

38. Ibid., p. 63.

39. See, e.g., Mark Sagoff, "Animal Liberation and Environmental Ethics: Bad Marriage, Quick Divorce," *Osgoode Hall Law Journal* 22 (1984): 303.

40. J. Baird Callicott, "Animal Liberation: A Triangular Affair," in *The Animal Rights / Environmental Ethics Debate*, p. 56.

41. Ibid., p. 60.

42. Gary L. Francione, *Introduction to Animal Rights: Your Child or the Dog?* (Philadelphia, Pa.: Temple University Press, 2000), p. 170.

43. Callicott, "Animal Liberation," p. 57.

44. Ibid.

45. Ibid., p. 58.

46. Ted Benton, *Natural Relations: Ecology, Animal Rights, and Social Justice* (London: Verso, 1993), p. 200.

47. See, in particular, the discussions of Pythagoras, Empedocles, Plutarch, Porphyry, and Schopenhauer in Steiner, *Anthropocentrism and Its Discontents*. See chapter 3 of that text for a detailed discussion of Aristotle and the Stoics.

48. Aristotle, *Nicomachean Ethics*, bk. X, chap. 7 at 1177b20–30, in *The Complete Works of Aristotle*, 2:1861.

49. Aristotle, *Nicomachean Ethics*, bk. III, chaps. 1–2 at 1111a20–1111b18.

50. Aristotle, *Politics*, bk. I, chap. 2 at 1253a7–17.

51. See Cleanthes, *Hymn to Zeus* (SVF 1.537), in *The Hellenistic Philosophers*, 2 vols., ed. and trans. A. A. Long and D. N. Sedley (Cambridge: Cambridge University Press, 1990), 541.

52. Epictetus, *Discourses* 2.10.3, in *The Discourses as Reported by Arian, Books I–II*, Greek with English trans. by W. A. Oldfather (Cambridge, Mass.: Harvard University Press, 2000), p. 269; see also 1.9.2 and Cicero, *De finibus* 3.64 in *De Finibus Bonorum et Malorum*, Latin with English trans. by H. Rackham (Cambridge, Mass.: Harvard University Press, 1999), pp. 284–85.

53. Cicero, *De natura deorum* (*On the Nature of the Gods*) 2.37–39, in *The Hellenistic Philosophers*, 54H. Cicero attributes this view to Chrysippus. See also Epictetus, *Discourses* 1.16.1–5 and 2.8.6–8.

54. Marcus Aurelius 5.16, in *The Hellenistic Philosophers*, 63K.

55. A. A. Long, *Epictetus: A Stoic and Socratic Guide to Life* (Oxford: Clarendon Press, 2002), pp. 233–34.

56. Cicero, *De finibus* 3.16, pp. 232–33.

57. Cicero, *De finibus* 3.62, pp. 281–82.

58. Epictetus, *Discourses* 1.23.8, p. 147.

59. Cicero, *De finibus* 3.62–63, p. 283. Here Cicero translates *oikeiosis* as *commendatio* and *conciliatio*.

60. Hierocles (Stobaeus 4.671,7–7.673,11), in *The Hellenistic Philosophers*, 57G..

61. Cicero, *De finibus* 3.63, p. 283; see also 3.65, pp. 285–86.

62. Cicero, *De officiis* (*On Duties*) 1.107, in *The Hellenistic Philosophers*, 66E.

63. Diogenes Laertius 7.129, in *Lives of Eminent Philosophers*, vol. 2, Greek with English trans. by R. D. Hicks (Cambridge, Mass.: Harvard University Press, 2000), p. 233 (describing the views of Chrysippus and Posidonius).

64. Cicero, *De finibus* 3.67, p. 287 (describing Chrysippus's view).

65. Karl Löwith, "Welt und Menschenwelt," in *Welt und Menschenwelt: Beiträge zur Anthropologie*, vol. 1 (Stuttgart: Metzler, 1981), p. 295.

66. Karl Löwith, *Heidegger: Thinker in a Destitute Time*, in *Martin Heidegger and European Nihilism*, trans. Gary Steiner (New York: Columbia University Press, 1995), p. 95.

67. Karl Löwith, *Meaning in History: The Theological Implications of the Philosophy of History* (Chicago: University of Chicago Press, 1962), p. 25.

68. Gary E. Varner, *In Nature's Interests? Interests, Animal Rights, and Environmental Ethics* (Oxford: Oxford University Press, 1998), pp. 7, 121.

69. Ibid., pp. 43–45.

70. Peter S. Wenz, *Environmental Justice* (Albany, N.Y.: SUNY Press, 1988), p. 316.

71. Ibid., p. 309.

72. Ibid., p. 328.

73. Francione, *Introduction to Animal Rights*, p. 159 (italics added).

74. Wenz writes: "According to the method of reflective equilibrium, one's particular judgments and general theories should be revised or modified until consistency among them is achieved" (*Environmental Justice*, p. 310).

75. Callicott, "Animal Liberation," p. 60.

76. Taylor, "The Ethics of Respect for Nature," p. 117.

77. Heidegger, "On the Essence of Truth," pp. 144–45.

78. Ibid., p. 148.

79. Arthur Schopenhauer, "On Religion," chap. 15, sec. 177, in *Parerga and Paralipomena*, 2 vols., trans. E. F. J. Payne (Oxford: Clarendon Press, 2000), 2:376, 372. Schopenhauer, however, does not entirely escape the influence of anthropocentrism. He considers practices such as the consumption of meat and vivisection permissible under some circumstances. See Steiner, *Anthropocentrism and Its Discontents*, pp. 188–89.

# 6. "COSMO-POLITICS"

1. Karl Löwith, "Welt und Menschenwelt," in *Welt und Menschenwelt: Beiträge zur Anthropologie*, vol. 1 (Stuttgart: Metzler, 1981), p. 303.

2. Ibid., p. 307.

3. Tom Regan, *The Case for Animal Rights* (Berkeley: University of California Press, 1983), p. 361.

4. Aldo Leopold, *A Sand County Almanac* (New York: Oxford University Press, 1949), p. 217; Regan, *The Case for Animal Rights*, p. 361.

5. Regan, *The Case for Animal Rights*, pp. 361–62.

6. Terence Ball, "Democracy," in *Political Theory and the Ecological Challenge*, ed. Andrew Dobson and Robyn Eckersley (Cambridge: Cambridge University Press, 2006), pp. 131–32.

7. Luc Ferry, *The New Ecological Order*, trans. Carol Volk (Chicago: University of Chicago Press, 1995), p. xxi. This is an oblique reference to the SA (*Sturmabteilung*, Storm Troopers or Brownshirts), the Nazi security force organized by Ernst Röhm in 1921.

8. Ibid., p. 89.

9. Ibid., pp. 67, 69.

10. Ibid,, p. 90. On Nazi environmental legislation, see Steiner, *Anthropocentrism and Its Discontents*, p. 228; for further remarks on Ferry's critique of environmentalism, see pp. 226–30.

11. Bryan G. Norton, "Democracy and Environmentalism: Foundations and Justifications in Environmental Policy," in *Democracy and the Claims of Nature: Critical Perspectives for a New Century*, ed. Ben A. Minteer and Bob Pepperman Taylor (Lanham, Md.: Rowman and Littlefield, 2002), p. 23. *Gleichschaltung* refers to the legal measures enacted by the Nazis to impose totalitarian control over German society.

12. Brian Barry, *Justice as Impartiality* (Oxford: Clarendon Press, 1995), pp. 99, 110.

13. Ibid., pp. 72, 77.

14. Ibid., pp. 160, 169.

15. Ibid., p. 129.

16. Immanuel Kant, "What is Enlightenment?" in *Political Writings*, ed. H. S. Reiss (Cambridge: Cambridge University Press, 2001), p. 57.

17. Immanuel Kant, *Grounding for the Metaphysics of Morals*, trans. James W. Ellington (Indianapolis, Ind.: Hackett, 1985), p. 45 (Ak. 441).

18. Immanuel Kant, *Critique of Pure Reason*, trans. Norman Kemp Smith (New York: Humanities Press, 1950), B xxx.

19. Barry, *Justice as Impartiality*, p. 171.

20. Ibid., p. 20.

21. Ibid.

22. Ibid., p. 22.

23. Ibid., p. 227.

24. Ibid., p. 234.

25. John S. Dryzek, *Deliberative Democracy and Beyond: Liberals, Critics, Contestations* (Oxford: Oxford University Press, 2000), p. 147.

26. Marcel Wissenburg, "Liberalism," in *Political Theory and the Ecological Challenge*, ed. Andrew Dobson and Robyn Eckersley (Cambridge: Cambridge University Press, 2006), p. 31. For a socialist approach to the moral status of animals, see Ted Benton, *Natural Relations: Ecology, Animal Rights, and Social Justice* (London: Verso, 1993).

27. F. A. Hayek, *The Road to Serfdom* (Chicago: University of Chicago Press, 1994), pp. 40–41.

28. Ibid., p. 63.

29. Ibid., p. 77.

30. Ibid., p. 78. Cf. John Gray, *Hayek on Liberty*, 3rd ed. (London: Routledge, 1998): "The kind of omniscience demanded of a socialist planner could be possessed only by a single mind, entirely self-aware, existing in an unchanging environment—a supposition so bizarre that we realize we have moved from any imaginable social world to a metaphysical fantasy in which men and women have disappeared altogether, and all that remain are Leibnizian monads, featureless and unhistorical ciphers" (p. 39).

31. Hayek, *The Road to Serfdom*, p. 182.

32. Hans Jonas, *The Imperative of Responsibility: In Search of an Ethics for the Technological Age* (Chicago: University of Chicago Press, 1984), pp. 146–47.

33. Ibid., p. 141 (translation altered).

34. Ibid., p 147.

35. Ibid., p. 98.

36. Ferry, *The New Ecological Order*, pp. 82–83.

37. Ibid., pp. 26–27, 112.

38. Ibid., p. 93.

39. Ibid., p. 89.

40. Peter Carruthers, *The Animals Issue: Moral Theory in Practice* (Cambridge: Cambridge University Press, 1992), p. 190.

41. Joe Bowersox, "The Legitimacy Crisis in Environmental Ethics and Politics," in *Democracy and the Claims of Nature: Critical Perspectives for a New Century*, ed. Ben A. Minteer and Bob Pepperman Taylor (Oxford: Row-

man and Littlefield, 2002), p. 85. Moreover, the suggestion that we include animals in a Rawlsian original position (see, e.g., Regan, *The Case for Animal Rights*, p. 171) begs the question by conflating cosmic and social justice. Whereas Rawls, Scanlon, and other liberal thinkers who start from an original position embrace a social (which is to say, a narrowly anthropocentric) conception of justice, the inclusion of animals in the original position presupposes a cosmic conception of justice (and hence a substantive, first-order conception of the good) that goes beyond the limits of the liberal ideal.

42. Hans Jonas, *The Gnostic Religion: The Message of the Alien God and the Beginnings of Christianity*, 2nd ed. (Boston: Beacon Press, 1991), p. 340.

43. Novalis, "The Universal Brouillon: Materials for an Encyclopaedia," in *The Early Political Writings of the German Romantics*, ed. Frederick C. Beiser (Cambridge: Cambridge University Press, 1996), sec. 857, p. 90.

44. G. W. F. Hegel, *Hegel's Philosophy of Right*, trans. T. M. Knox (London: Oxford University Press, 1967), pp. 20–22.

45. Charles Taylor, *Hegel* (Cambridge: Cambridge University Press, 1975), p. 365.

46. Cf. G. W. F. Hegel, *Introduction to the Philosophy of History*, trans. Leo Rauch (Indianapolis, Ind.: Hackett, 1988): "Nothing is more misguided than to look for models among the Greeks, the Romans, or Orientals for the constitutional structures of our own time ... [for these societies did not] see the state as the ethical whole and the reality of freedom, and hence as the objective unity of [knowing and willing]" (pp. 50–51). Hegel also writes that Greek society achieved only "the union of ethical custom with the subjective will" (p. 95)

47. Taylor, *Hegel*, p. 366.

48. Ibid., p. 388.

49. Hegel, *Hegel's Philosophy of Right*, sec. 5, p. 21.

50. Ibid., sec. 5, p. 22.

51. Ibid., sec. 6, p. 22.

52. Ibid., sec. 11, p. 25.

53. Ibid., sec. 7, p. 23.

54. Ibid., sec. 7, p. 24.

55. Ibid., sec. 13, p. 26.

56. Ibid., sec. 28, pp. 32–33.

57. Hegel, *Hegel's Logic*, trans. William Wallace (Oxford: Clarendon Press, 1975), sec. 86, p. 126; Hegel, *Hegel's Philosophy of Right*, sec. 270, p. 165. See also Hegel, *Introduction to the Philosophy of History*, pp. 10, 74

58. Arthur Schopenhauer, *The World as Will and Representation*, vol. 1, trans. E. F. J. Payne (Indian Hills, Colo.: Falcon's Wing Press, 1958), sec. 29, p. 164.

59. On "Besonnenheit," see Arthur Schopenhauer, *On the Fourfold Root of the Principle of Sufficient Reason*, trans. E. F. J. Payne (La Salle, Ill.: Open Court, 1974), sec. 27, p. 151.

60. Schopenhauer, *The World as Will and Representation*, vol. 1, sec. 7, pp. 30–31.

61. Ibid., sec. 6, p. 23. Cf. sec. 7, p. 34: The capacity for conceptual abstraction "belongs to man alone."

62. Arthur Schopenhauer, *On the Basis of Morality*, trans. E. F. J. Payne (Providence, R.I.: Berghahn Books, 1995), sec. 19, pp. 177–78.

63. According to Schopenhauer, animals live in the present, whereas humans also live in the past and future; hence the suffering of humans "far surpasses" that of animals (*The World as Will and Representation*, vol. 1, sec. 8, p. 36).

64. Porphyry, *On Abstinence from Killing Animals*, trans. Gillian Clark (Ithaca, N.Y.: Cornell University Press, 2000), 3.26.9, 3.27.2, pp. 98–99.

65. Ibid., 3.25.3, p. 96.

66. Ibid., 3.27.6, 4.1.1, pp. 99–100.

67. Some useful work in this area has already been done. See, e.g., Paul W. Taylor, *Respect for Nature: A Theory of Environmental Ethics* (Princeton, N.J.: Princeton University Press, 1986), and James P. Sterba, "Justice," in *Political Theory and the Ecological Challenge*, pp. 148–64.

68. Again, I leave aside those rare instances in which a human being's life might depend on consuming animal products.

# BIBLIOGRAPHY

Allen, Colin. "Animal Concepts Revisited: The Use of Self-Monitoring as an Empirical Approach." *Erkenntnis* 51 (1999): 33–40.

———. "Mental Content." *British Journal for the Philosophy of Science* 43 (1992): 537–53.

———. "Mental Content and Evolutionary Explanation." *Biology and Philosophy* 7 (1992): 1–12.

———. "Transitive Inference in Animals: Reasoning or Conditioned Associations?" In *Rational Animals?*, ed. Susan Hurley and Matthew Nudds, pp. 175–85. Oxford: Oxford University Press, 2006.

Allen, Colin, and Marc Bekoff. "Intentionality, Social Play, and Definition." In *Readings in Cognitive Ethology*, ed. Marc Bekoff and Dale Jamieson, pp. 229–39. Cambridge, Mass.: MIT Press, 1996.

Allen, Colin, and Marc Hauser. "Concept Attribution in Nonhuman Animals: Theoretical and Methodological Problems in Ascribing Complex Mental Processes." *Philosophy of Science* 58 (1991): 221–40.

Aristotle. *The Complete Works of Aristotle.* 2 vols. Ed. Jonathan Barnes. Princeton, N.J.: Princeton University Press, 1995.

Baerends, Gerardus Pieter. "Fortpflanzungsverhalten und Orientierung der Grabwespe *Ammophila campestris.*" *Tijdschrift voor Entomologie* 84 (1941): 68–275.

Ball, Terence. "Democracy." In *Political Theory and the Ecological Challenge*, ed. Andrew Dobson and Robyn Eckersley, pp. 131–47. Cambridge: Cambridge University Press, 2006.

Barry, Brian. *Justice as Impartiality.* Oxford: Clarendon Press, 1995.

Beiser, Frederick C., ed. *The Early Political Writings of the German Romantics.* Cambridge: Cambridge University Press, 1996.

Bentham, Jeremy. *Introduction to the Principles of Morals and Legislation*. New York: Hafner, 1948.

Benton, Ted. *Natural Relations: Ecology, Animal Rights, and Social Justice*. London: Verso, 1993.

Berkeley, George. *A Treatise Concerning the Principles of Human Knowledge*. Ed. Jonathan Dancy. Oxford: Oxford University Press, 1998.

Bermudez, José Luis. *Thinking Without Words*. Oxford: Oxford University Press, 2003.

Bishop, John. "More Thought on Thought and Talk." *Mind* 89 (1980): 1–16.

Bowersox, Joe. "The Legitimacy Crisis in Environmental Ethics and Politics." In *Democracy and the Claims of Nature: Critical Perspectives for a New Century*, ed. Ben A. Minteer and Bob Pepperman Taylor, p. 71–90. Oxford: Rowman and Littlefield, 2002.

Boyle, Deborah. "Hume on Animal Reason." *Hume Studies* 29 (2003): 3–28.

Callicott, J. Baird. "Animal Liberation: A Triangular Affair." In *The Animal Rights / Environmental Ethics Debate: The Environmental Perspective*, ed. Eugene C. Hargrove, pp. 37–69. Albany, N.Y.: SUNY Press, 1992.

Candland, Douglas Keith. *Feral Children and Clever Animals: Reflections on Human Nature*. New York: Oxford University Press, 1993.

Carruthers, Peter. *The Animals Issue: Moral Theory in Practice*. Cambridge: Cambridge University Press, 1992.

Cicero. *De Finibus Bonorum et Malorum*. Latin with English trans. by H. Rackham. Cambridge, Mass.: Harvard University Press, 1999.

Clayton, Nicola, Nathan Emery, and Anthony Dickinson. "The Rationality of Animal Memory: Complex Caching Strategies of Western Scrub Jays." In *Rational Animals?*, ed. Susan Hurley and Matthew Nudds, pp. 197–216. Oxford: Oxford University Press, 2006.

Crane, Tim. "The Intentional Structure of Consciousness." In *Consciousness: New Philosophical Perspectives*, ed. Quentin Smith and Aleksandar Jokic, pp. 33–56. Oxford: Clarendon Press, 2003.

——. "The Nonconceptual Content of Experience." In *The Contents of Experience: Essays on Perception*, ed. Tim Crane, pp. 136–57. Cambridge: Cambridge University Press, 1992.

Davidson, Donald. "The Emergence of Thought." *Erkenntnis* 51 (1999): 7–17.

——. "Rational Animals." In *Actions and Events: Perspectives on the Philosophy of Donald Davidson*, ed. Ernest LePore and Brian McLaughlin, pp. 473–80. Oxford: Basil Blackwell, 1985.

———. "Thought and Talk." In *Mind and Language*, Wolfson College Lectures 1974, ed. Samuel Guttenplan, pp. 7–23. Oxford: Clarendon Press, 1975.

DeGrazia, David. *Taking Animals Seriously: Mental Life and Moral Status*. Cambridge: Cambridge University Press, 1996.

Dennett, Daniel. *Brainstorms: Philosophical Essays on Mind and Psychology*. Cambridge, Mass: MIT Press, Bradford BooksMIT, 1978.

———. "Do Animals Have Beliefs?" In *Comparative Approaches to Cognitive Ethology*, ed. Herbert L. Roitblat and Jean-Arcady Meyer, pp. 111–18. Cambridge, Mass.: MIT Press, 1995.

———. "Intentional Systems in Cognitive Ethology: The 'Panglossian Paradigm' Defended." *Behavioral and Brain Sciences* 6 (1983): 343–90.

Descartes René. *Oeuvres de Descartes*. 12 vols. Ed. Charles Adam and Paul Tannery. Paris: Vrin, 1964–74.

———. *The Philosophical Writings of Descartes*, vol. 1. Trans. John Cottingham, Robert Stoothoff, and Dugald Murdoch. Cambridge: Cambridge University Press, 1985.

Dickinson, Anthony, and Bernard W. Balleine. "Causal Cognition and Goal-Directed Action." In *The Evolution of Cognition*, ed. Cecilia Heyes and Ludwig Huber, pp. 185–204. Cambridge, Mass.: MIT Press, Bradford/ Books, 2000.

Diogenes Laertius. *Lives of Eminent Philosophers*, vol. 2. Greek with English trans. by R. D. Hicks. Cambridge, Mass.: Harvard University Press, 2000.

Dretske, Fred. *Explaining Behavior: Reasons in a World of Causes*. Cambridge, Mass.: MIT Press, 1998.

———. "Machines, Plants and Animals: The Origins of Agency." *Erkenntnis* 51 (1999): 19–31.

Dreyfus, Hubert L., Stuart E. Dreyfus, and Tom Athanasiou. *Mind Over Machine: The Power of Intuition and Expertise in the Era of the Computer*. New York: Free Press, 1986.

Dryzek, John S. *Deliberative Democracy and Beyond: Liberals, Critics, Contestations*. Oxford: Oxford University Press, 2000.

Dummett, Michael. *Origins of Analytical Philosophy*. Cambridge, Mass.: Harvard University Press, 1994.

Epictetus. *The Discourses as Reported by Arian, Books I-II*. Greek with English trans. by W. A. Oldfather. Cambridge, Mass.: Harvard University Press, 2000.

Ferry, Luc. *The New Ecological Order*. Trans. Carol Volk. Chicago: University of Chicago Press, 1995.

Francione, Gary L. *Animals as Persons: Essays on the Abolition of Animal Exploitation*. New York: Columbia University Press, 2007.

———. *Animals, Property, and the Law*. Philadelphia, Pa.: Temple University Press, 1995.

———. *Introduction to Animal Rights: Your Child or the Dog?* Philadelphia, Pa.: Temple University Press, 2000.

———. *Rain Without Thunder: The Ideology of the Animal Rights Movement*. Philadelphia, Pa.: Temple University Press, 2004.

———. "Taking Sentience Seriously." *Journal of Animal Law and Ethics* 1 (2006): 1–18.

Frankfurt, Harry. "Freedom of the Will and the Concept of a Person." *Philosophical Review* 68 (1972): 5–20.

Franklin, Julian. *Animal Rights and Moral Philosophy*. New York: Columbia University Press, 2005.

Frege, Gottlob. *Die Grundlagen der Arithmetik: Eine logisch mathematische Untersuchung über den Begriff der Zahl/The Foundations of Arithmetic: A Logico-Mathematical Enquiry into the Concept of Number*. German with English trans. J. L. Austin. 2nd rev. ed. Evanston, Ill.: Northwestern University Press, 1968.

Friedmann, Herbert. "The Honey-Guides." *U.S. National Museum Bulletin* 208 (1955): 1–292.

Gadamer, Hans-Georg. *Wahrheit und Methode: Grundzüge einer philosophischen Hermeneutik*. Tübingen: J. C. B. Mohr (Paul Siebeck), 1975.

Glock, Hans-Johann. "Animals, Thoughts and Concepts." *Synthese* 123 (2000): 35–64.

Gould, James L., and Carol Grant Gould. "Invertebrate Intelligence." In *Animal Intelligence: Insights into the Animal Mind*, ed. R. J. Hoage and Larry Goldman, pp. 21–36. Washington, D.C.: Smithsonian Institution, 1986.

Gray, John. *Hayek on Liberty*. 3rd ed. London: Routledge, 1998.

Griffin, Donald R. *Animal Minds*. Chicago: University of Chicago Press, 1992.

Hampshire, Stuart. "Morality and Pessimism." In *Public and Private Morality*, ed. Stuart Hampshire et al., pp. 1–22. Cambridge: Cambridge University Press, 1978.

Harrison, Peter. "Do Animals Feel Pain?" *Philosophy* 66 (1991): 25–40.

Hayek, F. A. *The Road to Serfdom*. Chicago: University of Chicago Press, 1994.

Hegel, G. W. F. *Hegel's Logic*. Trans. William Wallace. Oxford: Clarendon Press, 1975.

———. *Introduction to the Philosophy of History*. Trans. Leo Rauch. Indianapolis, Ind.: Hackett, 1988.

———. *Hegel's Philosophy of Right*. Trans. T. M. Knox. London: Oxford University Press, 1967.

Heidegger, Martin. *Being and Time*. Trans. John Macquarrie and Edward Robinson. New York: Harper and Row, 1962.

——— *Discourse on Thinking*. Trans. John M. Anderson and E. Hans Freund. New York: Harper and Row, Harper Torchbooks, 1969.

———. *Die Grundbegriffe der Metaphysik: Welt-Endlichkeit-Einsamkeit*. Vol. 29/30 of *Gesamtausgabe*. Frankfurt: Klostermann, 1983.

———. *Logik: Die Frage nach der Wahrheit*. Vol. 21 of *Gesamtausgabe*. Frankfurt: Klostermann, 1975.

———. *Pathmarks*. Ed. William McNeill. Cambridge: Cambridge University Press, 1998.

———. *The Question Concerning Technology and Other Essays*. Trans. William Lovitt. New York: Harper and Row, Harper Torchbooks, 1977.

———. *Schellings Abhandlung über das Wesen der menschlichen Freiheit (1809)*. Ed. Hildegard Feick. Tübingen: Niemeyer, 1971.

Herrnstein, R. J. "Riddles of Natural Categorization." *Philosophical Transactions of the Royal Society of London* B 308 (1985): 129–44.

Herrnstein, R. J., Donald H. Loveland, and Cynthia Cable. "Natural Concepts in Pigeons." *Journal of Experimental Psychology: Animal Behavior Processes* 2 (1976): 285–302.

Heyes, Cecilia, and Anthony Dickinson. "The Intentionality of Animal Action." *Mind and Language* 5, no. 1 (1990): 87–104.

Hillix, William A., and Duane Rumbaugh, *Animal Bodies, Human Minds: Ape, Dolphin, and Parrot Language Skills*. New York: Kluwer Academic/Plenum Press, 2004.

Huber, Robert, et al.. "Serotonin and Aggressive Motivation in Crustaceans: Altering the Decision to Retreat." *Proceedings of the National Academy of Science* 94 (1997): 5939–42.

Hume, David. *Essays Moral, Political, and Literary*. Rev. ed. Ed. Eugene F. Miller. Indianapolis, Ind.: Liberty Fund, 1987.

———. *A Treatise of Human Nature*. 2nd ed. Ed. P. H. Nidditch. Oxford: Clarendon Press, 1981.

Jeffrey, Richard. "Animal Interpretation." In *Actions and Events: Perspectives on the Philosophy of Donald Davidson*, ed. Ernest LePore and Brian McLaughlin, pp. 481–87. Oxford: Basil Blackwell, 1985.

Jonas, Hans. *The Gnostic Religion: The Message of the Alien God and the Beginnings of Christianity*. 2nd ed. Boston: Beacon Press, 1991.

——. *The Imperative of Responsibility: In Search of an Ethics for the Technological Age*. Chicago: University of Chicago Press, 1984.

Kant, Immanuel. *Critique of Judgment*. Trans. Werner S. Pluhar. Indianapolis, Ind.: Hackett, 1987.

——. *Critique of Practical Reason*. 3rd ed. Trans. Lewis White Beck. Upper Saddle River, N. J.: Library of Liberal Arts, 1993.

——. *Critique of Pure Reason*. Trans. Norman Kemp Smith. New York: Humanities Press, 1950.

—— *Grounding for the Metaphysics of Morals*. Trans. James W. Ellington. Indianapolis, Ind.: Hackett, 1981.

——. *Lectures on Ethics*. Ed. Peter Heath and J. B. Schneewind. Trans. Peter Heath. Cambridge: Cambridge University Press, 1997.

——. *The Metaphysics of Morals*. Ed. Mary Gregor. Cambridge: Cambridge University Press, 1996.

——. *Political Writings*. Ed. H. S. Reiss. Cambridge: Cambridge University Press, 1991.

Kohak, Erazim. *The Embers and the Stars: A Philosophical Inquiry into the Moral Sense of Nature*. Chicago: University of Chicago Press, 1984.

Leopold, Aldo. *A Sand County Almanac*. New York: Oxford University Press, 1949.

Locke, John. *An Essay Concerning Human Understanding*. Ed. Peter H. Nidditch. Oxford: Clarendon Press, 1990.

——. *Two Treatises of Government*. Ed. Peter Laslett. Cambridge: Cambridge University Press, 1988.

Long, A. A. *Epictetus: A Stoic and Socratic Guide to Life*. Oxford: Clarendon Press, 2002.

Long, A. A., and D. N. Sedley, eds. and trans. *The Hellenistic Philosophers*. 2 vols. Cambridge: Cambridge University Press, 1990.

Löwith, Karl. *Martin Heidegger and European Nihilism*. Trans. Gary Steiner. New York: Columbia University Press, 1995.

——. *Meaning in History: The Theological Implications of the Philosophy of History*. Chicago: University of Chicago Press, 1962.

——. *Welt und Menschenwelt: Beiträge zur Anthropologie*. Vol. 1 of *Sämtliche Schriften*. Stuttgart: Metzler, 1981.

——. "Der Weltbegriff der neuzeitlichen Philosophie." *Sitzungsberichte der Heidelberger Akademie der Wissenschaften, Philosophisch-historischer Klasse* 44 (1960): 7–23.

Mackintosh, Nicholas J. "Abstraction and Discrimination." In *The Evolution of Cognition*, ed. Cecilia Heyes and Ludwig Huber, pp. 123–41. Cambridge, Mass.: MIT Press, Bradford Books, 2000.

Macphail, Euan M. "The Search for a Mental Rubicon." In *The Evolution of Cognition*, ed. Cecilia Heyes and Ludwig Huber, pp. 253–71. Cambridge, Mass.: MIT Press, Bradford Books, 2000.

Malcolm, Norman. "Thoughtless Brutes." *Proceedings and Addresses of the American Philosophical Association* 46 (1973): 5–20.

Martin, Michael. "Perception, Concepts, and Memory." In *Essays on Nonconceptual Content*, ed. York H. Gunther, pp. 237–50. Cambridge, Mass.: MIT Press, 2003.

McDowell, John. "The Content of Perceptual Experience." *Philosophical Quarterly* 44 (1994): 190–205.

——. *Mind and World*. Cambridge, Mass.: Harvard University Press, 1994.

——. "Reply to Commentators." *Philosophy and Phenomenological Research* 58 (1998): 403–31.

Mendelson, Joseph, III,. "Should Animals Have Standing? A Review of Standing Under the Animal Welfare Act." *Boston College Environmental Affairs Law Review* 24 (1997): 795–820.

Merleau-Ponty, Maurice. *Phenomenology of Perception*. Trans. Colin Smith. London: Routledge and Kegan Paul/N.J.: Humanities Press, 1978.

Mill, John Stuart. *"On Liberty" and Other Essays*. Ed. John Gray. Oxford: Oxford University Press, 1998.

——. *Three Essays on Religion*. New York: Henry Holt, 1878.

Millikan, Ruth Garrett. *On Clear and Confused Ideas: An Essay about Substance Concepts*. Cambridge: Cambridge University Press, 2000.

——. *Language, Thought, and Other Biological Categories: New Foundations for Realism*. Cambridge, Mass.: MIT Press, 1984.

——. "Styles of Rationality." In *Rational Animals?* ed. Susan Hurley and Matthew Nudds, pp. 117–26. Oxford: Oxford University Press, 2006.

——. *Varieties of Meaning*. The 2002 Jean Nicod Lectures. Cambridge, Mass.: MIT Press, 2004.

Morgan, C. Lloyd. *Animal Behavior*. London: Edward Arnold, 1900.

——. *Animal Life and Intelligence*. Boston: Ginn, 1891.

Murphy, Gregory L. *The Big Book of Concepts*. Cambridge, Mass.: MIT Press, 2002.

Nagel, Thomas. "What Is It Like to Be a Bat?" In *Mortal Questions*, pp. 165–80. Cambridge: Cambridge University Press, 1979.

Norton, Bryan G. "Democracy and Environmentalism: Foundations and Justifications in Environmental Policy." In *Democracy and the Claims of Nature: Critical Perspectives for a New Century*, ed. Ben A. Minteer and Bob Pepperman Taylor, pp. 11–32. Lanham, Md.: Rowman and Littlefield, 2002.

Nussbaum, Martha C. "Animal Rights: The Need for a Theoretical Basis." *Harvard Law Review* 114 (2001): 1548.

———. *Frontiers of Justice: Disability, Nationality, Species Membership.* Cambridge, Mass.: Harvard University Press, Belknap Press, 2006.

———. *Upheavals of Thought: The Intelligence of Emotions.* Cambridge: Cambridge University Press, 2001.

Papineau, David. "Human Minds." In *Minds and Persons*, Royal Institute of Philosophy Supplement 53, ed. Anthony O'Hear, pp. 159–83. Cambridge: Cambridge University Press, 2003.

Papineau, David, and Cecilia Heyes. "Rational or Associative? Imitation in Japanese Quail." In *Rational Animals?*, ed. Susan Hurley and Matthew Nudds, pp. 187–95. Oxford: Oxford University Press, 2006.

Peacocke, Christopher. "Does Perception Have a Nonconceptual Content?" *Journal of Philosophy* 98 (2001): 239–64.

———. *A Study of Concepts.* Cambridge, Mass.: MIT Press, 1992.

Pepperberg, Irene M. "Number Comprehension by a Grey Parrot (*Psittacus erithacus*), Including a Zero-Like Concept." *Journal of Comparative Psychology* 119, no. 2 (2005): 197–209.

Pitson, Antony E. "The Nature of Humean Animals." *Hume Studies* 19 (1993): 301–16.

Plutarch. *Plutarch's Lives*, vol. 2. Greek with English trans. by Bernadotte Perrin. Cambridge, Mass.: Harvard University Press / London: William Heinemann, 1985.

———. *Moralia*, vol. 12. Greek with English trans. by Harold Cherniss and William C. Helmbold. Cambridge, Mass.: Harvard University Press, 1995.

Porphyry. *On Abstinence from Killing Animals.* Trans. Gillian Clark. Ithaca, N.Y.: Cornell University Press, 2000.

Rawls, John. *Political Liberalism.* enl. ed. New York: Columbia University Press, 2005.

———. *A Theory of Justice.* Rev. ed. Cambridge, Mass.: Harvard University Press, 1999.

Regan, Tom. *The Case for Animal Rights.* Berkeley: University of California Press, 1983.

Ristau, Carolyn A. "Aspects of the Cognitive Ethology of an Injury-Feigning Bird." In *Readings in Cognitive Ethology*, ed. Marc Bekoff and Dale Jamieson, pp. 79–89. Cambridge, Mass.: MIT Press, 1996.

Rollin, Bernard. "Thought without Language." In *Animal Rights and Human Obligations*, ed. Tom Regan and Peter Singer, pp. 43–50. Upper Saddle River, N.J.: Prentice Hall, 1989.

Rolston, Holmes, III,. *Conserving Natural Value*. New York: Columbia University Press, 1994.

Routley, Richard. "Alleged Problems in Attributing Beliefs, and Intentionality, to Animals." *Inquiry* 24 (1981): 385–417.

Routley, R., and V. Routley. "Against the Inevitability of Human Chauvinism." In *Ethics and Problems of the 21st Century*, ed. K. E. Goodpaster and K. M. Sayre, pp. 36–59. Notre Dame, Ind.: University of Notre Dame Press, 1979.

Sagoff, Mark. "Animal Liberation and Environmental Ethics: Bad Marriage, Quick Divorce." *Osgoode Hall Law Journal* 22 (1984): 297–307.

Saint Augustine. *Confessions*. Trans. R. S. Pine-Coffin. London: Penguin, 1961.

Schopenhauer, Arthur. *On the Basis of Morality*. Trans. E. F. J. Payne. Providence, R.I.: Berghahn Books, 1995.

——. *On the Fourfold Root of the Principle of Sufficient Reason*. Trans. E. F. J. Payne. La Salle, Ill.: Open Court, 1974.

——. *Parerga and Paralipomena*. 2 vols. Trans. E. F. J. Payne. Oxford: Clarendon Press, 2000.

——. *The World as Will and Representation*, vol. 1. Trans. E. F. J. Payne. Indian Hills, Colo.: Falcon's Wing Press, 1958.

Searle, John R. "Animal Minds." In *Consciousness and Language*, pp. 61–76. Cambridge: Cambridge University Press, 2002.

——. "The Explanation of Cognition." In *Thought and Language*, Royal Institute of Philosophy Supplement 42, ed. John Preston, pp. 103–26. Cambridge: Cambridge University Press, 1997.

——. *Intentionality: An Essay in the Philosophy of Mind*. Cambridge: Cambridge University Press, 1983.

——. "Minds, Brains and Programs." *Behavioral and Brain Sciences* 3 (1980): 417–57.

Seneca. *Ad Lucilium Epistulae Morales*, vol. 3. Latin with English trans. by Richard M. Gummere. London: Heinemann/New York: G.. P. Putnam's Sons, 1925.

Sextus Empiricus. *The Skeptic Way: Sextus Empiricus's "Outlines of Pyrrhonism."* Trans. Benson Mates. New York: Oxford University Press, 1996.

Singer, Peter. *Animal Liberation.* 2nd ed. New York: New York Review of Books, 1990.

Sorabji, Richard. *Animal Minds and Human Morals: The Origins of the Western Debate.* Ithaca, N.Y.: Cornell University Press, 1993.

Steiner, Gary. *Anthropocentrism and Its Discontents: The Moral Status of Animals in the History of Western Philosophy.* Pittsburgh, Pa.: University of Pittsburgh Press, 2005.

———. *Descartes as a Moral Thinker: Christianity, Technology, Nihilism.* Amherst, N.Y.: Prometheus/Humanity Books, 2004.

Stephan, Achim. "Sind Tiere 'schwer vom Begriff'?" *Deutsche Zeitschrift für Philosophie* 52 (2004): 569–83.

Sterba, James P. "Justice." In *Political Theory and the Ecological Challenge,* ed. Andrew Dobson and Robyn Eckersley, pp. 148–64. Cambridge: Cambridge University Press, 2006.

Stich, Steven P. "Do Animals Have Beliefs?" *Australasian Journal of Philosophy* 57 (1979): 15–28.

———. *From Folk Psychology to Cognitive Science: The Case Against Belief.* Cambridge, Mass.: MIT Press, 1983.

Sunstein, Cass R. "Standing for Animals (with Notes on Animal Rights)." *UCLA Law Review* 47 (2000): 1333–68.

Taylor, Charles. *Hegel.* Cambridge: Cambridge University Press, 1975.

Taylor, Paul W. "The Ethics of Respect for Nature." In *The Animal Rights / Environmental Ethics Debate: The Environmental Perspective,* ed. Eugene C. Hargrove, pp. 95–120. Albany, N.Y.: SUNY Press, 1992.

———. *Respect for Nature: A Theory of Environmental Ethics.* Princeton, N.J.: Princeton University Press, 1986.

Terrace, H. S. "Animal Cognition." In *Animal Cognition,* ed. H. L. Roitblat, T. G. Bever, and H. S. Terrace, pp. 7–28. Hillsdale, N.J.: Lawrence Earlbaum, 1984.

———. "Animal Cognition: Thinking without Language." *Philosophical Transactions of the Royal Society of London* B 308 (1985): 113–28.

Thorndike, Edward L. *Animal Intelligence: Experimental Studies.* New Brunswick, N.J.: Transaction Publishers, 2000.

Varner, Gary E. *In Nature's Interests? Interests, Animal Rights, and Environmental Ethics.* Oxford: Oxford University Press, 1998.

Warren, Mary Anne. "The Rights of the Nonhuman World." In *The Animal Rights / Environmental Ethics Debate: The Environmental Perspective,* ed. Eugene C. Hargrove, pp. 185–210. Albany, N.Y.: SUNY Press, 1992.

Weiskrantz, L. "Thought without Language: Thought without Awareness?" *Thought and Language*, Royal Institute of Philosophy Supplement 42, ed. John Preston, pp. 127–50. Cambridge: Cambridge University Press, 1999.

Wenz, Peter S. *Environmental Justice*. Albany, N.Y.: SUNY Press, 1988.

Wilkes, K. V. "Talking to Cats, Rats and Bats." In *Thought and Language*, Royal Institute of Philosophy Supplement 42, ed. John Preston, pp. 177–95. Cambridge: Cambridge University Press, 1997.

Williams, Bernard. *Problems of the Self*. Cambridge: Cambridge University Press, 1973.

Wissenburg, Marcel. "Liberalism." In *Political Theory and the Ecological Challenge*, ed. Andrew Dobson and Robyn Eckersley, pp. 20–34. Cambridge: Cambridge University Press, 2006.

Wittgenstein, Ludwig. *Philosophical Investigations*. Trans. G. E. M. Anscombe. New York: Macmillan, 1968.

# INDEX

dolphins, cognitive abilities of, xi, 6, 33, 60

dominion: Aristotle on human, over animals, 35, 99, 133; Descartes on the mastery of nature, 35–36, 95, 124, 138, 141; Heidegger on letting beings be, 141; Heidegger on standing-reserve, 124; Kant on human, over animals, 97, 138; Locke on human, over animals, 93, 97; Mill on human, over nature, 98, 114; Stoics on human, over animals, 35, 99, 132–37, 140–41, 162

Dretske, Fred: on intentionality in animals, 151–54

duties, 92, 126, 129; of compassion versus, of justice toward animals, 117–20, 132, 143, 154; Kant on indirect versus direct, 94–96, 108, 111; Rawls on, toward animals, 117–18, 129

engaged practice: Heidegger on, 57, 64; need not involve concepts and intentionality, 9–10, 77–79

equal consideration, principle of, 152; Callicott on the impracticality of extending, to animals, 130, 141; extension of, to animals required by justice, ix–x, 102–3, 106, 129, 131; Francione on, 103; Regan and Singer on, 112

ethology: concept of association in, 74; Nagel's challenge to, 12, 49, 63; role of content in, 45; shift from behavioral to cognitive, 5–6, 31, 89

experience, perceptual, 10, 12, 31, 58, 63; animals are confined within, 66, 68, 70, 75–76; Bermudez on, 70–71; Crane on intentionality of,

74–75; Griffin on link between, and reflective experience, 32, 47, 66; Malcolm on nonpropositional character of animal perception, 23; McDowell on, 11, 14–15, 24, 67, 74; Millikan on, without concepts, 30, 34, 59, 63; Morgan on the difference between, in animals and in humans, 68–70, 73, 76; role of concepts in, 14; Rollin on link between, and reflective experience, 47, 66; as a sign of individuality, 129; sufficient for moral status, 91

experience, reflective, x, 8, 32, 38; animals incapable of, 66, 125, 127, 161; not presupposed by perceptual experience, 57, 59, 65; as precondition for moral status, 92; presupposed by perceptual experience, 47, 66. *See also* abstraction, self-awareness

experimentation on animals. *See* vivisection

fairness: Barry on justice as, 147–49; liberal conception of, 154

fascism, environmental: Ferry's charge of, against cosmic holism, 146, 155; Regan's charge of, against cosmic holism, 145, 152

feeling, role of: in moral commitment, 110, 111, 114, 154; *oikeíosis* and, 135–40; Plutarch on, 120. *See also* community, kinship, *oikeíosis*

Ferry, Luc: charge of environmental fascism against cosmic holism, 146, 155; critique of central planning, 153, 156; defense of Kantian autonomy, 146, 155

Francione, Gary: abolitionism, 91, 102; move beyond social justice

Hume: on association, 79–80; on the similarities and differences between animal and human rationality, 81; on the impossibility of genuine abstraction, 82; on the nature of belief, 83

Impartiality: Barry on second-order, of the liberal conception of society, 147–50; first-order versus second-order, 150, 152; totalitarian implications of first-order, 152
individualism, liberal: anthropocentrism of, 97, 99, 100, 105–6, 111, 114, 117, 121; basic commitments of, 144, 146; limits of, in the endeavor to secure the moral status of animals, 111, 121, 125, 144; priority of cosmic holism over, 121, 125. See also holism, cosmic; liberal political theory
inference, 46, 73–74; perceptual, in animals, 83–84; Chrysippus's dog, 42; perceptual, in honey guides, 85; Bermudez on, in animals, 70–71; Griffin on, in animals, 84; Hume on, 79–81; Morgan on the distinction between perceptual and conceptual, 68–69, 73; perceptual, in Chelsea the border collie, 86–87
inherent worth. See worth, inherent
instinct, ix–x, 4; in ants, crabs, and sand wasps, 19; Descartes on, in animals, 35; Griffin on, in animals, 33; in honey guides, 2; Hume on, 81, 83; inadequacy of appeal to, in the endeavor to explain animal behavior, 20, 37; Kant on, in animals, 94–96; Millikan on, in animals, 33–34; possible role of,

in deceptive behavior, 91. See also adaptability
intentionality, intentional states: defined, 3, 13–16, 29, 45–46, 71; first-order versus second-order, 71; in animals, 16, 19, 25–26, 32, 46, 50; Crane on intentional states without propositional form, 74–75; Davidson on lack of, in animals, 20, 22; DeGrazia on the role of content in intentional states, 49–50; Dennett on, 17–18; Dretske on presence of, in animals, 51–53; Glock on intentionality without concepts, 53; in humans, 8; Hume on the nature of belief, 78–84; lack of, in animals, 63, 66, 84, 86–87, 122; Millikan on intentionality without concepts, 30, 33–34, 53–54, 62; moral status of animals not dependent upon possession of, 55, 113; Nussbaum on, in animals, 38–39, 41; Regan on presence of, in animals, 50; Routley on intentionality without language, 53–54; Searle on intentionality in animals, 41; Williams on, in animals, 18; Wittgenstein on, in dogs, 82. See also judgment, propositional content, rationality
intrinsic worth. See worth, inherent

Jonas, Hans: charge of environmental fascism against, 153; defense of cosmic holism, 152, 155–56
judgment: role of propositional content in, 21; Kant on, 47–48; lack of capacity for, in animals, 20, 67, 75, 125

Morgan, C. Lloyd: Morgan's Canon, 65, 71; on the distinction between perceptual and conceptual inference, 68–69, 73; on the distinction between intelligence and rationality, 68–69, 73, 76; on the difference between perception in animals and in humans, 69–70

Nagel, Thomas: attribution of subjective awareness to animals, 29, 33, 75, 90–91; challenge to ethology, 12, 49, 63; McDowell's criticism of, 15

Nussbaum, Martha, 49, 109; appeal to anecdotal accounts of animal behavior, 40; on eudaimonistic character of animal behavior, 38; on the permissibility of horse racing, 107; on the moral status of domestic animals, 107; on predicative ability in animals, 38–39, 41

*oikeíosis*: Stoic conception of, 92, 132, 134–37, 140, 178n. 4; Wenz on, 139. *See also* community, kinship, Stoic philosophy

pain, 49, 58, 64; animal awareness of, 75–76, 113; Bentham on moral significance of, in animals, 36; Carruthers on moral insignificance of, in animals, 65–66, 68, 74, 154; Crane on the intentional character of, 75; Harrison on, in animals, 64–65; McDowell on, in animals, 11, 26, 67–68, 74. *See also* sentience

Papineau, David: on the nature of associations made by animals, 74; Papineau and Heyes on the role

of representations in associative behavior, 84

parrots. *See* Alex the parrot

Pepperberg, Irene. *See* Alex the parrot

perception. *See* experience, perceptual

planning, central: Ferry's critique of, 153, 155; Hayek's critique of, 150–51; Jonas's defense of, 152–53. *See also* totalitarianism, threat of

plover, piping. *See* broken-wing display

Plutarch: critique of Chrysippus, 42–43; on continuity between animals and humans, 60; on duties of compassion toward animals, 120; on duties of justice toward animals, 120; on rationality in animals, 43

Porphyry: on continuity between animals and humans, 60; on duties of justice toward animals, 162–63

predication, predicative ability: lack of, in animals, x, 10, 11, 27, 30, 38, 47, 51–52, 55, 61, 63; Nussbaum on predicative abilities of animals, 38–39

primates, higher. *See* apes

problem-solving ability. *See* adaptability, adaptation

property, animals as: Bentham on, 98; Francione on, 98, 102–3, 106, 109; Hume on, 81; Locke on, 93, 97

propositional content: role of, in beliefs and desires, 13–15, 20–26, 39, 54; Glock on propositional attitudes without concepts, 53, 167n. 23; lack of, in animal representations, 70, 75, 84. *See also* intentionality, rationality

proto-concepts, proto-subjectivity, proto-thought in animals, 34, 53, 84, 91, 125–26; Bermudez on protoinference, 71, 175n. 35;

Seneca: on horse's ability to envision a familiar road, 72–73, 87

sentience: as criterion for moral status, xi, 36, 103, 113, 114, 119, 126, 143, 147, 156; Bentham on, as basis for moral status, 97; Francione on, 102–3, 112–13, 128, 171n. 15; Kant on, in animals, 37, 97; Mill on, 98; as a sign of a larger life project, 38, 48, 102, 119, 126. *See also* pain

Singer, Peter: critique of, 90, 104, 112

social justice. *See* justice

Stephan, Achim: on non-rational intentionality, 23

Stoic philosophy: anthropocentrism of, 137, 140, 162; cosmopolitan ideal, 133–34; distinction between human and animal experience, 10, 17–18, 35, 38, 135–37; Chrysippus on lack of emotion in animals, 38; *oikeiosis* and the exclusion of animals from the sphere of rights, 35, 42, 92, 96–97, 113, 120, 133–36, 141, 160, 162

subjective mental states of animals: ultimately inaccessible, 4–5, 31–32, 50, 61; Nagel on, 12, 29, 33, 49; McDowell on subjectivity versus proto-subjectivity, 11, 15, 26. *See also* proto-concepts, proto-subjectivity, proto-thought in animals

subject-of-a-life: Regan's notion of, 10; Wenz on, 139–40

teleological behavior. *See* goal-directed behavior

things, animals as: Bentham on, 97–98; Francione on, 103; Kant on, 94–96, 112

Thorndike, Edward: on associations in animals, 73

totalitarianism, threat of: Hayek on, 150–53; liberal charge of, against cosmic holism, x, 145–46, 149, 153, 155–56. *See also* planning, central

utilitarianism: Bentham, 36, 97–99; critique of, 90, 112, 114; Singer, 90, 98, 104

Varner, Gary: axiological anthropocentrism, 139

veganism: duty of, toward animals, 163. *See also* justice, vegetarianism

vegetarianism: critique of, 130; Plutarch on, 120; Porphyry on, 162–63. *See also* justice, veganism

vervets: communicative abilities in, 6, 45–46

vivisection: Descartes on, 124; Kant on, 97; Schopenhauer on, 108, 186n. 79; welfarist on, 119

volition: Aristotle on, in animals versus choice in humans, 133; Hume on, 81; Kant on, in animals versus choice in humans, 94

welfarism, animal: contrasted with abolitionism, 101, 118–19; duties of compassion toward animals, 102, 119; Francione's critique of, 102; Plutarch on, 120. *See also* abolitionism

will. *See* volition

Wittgenstein: on dogs, 62–63; on language, 21; on lions, 63

worth, inherent: of animals in relation to that of humans, 110, 113, 155; Francione on, 129; Kant on, 89, 97, 100; Rawls on, 118; Regan on, 100, 101, 118; Taylor on, 126; Warren on, 125–26